Perestroika
for
America

PERESTROIKA FOR AMERICA

Restructuring U.S. Business-Government
Relations for Competitiveness in the
World Economy

George C. Lodge
Harvard Business School

Harvard Business School Press

Boston, Massachusetts

Printed in the United States of America

94 93 92 91 90   5 4 3 2 1

The paper used in this publication meets the requirements of the American National Standard for Permanence of Paper for Printed Library Materials Z39.49-1984.

Library of Congress Cataloging-in-Publication Data

Lodge, George C.
    Perestroika for America : restructuring U.S. business-government relations for competitiveness in the world economy / George C. Lodge.
        p.   cm.
    Includes bibliographical references.
    ISBN 0-87584-234-8
    1. Industry and state—United States.   2. Competition, International.   I. Title.
    HD3616.U47L65   1990
    338.973—dc20   90-33228
                                                               CIP

In memory of
Henry Cabot Lodge

CONTENTS

Acknowledgments, ix

Preface, xi

Introduction   Restructuring America, 1

Chapter 1   Roles and Relationships of Business and
               Government, 13

Chapter 2   Industrial Policy Comes to America, 65

Chapter 3   Power and Control: Who's in Charge?, 103

Chapter 4   Organizing the Interface, 121

Chapter 5   Governmental Affairs Managers: Masters of
               the Fine Line, 153

Chapter 6   Recovery, 201

Appendix I   Some Government Policies Affecting
               Business, 215

Appendix II   Japan versus America, 223

Index, 225

ACKNOWLEDGMENTS

Many have helped, guided, stimulated, and encouraged me in the writing of this book. My thanks go to the students in Harvard's MBA program and the participants in the Advanced Management Program who for more than twenty years have helped me to understand more fully and precisely what I was attempting to teach.

During most of that time I have had the pleasure of working closely with Bruce R. Scott, who has taught me much about the analysis of comparative national strategies. In particular, his work on the erosion of U.S. competitiveness in the world economy that began some fifteen years ago has helped me to see and understand the inexorable pressures forcing change on U.S. business and government.

I am grateful also to my colleagues Joseph L. Bower, for his research on Japan's Very Large-Scale Integrated Circuit (VLSI) research project, and Helen Shapiro, for her assistance in interviewing those involved in Brazil's informatics program.

I owe a particular debt to two research assistants. Barbara L. Jenkins, now a professor at Carleton University, Ottawa, helped me with French telecommunications policy, and Robert S. Williams, Harvard MBA 1988, helped me with Sematech, "Imaging the Earth from Space," and the Joint European Submicron Silicon Initiative (JESSI).

My thanks go also to those at Harvard who read and criticized all or parts of the manuscript: Harvey Brooks, J.

Ronald Fox, Rosabeth Moss Kanter, Richard E. Walton, David B. Yoffie, and research associate Jeffrey F. Rayport.

Dean John H. McArthur has given me continuing support and encouragement, as has Michael Y. Yoshino, Research Director.

My thanks go also to Barbara Feinberg, Richard Luecke, and Natalie Greenberg for the skill, care, and imagination with which they edited the manuscript. I am also deeply grateful to Rose M. Giacobbe and her associates in the Word Processing Division at the Harvard Business School for the perfection with which they handled many drafts of this work. And my secretary, Lois Smith, was indispensable in proofreading, coordinating, and keeping all my efforts on track.

Finally, I am profoundly grateful to my wife, Nancy, and to my children and grandchildren for their continuing love and support and for the understanding with which they withstood the petulance which sometimes attended composition.

PREFACE

This book evolved from my teaching in the Advanced Management Program at the Harvard Business School. There, the participants and I explored the strategies of governments—their goals and policies—in order to identify the significant and sometimes overwhelming effect those strategies have had on the fortunes of business. More competitive strategies—Japan's, for example—are forcing less competitive ones, like that of the United States, to change. The longer the change takes, the worse off the lagging nation becomes.

No teacher could have asked for better students. About two-thirds have been Americans; the rest have come from many countries, but mostly from Japan, Germany, France, the United Kingdom, and Scandinavia. When I started teaching, they seemed old enough to be my parents, and I approached them with the deference appropriate to their age and vast collective experience. Now, of course, they are more like younger siblings, but the deference is no less. I am still dazzled by the range of their accomplishments and skills—managers of manufacturing, research, finance, and marketing for General Motors, Philips, Fujitsu, and AT&T; planners and strategists from Citibank, the Industrial Bank of Japan, the government of the People's Republic of China, the U.S. Department of Defense. For the most part they teach one another; I act as an intellectual traffic cop.

The curriculum of the AMP follows that of Harvard's master's program. The faculty is composed of senior professors of finance, marketing, production, organization behavior, strategy, control, and information systems. We work more or less as a group, seeking to tie our separate academic disciplines together and so replicate the complexity of the manager's task, which can rarely be so neatly packaged. (The participants—we do not call them students—are more impressed by our success on this score than we are.) My own focus is on the political, social, and cultural context in which corporations work and from which they derive their legitimacy.

The course, called Business, Government and the International Economy (BGIE), starts with a comparison of national strategies, an analysis of how the goals and policies of different nations have evolved during the past fifty years or so and resulted in quite different outcomes. Germany and Japan, for example, determined to rise from the ashes of World War II and gain market share in the world, developed and followed coherent policies that encouraged savings and investment in critical industries and produced outstanding economic performance. At the same time, the more diffuse and sometimes contradictory goals of the United States—revitalizing the vanquished, defending the "free world," ensuring a rising standard of living at home—were accompanied by policies that encouraged consumption, kept markets open to all, and discouraged industry cooperation. The result was relative economic decline; by 1989, the United States had become the world's largest debtor.

A nation's strategy—its goals and policies—does not exist in a vacuum. It is the product of that nation's historical context, the social, political, cultural, and ideological foundation of the institutional roles and relationships that shape the strategy. The context constrains strategic change. So it is that nations can for some years suffer deteriorating performance— trade deficits in the U.S. case, shortages in the Soviet Union—without having the will or the means to change. Perestroika came to the USSR and the nations of Eastern Europe when those nations were determined to restructure, to remodel the roles and relationships of government and business, to break the old links with the context, and change their strategies. It is coming to the United States as the nation sees its ability to compete in critical sectors of the world economy deteriorate and its power and control thus decline.

Perestroika comes hard. It represents a departure from traditional ideology, from the principles that have determined how such values as justice, economy, individual fulfillment, and self-respect are defined and given institutional vitality, from old conceptions about the purposes of and justification for government and business. And although perestroika is undertaken for pragmatic reasons, it carries within it—unavoidably—the seeds of a new set of justifications, a new ideology. Practitioners of perestroika, whether in the United States or in the Soviet Union, are naturally loathe to make explicit the new ideology reflected in the new practice because it seems needlessly controversial to do so. In fact, however, the new ideology must be articulated if the changes are to be effective, acceptable, and legitimate.

BGIE—participants call it "biggy"—thus takes a holistic look at nations as systems moving through time, competing with one another in an increasingly interdependent world. Its techniques were introduced in 1971 at Harvard by Professors John Rosenblum, now dean of the Darden School of the University of Virginia, and Bruce R. Scott of the Harvard Business School. Since then, many others have developed and extended the course, and most of the world's major countries are now covered by BGIE case studies. As the strategies of nations collide and compete, they affect the fortunes of business—sometimes overwhelmingly—and so managers find this course relevant, although it can be disconcerting for those, like Americans, from nations whose strategies have been anything but competitive in the world economy.

The course moves beyond country analysis to an examination of global flows of oil, money, and trade among countries. We examine who the key players are in these international games, the rules by which they play, and how and why the players and rules change. The debt crises facing Brazil, Mexico, and, more recently, the United States have lent urgency to this pursuit.

Finally, we analyze the different and changing relation-

ships between government and business that characterize the
nations we have studied. A case taking General Motors from
about 1917 to 1985, for example, describes the systemic
changes that company has undergone, changes in relations
between managers and the managed as well as between the
corporation and the government, that have, in turn, changed
old conceptions of managerial prerogatives and, indeed, the
very conception of the purpose of business. A more recent
example of such systemic change in the United States is
Sematech, in which the relatively small and individualistic
semiconductor companies have banded together and joined
with the U.S. Department of Defense in an effort to withstand
the competitive onslaughts of the integrated Japanese electronics giants that work hand in hand with their government.

Implicit in the historical process described in the course is
an ideological inevitability. Briefly stated, what participants
from the United States discover is that America's individualistic ideology, with its emphasis on property rights, open
markets, and the limited state, which they generally take to
be the justification for their undertakings, the source of their
authority, and the manifestation of their values, is, in practice, eroding. Less and less do Americans practice what they
preach—indeed, it would be disastrous if they did. Their corporations and their government—even under Ronald Reagan
and George Bush—are departing, however hesitantly, from
the laissez-faire ideology they cherish because there is no
choice. The choice now is which of the wide variety of communitarian options the United States will select. It is urgent,
the participants realize, to formulate a new doctrine that
reflects what they are doing and must do.

This realization evokes a complex array of responses among
the course participants. The non-Americans take this need for
change pretty much for granted. "This is what we have been
trying to tell you people," they say, sometimes with the exas-
peration of friends whose sage advice has been ignored. The
Americans are for the most part ambivalent. On one hand,
they are relieved to hear an undeniably plausible explanation
for the confusion, tensions, and—in some industries—failure

they have experienced. But they also feel frightened and frustrated. "If perestroika comes to America, if a new ideology is in fact implicit in practice, and if effective and competitive management depends upon its articulation and refinement, then how," they wonder, "do I tell the boss, and what do I do about it?" This book is an attempt to answer that question.

Boston, Massachusetts   *George C. Lodge*
November 1989

Perestroika
for
America

INTRODUCTION

Restructuring America

As the 1980s drew to a close, the roles and relationships of government and business in the United States were being remodeled by crisis, caused especially by competition from abroad; some industries, such as steel and machine tools, were actually withering. The choices seemed to be to remodel in order to recover economic competitiveness, or to reduce and retrench in the hope that what remained would survive. As in the Soviet Union, perestroika is coming to America because the alternative is unthinkable. In fact, there *is* no choice, for without restructuring there will be economic, political, and social deterioration.

The speed and effectiveness with which restructuring occurs depend on how well the leaders of government and business understand what they are doing and what they must do. Because remodeling threatens tradition, there is a tendency to think it is unnecessary—after all, if the remedy seems worse than the disease, the patient naturally will deny the disease. Even after remodeling has begun, there is a further tendency to deny that it is occurring, to regard it as a one-time aberration rather than a fundamental and irreversible change that must be managed. For example, as we shall see in Chapter 2, cooperation between government and business in the microelectronics industry was entered into slowly and with considerable hesitation and confusion on both sides. Bit by bit, the players perceived that what had been regarded as a problem confined to the semiconductor industry was in fact a far larger matter requiring governmental action to salvage

1

the entire electronics "food chain"—suppliers of the equipment needed to make the chips, and customers, such as makers of high-definition televisions, who buy them—upon which the semiconductor manufacturers depended. The government had to help identify and sustain that food chain because no one else was in a position to do so. But since reality threatened traditional relationships between government and business, the change proceeded slowly, retarded by ambivalence and skewed by inadvertence.

There are three requirements for the effective management of remodeling:

First, government and business leaders must understand that government policies profoundly affect the ability of business to compete in the world. They really count.

Second, there must be an understanding that government policies arise from national systems, and that they differ widely among countries, some of which are more competitive than others. The remodeling that America has undertaken in order to become more competitive threatens the old system. Moving to a new system requires a comprehensive understanding of what is at stake. Remodeling cannot succeed unless the systemic nature of the transition is perceived.

Third, far more importance must be ascribed to the task of managing business-government relations than it has generally been accorded in the past. That task is central to the fulfillment of both corporate and governmental strategy.

THE EFFECT OF GOVERNMENT POLICIES

The first step is not as easy as it seems. In the United States and perhaps a few other countries such as the United Kingdom, traditional theory is that the competitive position of nations in the world economy is a function of firms competing with firms. Businesses may benefit from the comparative advantages of the home country, but all will benefit, according to the theory, if markets are open and government does not interfere. Government may be a referee, blowing the whistle now and then, but it should not be a coach and certainly never a player.[1]

The fact is that, for better or worse, governments—all governments—intervene in the workings of business, some in such a way as to promote commercial interests, others to distort or retard those interests. Our two withering industries—steel and machine tools—illustrate the point.

Between 1974 and 1976, steel output in the United States, the European Community, and Japan declined by 122 million metric tons. One-half of the decline occurred in the United States.[2] The result was that, by the early 1980s, the United States had become a net importer of steel, while Europe and Japan retained their self-sufficiency and were net exporters.[3] The U.S. contraction, desirable or not, was painful. Twenty-eight companies filed for bankruptcy. Employment was cut 60% between 1980 and 1987; more than 200,000 high-paying jobs were lost. From 1982 to 1985 alone, the industry lost $12 billion. By 1987, the U.S. industry—what was left of it—was once again competitive, with costs 31% less than those in 1982.[4]

Why did U.S. production decline more than that of Europe and Japan? Government policies were a major cause. For example, European government subsidies for the modernization of steel-making capacity totalled $44.8 billion between 1975 and 1985, $35 billion in the last five years (1980–1985).[5] As Alan Wolff noted: "The European governments desired an outcome that the market was unwilling to provide, namely greater steel-making capacity."[6] The United States ignored the strategic roles of other governments. When forced by the steel industry, the government sought to punish those whom it considered to be cheating, in this case, the Europeans. To settle the matter, the Europeans agreed to "voluntary" restraints, as had other nations, to preserve a share of the U.S. market for Americans.

Government policies have made a difference in machine tools also, as David Collis's comparative study of the industry demonstrates.[7] They have affected the industry's structure, its products, the cost of its capital, its technologies, and its standards, and the results have been striking. Between 1955 and 1985, the U.S. share of world machine-tool production declined from 40.4% to 11.7%, Japan's rose from 0.6% to 24%, Germany's held steady at 14%, and the United Kingdom's declined from 8.7% to 3.3%. The Japanese government used a full range of policies—trade, investment, subsidization, research and development, tax incentives, easy credit, and more—to encourage the industry to collaborate, set common standards, move from simple to complex machines, and acquire market share, first at home and then in the world. The United States did very much the opposite. The Department of Defense, which had invested $1.5 billion in the industry by 1970, encouraged the development of extremely complicated and expensive machines that were fine for making jet fighters but had little commercial value, thus delaying the introduction of low-cost, numerically controlled machine tools for the mass market. Antitrust policy discouraged industry cooperation, and capital costs in the United States were twice those in Japan.

On numerous occasions during recent decades, the U.S. government sought to protect endangered industries—textiles, apparel, footwear, and television sets, for example—by using voluntary export restraints, as in steel, or orderly marketing arrangements. David B. Yoffie has described these forms of U.S. protectionism as short-term, narrowly focused, ad hoc responses to the particular problems of an eroding domestic industry confronting aggressive foreign competitors. Invariably and ironically, these policies are undertaken in the name of free trade as temporary devices, exceptions to the norm, in order to ward off more blatant protectionism. As Yoffie has shown, however, they have generally failed on all counts. They have tended to preserve an uncompetitive status quo at home while actually fostering increased competitiveness abroad, forcing foreign exporters to scale up their technologies, to diversify, and to exploit loopholes in the restraints, which often leads to lucrative new opportunities. These effects stem in large part from the refusal of the United States to regard trade policy as part of an integrated, long-

term scheme for "positive industrial adjustment."[8] Declining
industries get protection which does not help much, and
emerging industries are neglected or burdened by policies
that are uncoordinated and contradictory.[9]

It is not only national government policies that make a
difference. In 1989, as Europe headed for unity, 12,000
"Eurocrats" were working with tens of thousands policymakers from the twelve member-states of the European Community to develop the rules that would govern the world's biggest
market and make winners or losers out of American companies competing in Europe, rules on local content, antitrust,
auto emissions, banking, and more that would shape the conduct of business.[10] (See Appendix I for more detail on government policies affecting business.)

DIFFERENCES AMONG GOVERNMENT POLICIES

Government policies vary from country to country
because they are the products of markedly different national systems, which in turn arise from different historical patterns. Today, these disparate national systems con-
front one another and vie for a share of the global economic
pie.

It is difficult to say which of these systems is "best" because
they reflect quite different definitions of values. It is not as
difficult, however, to discern which produce the most competitive firms and industries; which gather and focus resources
most effectively for achievement in the high-tech endeavors of
tomorrow; which, in short, produce the most competitive economies. Clearly, in these terms, the U.S. system is not "best."
In 1989, the United States was the world's largest debtor.
Between 1982 and 1988, it had been forced to borrow $700
billion from foreign sources to sustain its standard of living
and to meet its governmental commitments, such as defense.
The United States faced the possibility that the enthusiasm of
foreign lenders might wane, or that foreign interests might
withdraw the $1.5 trillion in liquid assets that they held in

the United States in 1989. This deterioration of national power and control was provoking change, albeit slowly.[11]

It is the realization of forced change that causes American executives such concern. The new reality is undermining cherished myths. The United States is in fact moving from one ideological paradigm to another, not because it wants to, but because it must in order to sustain its economy and thus its political and social principles.

The old idea that firms compete with firms, unencumbered by government intervention, is shattered by reality: governments intervene. There is every reason to believe they will do so increasingly.

This fact destroys a second myth, that of the limited state. The old belief is that the least government is the best and what there is of it should be kept checked, balanced, and divided. Government should respond to crises as they arise and to the pushing and shoving of interest groups, but never should it plan, think ahead coherently about community needs, provide a vision of where the country is going. That government *is* planning and must do so for better or worse fills some with dread, partly because it threatens a third myth, that of property rights.

According to the idea of property rights, corporations are property and the fundamental aim of their managers is to satisfy the property owners, the shareholders. Doing so will be good for the community. Once, when shareholders were a relatively small number of easily identifiable persons, the idea made sense. The manager could ask them what they wanted—long-run market share or short-run financial returns—and act accordingly. Today, managers of the *Fortune* 500 are forced to discern shareholders' desires from the transactions of gifted traders on Wall Street whose objectives are purely financial: a return—and a quick one at that—on what they have invested for their clients, the owners. These traders could scarcely have less interest in the long-run health of the firms their actions sustain or destroy.

Many managers acknowledge the negative effect of the myth of shareholder ownership, but they continue to hold to it because it has been the source of their authority. If that idea goes, from where do they derive their authority? In practice, the answer is clear: It comes from those whom they manage and from the community in which they operate. This is the new reality, and it is fearful. If authority comes from the managed, then relationships with employees cannot be adversarial and contractual; they must be participative and consensual. If authority comes from the satisfaction of community needs, then those needs must be efficiently defined in a reliable way by government. If community needs require cooperation within and among industries to generate the economies of scale and marshal the financial and technical resources needed to compete with other systems, the sacred principles of marketplace competition as defined in the antitrust laws must be replaced. If it is government's role, then, to define community need reliably over time and facilitate its fulfillment, the idea of the limited state is dead.

Another myth that American managers see eroding is the desirability of functional and technological specialization, the idea that knowledge, especially technological knowledge, may be pursued narrowly by experts and that this process will lead invariably to acceptable outcomes. The manufacturers of nuclear power equipment, Freon, and toxic chemicals have learned that this idea is fundamentally flawed. We have become acutely aware that we live in a fragile biosphere, a "big blue bubble" in which our actions may have global consequences. Holism is here to stay, and without a sense of how the pieces affect the whole, the pieces themselves are illegitimate.

Elsewhere I have called the two ideologies reflected in this paradigm shift *individualism* and *communitarianism*. Since "individualism" is a word that has great appeal to Americans and "communitarianism" very little, U.S. executives may not find the terms helpful in explaining the transition. So the explanation of what is occurring must be made carefully and in terms of clearly recognizable corporate interests. Nevertheless, ideological analysis is essential for those who are managing the change and trying to convince others of its necessity because such an analysis reveals the dimensions of what are at stake—the myths, the mindsets, the hierarchies, and the interests that are threatened by the transition from one paradigm to another.

Proper analysis is needed to recognize and resolve the ambivalence, inadvertence, and anger that accompany the transition from individualism to communitarianism. There is ambivalence about making a change that is so radical and seems to many so wrong, which causes the transition to occur haltingly and only when the crisis is severe. There is inadvertence—seeing the change only in pragmatic terms, without examining the ideological consequences, adjusting the mindsets, or articulating the new rules of legitimacy—so the transition tends to be incomplete, fragile, and highly suspect to many. Finally, there is a good deal of irrational anger directed toward the foreigners—especially the Japanese—who are forcing Americans to depart from their valued ways. Anger only begets anger; it is important, therefore, that all parties understand its causes so that it may be controlled.

MANAGING GOVERNMENT-BUSINESS RELATIONS

We come now to the third step in the effective management of remodeling the roles and relationships of American government and business: the management of the relationship itself.

Because government policies are important to business, business has a keen interest in what those policies are and what they are becoming. This interest has two dimensions: first, the corporation would like to help shape government policies, and second, it would like to be able to align corporate strategy readily and expeditiously with those policies as they are finally determined.

These two dimensions constitute the function of corporate governmental affairs management, a function that has been sadly neglected by American firms. With some exceptions, governmental affairs (GA) is conceived of in narrow and limited terms. Too often it is left to "the Washington office," disconnected from headquarters where decisions are made, and viewed merely as an order-taker, carrying out instructions to kill this or promote that. Its operations are akin to those of fire fighting—defensive, ad hoc, with no long-run strategy. The GA manager is supposed to know how to influence members of Congress and Cabinet officers in order to achieve the aims of the corporation, which have already been determined, with little contribution from GA. Frequently, the GA manager reports to the firm's general counsel, which casts the job in legalistic, formal, and generally adversarial terms. The GA manager is supposed to fight the company's battles in Washington with little room for maneuver or compromise.

Business has much to contribute to the shaping of public policy. It is a vital repository of information and competence that legislators and executive officials need and want. At the same time, government has authority over many matters critical to business. The effective GA manager helps government by making available the competence and knowledge of the company or industry while shaping the strategy of the corporation so that it will be harmonious with community needs. It is a two-way street, and the GA manager cannot be influential one way if he or she is not effective the other way. Influence in Congress depends not only on the reliability of the information provided, but also on how sensitive the corporation is to congressional concerns. To put it briefly—and ideologically—Congress will respond favorably to corporate interests if they are in the interest of the community. If, on the other hand, corporate interests are conceived only in terms of the interests of the shareholders, they will naturally lack legitimacy in Congress. There need be, of course, no conflict between community interest and shareholder interest, especially if the latter is defined over the long run. So in many instances, it is merely a matter of mindset and approach rather than of substance.

The purpose of this book is to help Americans understand, explain, and manage what I argue are essentially inevitable developments in the roles and relationships of business and government around the world.

Chapter 1 takes a broad look at the different systems of business-government relations as they compete with one another over time in an increasingly interdependent world. It describes some concepts that will be used throughout the book to explain differences among national systems and changes occurring within a particular system, especially that of the United States. These concepts include:

- "Ideology" and two ideological types—"individualism" and "communitarianism";
- The "legitimacy gap," which separates institutional practice—the behavior of government or business, for example—from the dominant ideology;
- "Community need," together with alternative modes of aligning business with community need, and different patterns of decision making regarding what it and the "relevant community" are at different times; and
- "Alternative sources of management authority," leading to different conceptions of the purpose of business.

Chapter 2 presents concrete examples of the remodeling that is actually occurring in the United States, and an analysis of what the managerial implications of these events are. These examples include the debate that attended the FSX fighter plane deal with Japan in the spring of 1989 and the resulting recognition of an implicit industrial policy for aerospace; the decline of the semiconductor industry and the rise of Sematech; similar developments in superconductivity and high-definition television; and competing developments in Europe, such as the Joint European Submicron Silicon Initiative (JESSI). Again, the conclusion is that the success of such efforts requires careful inspection and sweeping renovation of old assumptions about government and business.

Chapter 3 delineates the extent to which the ability of the

United States to control its economic and political life depends on remodeling and renovation. The deterioration of the American lead in commercial imaging of the earth from satellites in space is offered as an example. In this case, it is the French, not the Japanese, who now have the more competitive system, even though the United States had a long-standing lead in the technology. In this chapter, we take a detailed look at the actual interface between business and government in Washington and begin an analysis of some of the key players and their interests and relationships.

Chapter 4 continues the description and analysis of the interface, focusing on the health equipment industry, Congress, the Food and Drug Administration, and the Health Care Financing Administration. The earlier chapters suggest the growing importance of collective industry action in America; in this chapter, we look in some detail at one of the more innovative industry associations, the Health Industry Manufacturers Association (HIMA), taking such action. We continue the consideration, begun in Chapter 2, of what it takes to manage the relationships between an industry and the federal government.

Chapter 5 moves from the industry level to that of the firm. It focuses on corporate management of the governmental affairs function, analyzing what "the Washington office" has to do. It examines in some detail the organization and operation of the Governmental Programs Office of IBM, and describes how the office functioned in two situations: Brazil's attempts in the 1970s and 1980s to reserve its domestic market for Brazilian producers of minicomputers, and Japan's procedures in the 1980s for developing its telecommunications network. The operations of other corporate government affairs offices are also considered.

Chapter 6 summarizes the themes of the book, gathers together lessons learned, and recommends actions for U.S. managers and government officials.

Although the transition with which this book is concerned is pervasive, extending into every kind of business, we will illustrate the changes and their implications by focusing on large, publicly held corporations and their industries. In particular, we will concentrate on those sectors in which the need for change is most apparent and most urgent if the United States is to regain global competitiveness and recover its strength.

NOTES

1. Bruce R. Scott, "U.S. Competitiveness: Concept, Performance, and Implications," in Bruce R. Scott and George C. Lodge, eds., *U.S. Competitiveness in the World Economy* (Boston: Harvard Business School Press, 1984), Chapter 1.
2. Thomas R. Howell, William A. Noellert, Jessi G. Kreier, and Alan Wm. Wolff, *Steel and the State: Government Intervention and Steel's Structural Crisis* (Boulder and London: Westview Press, 1988), p. 15.
3. Ibid., p. 542.
4. Ibid., pp. 501–503.
5. Ibid., p. 55.
6. Ibid., p. 537.
7. David Collis, "The Machine Tool Industry and Industrial Policy, 1955–1982," in A. Michael Spence and Heather A. Hazard, eds., *International Competitiveness* (Cambridge, MA: Ballinger, 1988), pp. 75–114.
8. David B. Yoffie, *Power and Protectionism: Strategies of the Newly Industrializing Countries* (New York: Columbia University Press, 1983), p. 19 and elsewhere.
9. David B. Yoffie, "American Trade Policy: An Obsolete Bargain?" in John E. Chubb and Paul E. Peterson, eds., *Can the Government Govern?* (Washington, DC: The Brookings Institution, 1989), p. 101.
10. Philip Revzin, "European Bureaucrats Are Writing the Rules Americans Will Live By," *The Wall Street Journal,* May 17, 1989, p. 1.
11. Edward Hamilton, *American Global Interests* (New York: W.W. Norton, 1989), p. 11.

CHAPTER 1

Roles and Relationships of Business and Government

The impact of business-government relations on the welfare of corporations and communities became critical during the 1980s. For some industries, as we shall see, they were devastating. The increased importance of business-government relations arose from three phenomena. The first was the extraordinary performance of countries such as Japan, Korea, Taiwan, and Germany, whose national strategies were characterized by close cooperation between business and government to gain world market share in selected industries. Those countries whose strategies were more inward-looking, marked by incoherent, rigid, or antagonistic business-government relations, were less successful.

The second phenomenon was the globalization of business, the formation of intricate coalitions of multinational enterprises, often aided by governments. These coalitions appeared to challenge the ability of nation-states—especially those that were losing world market share—to control business or even their own territories. The second phenomenon, unlike the first, was eroding governmental power. Indeed, Michael Porter could refer to nation-states as mere "platforms" on which the multinational corporations play, exploiting the strengths of some states and the weaknesses of others.[1] Nevertheless, governments do not give power away easily, and the importance of business-government relations increased.

The third phenomenon, an outgrowth of the other two, was the increased importance of technology to the political as well as economic development of countries. Although technology itself ensured its own rapid spread throughout the world, the ability to harness and exploit it varied by country. Through globalization, business might capture the benefits of technology, but nations, particularly those from which business had departed, risked being left behind with declining living standards. The rapid development of technology and of the expertise required to exploit it made it difficult if not impossible for nations that had fallen behind to catch up. Many governments assisted, directed, guided, or controlled business in an attempt to ensure that their nation had a particular technological edge: Brazil in minicomputers, for example, Japan and the United States in microelectronics. At the same time, and to varying degrees, national governments were becoming concerned about the threats that technology presented to the earth's fragile ecology and there was growing pressure to increase controls over its application.

In the face of these phenomena—intensified world competition, the globalization of business, and the politicization of technology—governments were generally anxious. In 1986, for example, Jacques Dondoux, head of the French government's Direction Générale des Télécommunications, put the case this way:

> If we want to retain our identity as Frenchmen, in the context of Europe, of course, the state really must intervene. There comes a point when the state must take risks so that on the vast world economic scene, Frenchmen can get a small piece of the action.[2]

The management of business-government relations requires an understanding of the sharp differences in the behavior of government and business in different countries as well as of prevailing views about how they are supposed to behave. In this chapter we shall examine a range of roles and purposes of government and business in selected countries, and we shall see that the roles and purposes seem to be accompanied by comparable forms of organization and structure. Those nations whose governments are expected to think coherently over time about the nation's priorities, for example, tend to be centralized and dominated by a prestigious and powerful bureaucracy. They are invariably related in some cooperative way to business, which itself is organized into influential industry associations. On the other hand, those national governments whose functions are more constrained and limited tend to be more fragmented and decentralized, led by bureaucrats who may not even have the respect of their political leaders. They are usually accompanied by loosely organized business groups with which they have distant, if not adversarial, relations.[3] Along with an analysis of roles, purposes, and structures, we shall also compare some of the more important tasks that governments perform and the tools they use.

THE ROLES OF GOVERNMENT

There are two ideological paradigms concerning the role of government: *individualistic,* which stresses the individual over the community, and *communitarian,* in which the reverse is true. In actual practice, most nations display a mix of these two types.

In an individualistic society, the role of government is limited. Its fundamental purposes are to protect property, enforce contracts, and keep the marketplace open so that competition among firms may be as vigorous and as free as possible. Government is essentially separate from business. It intervenes in the affairs of business only when the national health and safety are involved. Intervention thus hinges on crisis—epidemics, pollution, economic disaster, war—and is temporary, an exception to the normal state of individual and business autonomy. The purpose and direction of government are left to the play of interest groups, which fix government's priorities. An individualistic society is inherently suspicious of government, anxious about centralized power, and reluctant to allow government to plan, especially over the long term.

The role of government in a communitarian society is quite

different. Here, government is prestigious and authoritative, sometimes authoritarian. Its function is to define the needs of the community over the long as well as the short term, and to see that those needs are met (although not necessarily through its offices). It sets a vision for the community; it defines and ensures the rights and duties of community membership, and it plays a central role in creating—sometimes imposing—consensus to support the direction in which it decides the community should move. Consensus-making often requires coercion of one sort or another, which may occur in either a centralized or decentralized fashion, flowing down from an elite or up from the grass roots. Communitarian societies may be hierarchical or egalitarian. If the former, the nature of the hierarchy will vary. It may, for example, be meritocratic, oligarchic, ethnocratic, theocratic, or aristocratic.[4]

To oversimplify, among the so-called capitalist countries, the United States has tended traditionally to be the most individualistic, Japan the most communitarian. Other nations can be placed somewhere along the continuum between these two extremes. Germany is more communitarian than the United Kingdom, but still less so than Japan. France is a complex mix that in the 1980s allowed a communitarian president and a more individualistic prime minister to share power effectively. Brazil and Mexico are also ideological mixtures, but they are less well integrated than France.[5] Mikhail Gorbachev's USSR may, with luck, move out of its dark ages to a more Japanese-like version of communitarianism if perestroika succeeds in removing "the rust of bureaucratism from the values and ideals of socialism."[6]

Individualism tends to produce what Chalmers Johnson calls a "regulatory" state in which the market shapes business activity and government regulates business only in order to achieve ends that the market cannot meet. Communitarianism on the other hand is characterized by a "developmental" state in which government's task is to define the nation's priorities and see that they are met. The developmental state is associated with such historical patterns as economic nationalism and mercantilism.[7] Government in individualistic societies is invariably democratic, whereas communitarian government may be democratic or autocratic. We shall consider later the variety of governmental structures associated with these different roles.

These broad categories may be further distinguished by the strategies that governments pursue and the priorities that they set. For example, they may be inward-looking, focused on domestic considerations, or outward-looking, aimed at achieving global political or economic position.[8]

Traditional Western economics is rooted in individualism, holding that free trade among independent firms unconstrained by the hand of government results in the best outcome for all concerned. Firms benefit from their country's natural endowments or its comparative advantage.

The dramatic success of Japan and other Asian countries in the past twenty years, however, has called this ideology into question. These nations and their companies have benefited greatly by acting contrary to the tenets of individualism. Their governments and companies practice neither free trade nor free enterprise, as traditionally conceived, and they are quite prepared to restrict the freedom of the market when it serves their purposes. Furthermore, they are unwilling to accept comparative advantage as a static notion, deriving only from nature's gifts. Rather, they are determined to *create* comparative advantage to suit national goals.[9] Indeed, according to one estimate, "nearly 75% of world commerce is conducted by economic systems operating with principles at odds with" American individualism.[10]

It took until the mid-1980s for Western economists to realize the discrepancy between their theory and the global reality. Paul Krugman of MIT notes that some nations, notably Japan, had clearly advanced their interests by adopting a national strategy in which government acted in concert with business to encourage certain industries. "At least under some circumstances," writes Krugman, "a government, by supporting firms in international competition, can raise national welfare at another country's expense."[11] This support, he finds, took the form of promoting exports while protecting, more or less discreetly, certain domestic markets.

Krugman goes on to caution that industry "targeting" by government for the purpose of promoting the national interest succeeds only under certain conditions: the government must know what its national interest is, the definition of that interest must be economically beneficial, key actors—business and labor—must be willing to be coerced to abide by the definition, and the community must in general be prepared to make the sacrifices entailed in the national strategy to achieve its goals. He points to many instances in the West where government, for political reasons, sustained ailing industries—coal, steel, shipbuilding, autos, textiles—with questionable results for the economy as a whole. Other countries, he acknowledges, have allowed uneconomic industries to decline while encouraging new ones—computers, semiconductors, and aircraft, for example—thereby helping those industries to attain world leadership in technology and in manufacturing processes. These countries have thus acquired world market share in the industries of the future, earned substantial incomes from exports, and achieved high rates of growth.

However, Krugman also notes a variety of problems with government intervention on behalf of domestic industry:

- There are no standards by which to measure—that is, quantify—the benefits and costs of such strategies. "Will a dollar of R&D in the semiconductor industry convey ten cents worth of benefits, or ten dollars? Nobody really knows."[12]
- The political risks may outweigh possible economic gains. Interest group pressures in a pluralist democracy are likely to tilt government policy away from long-run future benefits and toward the short-run preservation of the status quo. "A country cannot protect everything and subsidize everything."[13] Some industries must suffer in order for others to prosper, and in a democracy this does not occur easily.

• Government lacks the competence to understand all industries in the economy and to measure accurately the costs and benefits of a strategy to benefit particular ones. "Suppose the glamorous high-technology sectors yield less external benefit than the government thinks, and boring sectors more. Then a policy aimed at encouraging external economies may prove actually counterproductive."[14]

Japanese planners have argued that these difficulties can be overcome and that it is clearly the role of government to do so. Myohei Shinohara, an architect of Japan's postwar development, writes that during Japan's miracle growth period, the Ministry of International Trade and Industry (MITI) applied two consistent criteria in selecting particular industry sectors for promotion and protection: "an income elasticity criterion" and "a comparative technical progress criterion." He writes, "MITI's industrial policies were expected to foster the industries in which demand growth and technical progress were comparatively high."[15]

Japan believed that it was "a function of the state . . . to induce, guide, and accelerate the structural changes needed for long-term growth. Japanese industrial policy thus involves a commitment to long-term planning and programming of the nation's economy. . . ."[16] Although MITI's involvement had eased by the late 1980s, industry leaders in Japan acknowledged that the role of government as described by Shinohara had not changed.[17] Western economists have looked at the Japanese trend with growing interest. Chalmers Johnson's opinion is that foreign enterprises "haven't a chance unless foreign nations compete with Japan on the level of government-business relations."[18]

In a 1988 "White Paper on Industrial Technology," MITI declared that the nation needed "to make a stronger commitment" to technological innovation, and "more extensive efforts which adequately reflect its economic power and technological potential." And, it continued: "Because the private sector is limited in the measures it can take to conduct basic and fundamental research, the government will be called on to play a more significant role than in the past in this research field." The ministry included a chart comparing Japanese and American "ability to develop high-tech products." The chart showed where Japan was ahead, about equal, and behind. Arrows extended from the latter two categories into the first to indicate the ministry's intentions. (See Appendix II.)[19]

It should be noted that this notion of government as a strategist and as a partner with business for global competition does not necessarily have anything to do with the size of government or with government ownership. Both Japan and the United States rank well below other major industrial countries in these two areas. Nor is the issue one of state intervention in the economy per se. All governments intervene for one reason or another. What is significant is the purpose and method of the intervention. Johnson says, "There could be no more devastating weakness for any major nation in the 1980s than the inability to define the role of government in the economy."[20]

James C. McGroddy, an IBM group executive in manufacturing, spoke of this role at the Harvard Business School in 1987 in connection with the difficulties of the American semiconductor industry: "When it comes to emerging technologies, where lead times are short, results uncertain, and capital investment required is very big, there are problems which are beyond the powers of business." He gave as an example the use of X-rays in lithography for the manufacture of semiconductors, a long-range, high-risk project: "Whoever gets it will have a definite advantage. Government help in these areas is important to coordinate industry competition for research and development and to provide funds. America needs such a national effort, but it is not on the agenda. Defense Department programs for military needs are fine, but they are irrelevant to global competitiveness. We need sharing and subsidies."[21]

Echoing McGroddy two years later, the Defense Department in 1989 identified twenty-two technologies critical to the military needs of the United States. Most were also commercially significant. In six of these industries—microelectronic

circuits, robotics, semiconductors, fiber optics, biotechnology
materials and processing, and superconductivity—Japan was
found to be "significantly ahead," at least in certain technological niches.[22]

In Johnson's terms, if Japan's government is developmental
in nature, that of the United States is regulatory.[23] If Japan's
purpose is to use marketplace competition as one of several
procedures for ensuring that business activity serves the
needs of the community as determined by government, the
United States tends to suppose that a market kept open by
antitrust laws will, for the most part, define and fulfill community needs single-handedly.

I see four ways in which governments can bring business
activity into line with the needs of the community (see Figure
1-1):

(1) Promoting marketplace competition, a route that has
    the unique virtue of both defining and fulfilling com-
    munity need;
(2) Regulating the marketplace in instances where com-
    petition by itself is unreliable or unacceptable;
(3) Establishing a partnership with business; and
(4) Requiring in the corporate charter granted by the
    community to the corporation that the corporation
    serve a predetermined need as, for example, the U.S.
    government did with the Tennessee Valley Authority
    and COMSAT.

Individualistic communities tend to prefer the first two
methods, communitarian communities, the third and fourth.
One of the Japanese government's most striking features—
and the one that distinguishes it from old-fashioned European
socialism—is its heavy use of the first method and almost
total nonuse of the fourth. But the third method is the preva-
lent means in Japan, because it has proven most efficient in
meeting community need.

Government's selection of an appropriate method from
among these four choices requires a clear definition of community need. Here the critical questions are, Who decides what

Figure 1-1 *Community Need: Defining It and Procedures for Aligning Business with It*

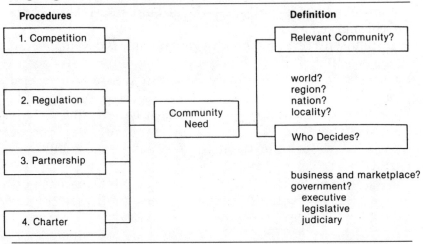

Source: George C. Lodge, *The American Disease* (New York: Alfred A. Knopf, 1984), p. 66.

the community needs? What is the role of government in deciding, and what is the role of business?

The Purposes of Government

To the extent that communities rely on government—not the marketplace—to define community needs, government's role is shaped by that definition. In post–World War II Japan and Germany, for example, the purpose of government was clearly to strengthen the economy to compete in the world. In the United States, the purpose of government was to build geopolitical strength against the Soviet Union, a purpose that was augmented in the 1960s and 1970s to include eliminating poverty, preventing ecological degradation, promoting consumption, and sustaining pluralistic democracy. The roles of all three governments were shaped by these purposes.

To examine the point in greater detail, consider welfare. Virtually every government is concerned in one way or an-

Figure 1-2   *Handsome Handouts*

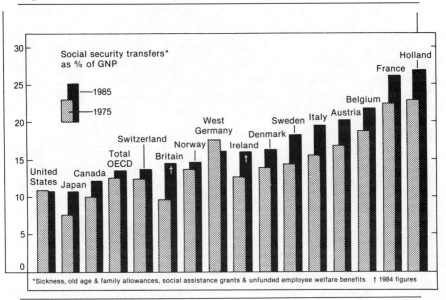

Source: OECD, as used in "Welfare Paradise: Survey of the Dutch Economy," *The Economist,* September 12, 1987, p. 10.

other with the welfare of its people, but the concern takes different forms. The tradition in the West has been to focus on income security, and government's role has been to provide for unemployment insurance, assistance to families, and social security. In Japan, the traditional focus has been on employment security, which has been reflected in distinctly different roles for government and business in providing jobs and job tenure. By 1985, however, as the value of the yen soared, it appeared that income security, even in Japan, was becoming more important. (See Figure 1-2.) This change in purpose will inevitably affect roles.

The success of nations in meeting their welfare objectives depends a good deal on their ability to adapt quickly to external changes that require having to make choices among competing community needs. Income transfers must be balanced against other needs such as current account surpluses, the availability of capital for business investment, the acquisition and application of new technology, education, and access to world markets.[24]

Oxford professor Andrew Shonfield, looking back at the postwar policies of the United Kingdom in which a commitment to a strong currency was combined with a commitment to the "abolition of want, disease, ignorance and squalor,"[25] remarks:

> One of the strangest aspects of British politics now appears to be the mood of insouciance in which a whole series of political decisions was taken, regardless of their effect in adding to the existing overload of economic burdens on the country. The politicians and even more the officials responsible, just assumed grandly that "a way would be found" of paying for the decisions that were taken in the interest of the nation.[26]

Jorge Domínguez of Harvard, considering the gap between the Mexican government's purposes as set during its Revolutionary period and the country's needs in the 1980s—for competitive enterprise, foreign investment, and a skilled and motivated work force—writes:

> Mexico's central dilemma is the conflict between the Revolution's goals and the performance of those who have ruled in its name. Because so much can be justified in the Revolution's name, the country's once-central legitimating myth no longer serves as the criterion for choosing among plausible alternatives.[27]

France, too, experienced the need for a policy reevaluation in the 1980s. French policies, which in the early 1980s involved nationalizing major industries while promoting the rights of French labor in pursuit of both prestige and income distribution, had to change in 1983 because of world competition.

By the end of the decade, the West in general had come to

appreciate that if government had an obligation to ensure citizens' rights, it had, partly as a consequence, as much of an obligation to insist that those citizens perform certain duties. Asian nations, long preoccupied with duties more than with rights, were forcing this appreciation on the West. Even in the traditionally individualistic United States, there has been a growing trend toward the communitarian notion of citizens' duties as defined not by the individual but by the community. By 1988, thirty states had a form of "workfare," which requires those on welfare to work or train for a job. It was even suggested that the right to health care ought to be contingent on a duty not to smoke.

Government and Global Industries

As governments are being forced to adapt their roles and purposes to the new reality of global competition, they are also competing among themselves to attract foreign firms and to make those firms within their borders more competitive. Between 1980 and 1985, the number of global agreements—joint ventures, partnerships, and alliances among firms across national borders—increased one hundredfold. Global industries thus gained substantial leverage over nation-states. No longer were firms bound to one country or two. They could shop around, and they did so, seeking the most inviting "platforms" from which to do their work.

Michael Porter writes,

> A country is a desirable global platform in an industry if it provides an environment yielding firms domiciled in that country an advantage in competing globally in that particular industry. . . . An essential element of this definition is that it hinges on success outside the country, and not merely country conditions that allow firms to successfully manage domestic competition.[28]

As countries compete for the blessings of global industries, governments that have clearly defined their community needs will do better than those that are less certain. A government that knows its priorities can move quickly to a bargain and will also be better prepared to take collective action in terms of the package of inducements it is prepared to offer, thus protecting itself from being whipsawed by global firms. Politics, in any case, will play an increasingly important role.

For the global firm, an obvious need emerges to manage governmental relations in a far more sophisticated way than in the old days when government was regarded as merely an obstacle to be hurdled. Today, good government relations can be an important competitive advantage.[29] For example, increasing numbers of multinational firms, which traditionally favored unrestricted free trade, are pressing their governments for strategic trade policies, demanding barriers at home until those abroad are removed. The U.S. semiconductor industry, for instance, has urged the American government to impose sanctions against Japan unless Japanese firms buy more U.S. chips. U.S. commercial aircraft manufacturers have taken a similar tack toward their European rival, Airbus. Furthermore, as these examples demonstrate, a company's relations with one government, i.e., the United States, can profoundly affect its relations with another, i.e., Japan.[30]

THE STRUCTURES OF GOVERNMENT

Neither the state, a nation's ultimate political authority, nor the government, the changing collections of institutions that manages its affairs, is a unitary concept. Neither is a monolith. Governments everywhere, in fact, are collections of competing executive agencies, legislative bodies, and courts that are being lobbied by countless interest groups at home and from abroad. To understand what governments do, it is necessary to look inside and examine the structures, the people who work them, the networks that influence them, and the tensions that separate them. In the United States, the interests of the departments of State and Commerce are often at odds, the former worrying about foreign policy, the latter about access to foreign markets. Similarly, the German Foreign Office has argued that foreign economic policy is an instrument of foreign policy and it should not be surrendered to free trade, an idea that is dear to the Economics Ministry.[31] And in Japan, as we shall see, consensualism scarcely mutes the disputes among MITI, the Ministry of Post and Telecommunications, and the Ministry of Finance (MOF).[32]

Furthermore, effective government rarely rules by fiat; it listens carefully to business, labor, and other interest groups and seeks a harmonious synthesis of those views and its own. And whatever the formalities may be, personalities are important in shaping the behavior of government. As President Nixon's one-time assistant, John D. Ehrlichman, put it, "The presidency is, of course, a constitutional institution, but it is also a baggy suit of clothes that molds itself to the man who is sitting in the chair. . . ."[33]

The Paradigms Revisited

The polar paradigms of individualism and communitarianism mentioned earlier also provide a way to consider the structures of government: where power lies, how it is used, and who uses it. The communitarian state, with its planning and vision-setting functions, tends to be relatively powerful, coherent, and centralized. The executive bureaucracy is more important than the legislature and attracts to its ranks society's best and brightest. It therefore commands the respect of business and the general public.

Communitarian systems are often characterized by strong political parties, with one party or a coalition of parties retaining control over a long period of time. Some examples are the various party coalitions that have governed Germany since World War II, the Liberal Democratic Party in Japan, and the Social Democratic Party in Sweden. More authoritarian variations of one-party rule have prevailed in South Korea, Taiwan, and Singapore. Communitarian government's

structure is thus consistent with its overriding role: to establish a consensus behind a coherent strategy for the nation's
development.

There are, of course, examples of communitarian states
where some of these characteristics are not clearly in evidence. Mexico has long had strong one-party rule, yet its government bureaucrats often do not command the same respect
as those of Japan or Sweden. Its consensus-making capabilities are therefore weakened. Indeed, when one element of a
communitarian system is weak, the whole is disproportion-
ately weakened.

In contrast, the individualistic state sees government's role
as essentially limited. In the United States, for example,
power is widely dispersed, checked, and balanced. The power
of the legislature is at least as great as and perhaps greater
than that of the executive or the judiciary, which was the
intent of the nation's founders. Federalist Paper No. 51 spoke
in the 1780s, for example, of the need to design controls over
the power of government so "that the private interests of
every individual may be a sentinel over the public rights."[34]
Samuel Huntington echoed that idea when he wrote, "Because of the inherently anti-government character of the
American Creed, government that is strong is illegitimate,
government that is legitimate is weak."[35] The exploits of CIA
Director William Casey and Lt. Col. Oliver North in the early
1980s were only one of many examples of executive impa-
tience with this creed.

Communitarian governmental structures evolved from
those of feudalism, in which the stratification of the "estates"
and the obligations of both rulers and ruled were clear and
accepted. The governmental structures associated with individualism either emerged from the feudal forms and were
affected by them, or grew fresh in soil virtually uncontaminated by old forms. Since the United States stands alone
in the world in its degree of independence from feudal traditions, individualism and its governmental structures exist in
their purest form. That is not to say that U.S. practice never
departs from its ideal; indeed, it does so frequently, especially

Figure 1-3   *The Legitimacy Gap*

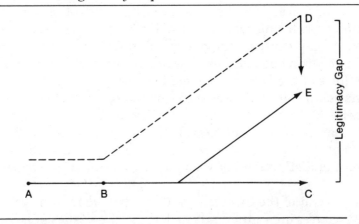

The solid line ABC represents a traditional ideology proceeding through time. The dotted line represents institutional practice—that is, what government, business, and labor are actually doing and how they are related to one another. During time period AB, institutional practice conforms to the prevailing ideology and, after that, departs: changes in the real world compel the institutions to behave differently than they did. By time C, institutional practice is very different from what the ideology presumed: the old hymns are being sung, but they are not being practiced. There is a gap, DC, which may be called a "legitimacy gap." There is an ideological schizophrenia: the new practice brings forth a new ideology to justify itself, but loyalty to the old ways discourages its articulation. As the legitimacy gap widens, two conflicting pressures converge on managers: one seeks to force errant institutions back into conformity with the ABC ideology; the other argues for a more forceful and articulate expression of the new ideology, which is the only means of legitimizing what is actually occurring (ABE).

Source: George C. Lodge, *The American Disease* (New York: Alfred A. Knopf, 1984), p. 34.

in times of crisis. During the Great Depression, for example, the National Recovery Administration sought to convert the structures of government into something capable of industrial planning in cooperation with big business. But the quick and ignominious death of the NRA at the hands of the Supreme Court serves for many as a reminder that such ventures are not for America.

American departures from the individualistic mode are regarded as suspect, illegitimate, and likely to fail. These departures create a "legitimacy gap" between ideology and practice (see Figure 1-3). As a result, authority falters and the community faces two choices: pull the wayward institutions back into line and practice what you preach, or install a new ideology and preach what you practice. However it is resolved, a legitimacy gap causes ambivalence on the part of decision makers in government and business, as exemplified by the uncertain efforts of the U.S. government in 1987 and 1988 to encourage national competitiveness in certain key industries, especially semiconductors, superconductivity, and biotechnology.

Harvard professor Steven Kelman in his study of government regulation in Sweden and the United States elaborates on the distinction between these governmental structures:

> Out of the Swedish tradition grew dominant values encouraging individuals to defer to the wishes of government and encouraging leaders to be self-confident in charting a course of how people should behave. Out of the American tradition grew values encouraging self-assertion and refusal to bow before the desires of rulers.

It was this difference that made agreement between government and business about such issues as health and safety regulation much more difficult in the United States than in Sweden. Kelman explains further:

> Contemporary Swedish society, like many European societies, emerged from a history of brutally sharp distinctions between ruler and ruled. The Swedish word *overhet* is a generic term for those on top of society, seen as an undifferentiated presence by those at the bottom. . . . It translates literally as "those over us" and consisted of those—kings, aristocrats, bishops—born to rule over others.[36]

Even with Sweden's contemporary democratic structures, elements of *overhet* can still be seen in the deference that citizens show to government. This is not unlike the respect the Japanese have for the young "summa cum laudes" who run the Ministry of Finance or the Ministry of International

Trade and Industry. In Japan and Sweden, the words of the Swedish poet that mark the entrance to Uppsala University ring a responsive chord: "To think freely is great, to think correctly is greater."[37] Such expressions are not found in America, where the supremacy of individual rights over the rights of the state is woven deep into the fabric of national thinking.

Strong and Weak States

In such places as Japan and Sweden, a strong government is associated with virtue. In the United States, as Huntington points out, it is at least a cause for suspicion if not an outright sign of evil. Other countries are arrayed between these extremes.

It cannot simply be said that communitarian governments are strong and individualistic ones weak, for such is clearly not the case. For example, no one would attribute strength to Lebanon's communitarian government. We must look further for traits consistent with strength and weakness.

We might say that a government is strong if it can (1) create a consensus in society sufficient to allow government to design and implement goals for the community as a whole; (2) change the behavior of important groups, such as business, to further its policies; and (3) change the structure of society—the nature of ownership, the degree of industrial concentration, and the importance of particular sectors—in pursuit of its goals.[38]

Japan. Let us take Japan as an example of a country in which government has, since World War II, shown its capacity to meet all three of those criteria. Until recently, we might have selected MITI as the most dramatic exemplar of governmental power in Japan. With a staff of fewer than 10,000 employees, it has done what the much-larger Commerce Department, United States Trade Representative, and Small Business Administration in the United States are supposed to do.[39] Today, however, without denying MITI's continuing influence, it is probably the Ministry of Finance that has the lead in Japanese governmental power. It is the MOF that now attracts the University of Tokyo's top graduates.

The following is an excerpt from *The Economist* describing the work of "Japan's men [never women] of MOF":

> Japan's most powerful economic policymaker is not a politician, but a civil servant—the top career bureaucrat in the Ministry of Finance. . . .
>
> It suits the Japanese pursuits of harmony and consensus to see policy disputes as politically neutral technicalities. It suits the economic bureaucrats, drawn from the top graduates of the best universities, even more. MOF, which is legally responsible for the financial management of Japan's central government, is thereby granted great power. It raises the government's money and decides how it will be spent. Policy initiatives, big or small, from any other part of the government have to win the approval of MOF.
>
> *The guiding hand*
>
> Within Japan, the ministry's role is often likened to that of a village elder who decides the shape of the annual harvest and then shares it in the way that is best for the village as a whole so as to preserve social order and cohesion. This perception gives it an authority far beyond its legal responsibility and makes its guidance—channelled through a network of informal instructions to financial institutions—a policy instrument in its own right.
>
> This is not to say that the process is simple. Far from it. Three factors complicate things:
>
> - Internal organization. The ministry is composed of different parts which compete with each other for influence and resources. . . .
> - Relations with other ministries. MOF has to deal with all the other ministries and official agencies

. . . [each of which] has its own economic divisions.
Some occasionally bid for parts of the finance
ministry's power over economic policy. The Ministry of International Trade and Industry, for instance, sets industrial policy; it controls some useful instruments of economic policy such as the
Export-Import Bank and the Japan Development
Bank. It also has some responsibilities concerning
foreign exchange. . . .

- Relations with parliament. Bureaucrats have long
been accustomed to primacy over politicians. (MOF
was established in 1870, and is therefore an older
institution than the cabinet.) Only in recent years
has the pendulum started to swing towards the parliament.

However, MOF cannot push through policies which
arouse broad opposition among politicians. For example,
the ministry has been trying since the late 1970s to introduce a new indirect tax. So far it has failed. Earlier
this year a planned sales tax was torpedoed. It was opposed for varying reasons by a broad coalition that encompassed some of the governing party's core supporters
as well as the opposition parties. This opposition was
sufficient to kill it.

Old pals

However, the fate of MOF's tax reform effort is the exception rather than the rule. There are many other institutional reasons why politicians rarely present a challenge to the authority of the bureaucrats. Both the
leaders of the Liberal Democratic party and senior
officials at the finance ministry tend to come from the
same highly educated elite, which gives them a similar
outlook.

Senior bureaucrats usually retire in their 50s to take
second jobs in companies or with influential industry associations and quasi-official business research organiza-

tions. This means that much of the outside advice offered on economic policy remains heavily influenced by the finance ministry's old boys. As a back-up, some 40 former MOF officials who are now members of parliament act as a cabal on economic-policy issues, irrespective of the faction of the party that they belong to.[40]

Germany. What we see in Japan is an interministerial apparatus, closely tied to big business and presided over by senior civil servants who descend to companies at about the age of fifty; it is an apparatus that surpasses parliament in power and influence. In a real sense, business generally is a part of government—perhaps even a controlling part. Much the same can be said of Germany where, as Peter Katzenstein points out, "Parliament is more or less eclipsed by the direct cooperation between interest groups and the ministerial bureaucracy."[41] The interest groups include the country's major banks, which are the "quarterbacks" of the German system because of their pervasive presence at all major decision-making points, holding in proxy 85% of all privately held shares.[42] They are early-warning systems, identifying weaknesses in German industry and, on occasion, organizing rescue operations.[43] Interest groups also include the numerous, well-organized, and powerful German business associations, which—like similar associations in Japan—have intimate relationships at all levels of the bureaucracy. In both Germany and Japan, labor organizations are powerful and well represented in government decision-making bodies. The power of business in the governance of both countries has led one observer to apply to them the term *nonstatist communitarianism.*[44]

The "commanding heights" of state power are occupied in both countries by carefully selected, widely respected individuals. "The state thus offers to a particular class of people a mechanism of political organization and control which it denies to others."[45] This does not mean that government policy will necessarily reflect the narrow concerns of the group, but it does mean that the group can define the national interest, relatively confident that its definition will be backed by a national consensus.

The structure of government in Germany differs from that of Japan in one important respect: It is more decentralized. Policymaking involves a constant struggle among three main rivals: the federal government in Bonn, the governments of the regional states (the Länder), and the independent central bank (Bundesbank).[46] The federal budget represents less than half of total public spending. The federal government and the regions try to coordinate policy through advisory bodies, but Bonn's capacity to control Germany depends on the cooperation of the Länder. And the Länder have power through their 45-member chamber (the Bundesrat) in the Bonn parliament. The Länder have veto power in matters involving their interests, such as taxes. The Bundesbank has control, too, through its sole authority over monetary policy and its great prestige as the principal bulwark against the inflation Germans dread most of all.[47]

France. French governmental structures, dominated by a well-respected, relatively autonomous, and strong (sometimes autocratic) bureaucracy, reflect what is perhaps the world's most sophisticated mixture of individualism and communitarianism. Janice McCormick of the Harvard Business School finds in France two ideological versions of each paradigm, which she labels liberalism and jacobinism, authoritarianism and social democracy.[48] The common belief around which all parties rally, however, is that government is "the reflection of the general will," as defined by Jean-Jacques Rousseau, "a will that is superior to that of any business or individual interest."[49] Until the early 1980s, that will was inspired by a desire to keep France uncontaminated by the world. More recently, it has been informed by the reality that competitiveness in the world economy is a prerequisite for all else. Toward this end, the state has become the partner of business.

John Zysman of Berkeley sees the French state as "an almost metaphysical notion . . . the unified authority of the society." The bureaucracy, created by kings to control unruly nobles, retains its power today as an instrument of collective power, insulated from interest groups and administered by the *Grands Corps,* which is composed of the top-ranking graduates of the two *Grands Ecoles,* the Ecole Nationale d'Administration (l'ENA) and the Polytechnique. "At the heart of this centralized system is the Direction du Trésor in the Ministry of Finance, what more than one ranking official has called the sanctuary in the temple, the holy of holies."[50] Here is centered the control of capital markets, credit allocation, public enterprise financial policy, and lending to private firms. In exercising its control, the French state uses three tools. The first is direct state action, what Zysman calls *faire.* The second is incitement to others to act (*faire faire*). And the third is simply to leave be (the traditional *laissez faire*).[51] In government's attempts to equip France for growth in the industries of the future—electronics, computers, telecommunications—all three tools have been used. In the 1980s, the role and structure of government in France was shaped by the need to link domestic economic management to the international economy.

Britain and the United States. In attempting to group nations by governmental roles, Katzenstein notes that Japan, Germany, and France are quite distinct from the United States and Britain. The former, in varying degrees, pursue their objectives using a wide range of relatively sharp instruments with which they can operate on particular sectors of the economy and even on individual firms.[52] The latter, the offspring of individualism, rely on a limited number of relatively blunt policy instruments that affect the entire economy rather than particular sectors or firms. From the end of World War II to the early 1960s, government policymakers in Britain, for example,

> tried to minimize government's role in the entire range of
> decisions affecting investment, the determination of
> wages and the conditions of work, and industrial rela-
> tions. They attempted to limit the government's economic

policy instruments to global mechanisms which would
minimize administrative discretion. [Fiscal and monetary
policy, for example.] Government's economic policies, it
was widely believed, should function globally as simply
and as automatically as possible. It was this dramatic
reassertion of the liberal state . . . that prompted Andrew
Shonfield to remark . . . that "The striking thing about
Britain is the extraordinary tenacity of older attitudes toward the role of the state."[53]

When in the 1960s the British government sought to collaborate with business and labor to formulate something like an
industrial policy, neither the institutions, the instruments,
the personnel, nor the ideology were there to make it work.
Furthermore, the policy itself was flawed because it assumed
the competitiveness of British exports and persisted in defending the value of sterling in world markets.

Among the most important factors in Britain's planning
failures is the role of organized labor, the Trades Union Council (TUC). The TUC has had a very different mission than
have the union movements of Germany, Japan, and the
United States. Traditionally, it has seen itself as a leader of
the working class pitted against the capitalist, owning class,
"the enemy within." Not only has the TUC been loath to share
decisions with business and government, but some of its more
extreme segments have perceived the destruction of business
and government as almost a patriotic duty. In Germany and
Japan, on the other hand, the interests of labor unions are
tied inexorably to the competitiveness of firms and to the
economy as a whole. In the United States, the role of unions in
the 1980s was uncertain. The old adversarial role embodied in
the idea of the collective contract was being challenged by a
new role in corporate governance not unlike that of Japan and
Germany.

Planning impediments for the United States government
start with a fundamental principle: The responsibility for
linking domestic economic management with the international economy is not an appropriate role for government.

When such linking does occur, it does so with little, if any, coordination among a disparate group of departments and agencies, including, for example, the Departments of Commerce, State, Defense, Treasury, and Agriculture; the White House Office of the United States Trade Representative, Office of Management and Budget, and Council of Economic Advisers; and a welter of congressional committees and subcommittees. The link is considered to evolve automatically from the interplay of market forces in a world of free trade and free enterprise; that is to say, it is taken for granted. It is significant that in the three years during which the 1986 tax bill was being framed, the inner circles of government never discussed its effect on national competitiveness in the world.[54]

During the 1980s, inaction and budgetary pressures in Washington forced increased planning activity at the state level. For example, in Michigan, which was hard hit by foreign competition, state government, working with business and labor, developed strategies for competitiveness. Interest groups also went to the states seeking action on a variety of fronts, including boycotts of companies doing business in South Africa, plant closings and antilayoff restrictions, pay based on "comparable worth," and safety and health regulations.[55]

Strategy versus Structure

In government, as in business, strategy often dictates structure.[56] But the reverse may also occur. The structure—personified, for example, by the young men of Japan's MOF or by the traditional economists of the President's Council of Economic Advisers—conditions and constrains strategy.[57] Furthermore, in both business and government, different structures may serve the same strategy, some more efficiently than others. The governments of the United States and Japan promote exports, but they employ quite different structures and tools to do so.

Finally, there is the question of what happens when old structures meet new challenges. Japan's emphasis on employment security, respect for elders, and consensualism through bottom-up decision making may have worked in periods of rapid growth. But will it serve as well the needs of contraction, conversion, and restructuring that the nation faces now? "There is no harmonious way to move 3,000 jobs offshore," wrote Bernard Wysocki, Jr., Tokyo bureau chief of *The Wall Street Journal*. Furthermore, Wysocki notes, pushing decision-making control down to the level of assistant section chiefs may have given government offices an atmosphere of collegiality, "but it also has produced ministries that are highly turf-conscious, inbred, and inflexible. . . ." When a nation confronts tough choices about which there is no consensus—taxes, land prices, and so forth—does it not need strong, tough, quick leadership? In this regard, Wysocki likens Japan's prime minister to the king in a game of chess. "He is surely important, but his own power is limited. He can only move one space at a time. To succeed, he has to persuade other, more powerful and agile players to move on his behalf."[58]

THE ROLES AND STRUCTURES OF BUSINESS

Comprehending the relations between government and business requires not only an awareness of how the roles and structures of governments vary throughout the world, but also an appreciation of similar variations in the roles and structures of business. For the purposes of this book, I shall concentrate on the large, publicly held companies that have increasingly allied themselves with other firms like themselves through joint ventures of one sort or another, and with governments both at home and abroad.

Again, our ideological paradigms—individualism and communitarianism—will be helpful. But let us first denude the corporation of ideology and see what it looks like. It is a collection of people and material brought together in order to complete a process: it gathers resources, designs, and produces goods or services that it distributes to the communities it serves. To do this, it must develop skills among its employees, motivate them, and exert organizational control over them. It should do this as efficiently as possible, maximizing benefits and minimizing costs.

Now let us introduce ideology. Externally, what goods does the corporation make? What resources does it use? What are the effects of its functions on the surrounding communities? Who decides the external issues? Internally, what are acceptable and effective methods of motivation and control? Who is admitted to the organizational hierarchy? Who succeeds, and how? Who decides the internal issues? Finally, how are costs and benefits defined? What happens to the surplus of benefits that it is the corporation's purpose to accrue? Again, who decides?[59]

The Roles of Business

The answers to these questions depend on the role the corporation plays in society and the sources from which it derives its legitimacy. Considering the various national communities we have observed, there are four possible sources of legitimacy, four sources of authority for corporation managers: (1) the owners, the shareholders who obtain authority via the idea of property rights, which in individualistic communities is almost sacred; (2) the banks and other debt holders that have an interest in safeguarding their loans; (3) the managed, the corporate membership; (4) the community, as represented by its government (see Figure 1-4).

Corporate raiders, such as T. Boone Pickens, argue forcefully that legitimacy derives from the owners. Indeed, many American managers would agree with him, in thought as well as deed, that the fundamental purpose of the corporation is the satisfaction of shareholders. Incentive systems, corporate allocation of resources, market strategies, and personnel policies are tied to this overriding purpose. It is indeed the primary source of authority that emerges naturally from the individualistic paradigm. Debt holders have a secondary position, employees are hired and fired as they are needed to max-

Figure 1-4   *Sources of Management Authority*

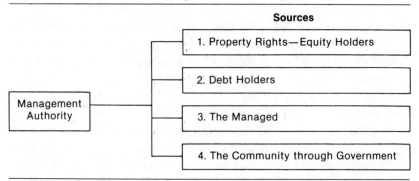

Source: George C. Lodge, *The American Disease* (New York: Alfred A. Knopf, 1984), p. 71.

imize return to shareholders, and government is an adversary to be kept at arm's length, and avoided entirely if possible.

Other American managers, however, especially those who have felt the fierce bite of Asian competition, are not so sure. General Motors, for instance, entered into a joint venture with Toyota in part to learn a different conception of the corporation, one in which the authority of the managers derives from the managed.[60] It turns out that employee motivation, productivity, and efficiency are greater when employees participate in decisions that affect their work and when they have enough of a sense of employment security to make a sacrifice today for gains tomorrow. And the U.S. semiconductor industry, on the ropes in its contest with Japan, is moving toward industry cooperation in partnership with government in the hope of attracting several billion dollars in subsidies that are presumably in the national interest.

Thus in America, there is doubt and even conflict about corporate purpose.* In Germany, however, corporate purpose

---

*There is nothing new about this conflict, as the following quotations from *The Modern Corporation and Private Property* by Adolf A. Berle, Jr., and Gardiner C. Means, published in 1933, reveal:

Power over industrial property has been cut off from the . . . legal right to enjoy its fruits. . . . The explosion of the atom of property destroys the basis of springs from a well-ordered combination of all four sources. Banks, having dominant positions on corporate boards of directors, exert control as holders of both shares and debt. Employees participate in corporate decision making through codetermination. Unions, banks, and corporate executives are informed about and responsive to the national interest as defined in numerous governmental forums in which the four are well represented.

Similarly, in Japan, corporate legitimacy has always derived from a clear combination of all sources. An executive of Mitsui, Japan's giant *soga shosha*—with sales of $120 billion in 1986, the largest company in the world—described Mitsui's purpose as follows, emphasizing the order: (1) to contribute to Japanese society, to serve the greater glory of Japan; (2) to realize profit for the company so as to promote the welfare and happiness of its employees; and (3) to foster and strengthen the spirit of Mitsui for the future, as that spirit is set forth in the company motto, *"Ten, Chi, Jen"* [heaven, earth, and human beings]. The satisfaction of shareholders, he said, is but a means to these ends (see Figure 1-5). The sources of authority are thus clearly the managed and the community from our previous list, as well as a spiritual something beyond the community that requires a bit of history to understand.

Mitsui was founded in 1671 as a merchant house at a time

---

the old assumption that the quest for profits will spur the owner of industrial property to its effective use . . . the very foundation on which the economic order of the past three centuries has rested.

The rise of the modern corporation has brought a concentration of economic power which can compete on equal terms with the modern state—economic power versus political power, each strong in its own field. . . . The future may see the economic organism, now typified by the corporation, not only an equal with the state, but possibly even superseding it as the dominant form of social organization.

The net result of stripping the stockholder of virtually all of his power within the corporation is to throw him upon an agency lying outside the corporation itself—the public market. . . . The fact appears to be that liquid property obtains a set of values . . . represented by market prices, which are not immediately dependent upon the underlying values of the properties themselves.[61]

Figure 1-5   *Ranking of Corporate Objectives: U.S. and Japan*

	U.S.	Japan
Return on Investment	8.1	4.1 (2)
Share Price Increase	3.8	0.1
Market Share	2.4	4.8 (1)
Improve Product Portfolio	1.7	2.3
Rationalization of Production and Distribution	1.5	2.4
Increase Equity Ratio	1.3	2.0
Ratio of New Products	0.7	3.5 (3)
Improve Company's Image	0.2	0.7
Improve Working Conditions	0.1	0.3

Note: Two hundred ninety-one Japanese companies and 227 U.S. companies ranked factors weighted 10, for first importance, to 1, for least importance.

Source: Adapted from Economic Planning Agency, Japanese Government, "Economic Survey of Japan 1980/1981" (Tokyo: *Japan Times,* 1982), p. 196, as used in James C. Abegglen and George Stalk, Jr., *Kaisha, The Japanese Corporation* (New York: Basic Books, 1988), p. 177.

when society was controlled by the local shogun and his government bureaucracy. The population was ranked in order: Samurai (retainers of the feudal lord) came first, then peasants, followed by artisans and, finally, merchants. The highest value was placed on learning, albeit of a sort restricted by Confucian orthodoxy.

Mitsui managers of the day made no bones about their desire for profits, but profits were pursued in a spirit of ancestral obedience and loyalty, in the knowledge that the stuff of this world was not their (or anyone else's) personal property, but had to be handed over, increased, to future generations of Mitsui men. Furthermore, since they were of a lowly order in the scheme of things, their activities had to be sanctioned by government.

When the Meiji modernization came in 1868, Mitsui's purpose was to serve the interests of government. The industrialization of Japan was in no sense marked by a flourishing of individualism. Indeed, it was carried out "for the sake of tradition itself, because, in the Japanese context, tradition had divine meaning and was symbolized in the Emperor." The modernization was necessary to protect Japan from foreign predators and to preserve its "innate superiority to any other nation."[62]

The legitimacy and purpose of Mitsui and the other great zaibatsu were thus closely tied to the purposes of government, and government provided protection and prestige. Mitsui operated the Osaka mint for the government, established banks, managed factories and mines. This conception of the firm was not only necessitated by the social and political context, it was also essential to the company's ability to attract top-notch young talent who sought prestigious careers.

Michael Jensen finds the large publicly held corporation being "eclipsed" in America by new "organizations that use public and private debt, rather than public equity, as their major source of capital." Their owners are "large institutions and entrepreneurs that designate agents to manage and monitor on their behalf" who have taken over through such transactions as the leveraged buyout (LBO). Jensen says the "evolving U.S. system of corporate governance and finance exhibits many characteristics of the Japanese system. LBO partnerships act much like the main banks (the real power center) in Japan's *keiretsu* business groupings." Jay O. Light adds that the new system also resembles "ownership systems in Germany" where the three major banks hold commanding accounts of debt and equity.[63]

The comparison with Japan and Germany raises a critical question: What is the purpose of the LBO corporation (Kohlberg Kravis Roberts, for example, which engineered the megabillion-dollar RJR Nabisco deal)? Is it comparable to that of the banks of Japan and Germany? Jensen says that the presence of the new LBO entrepreneurs in corporate governance "resolves the central weakness of the public corporation—the conflict between owners and managers over the control and use of corporate resources" because the new owners can and do exert control, which the old owners, dispersed as they were, did not. But what will the new owners seek? In Japan and Germany, the controlling banks have had a priority concern for the welfare of the country and its international competitiveness, a concern sharpened by intimate and often dependent relations with government. Are the new owners of American corporations similarly inclined, or is their goal quick returns whatever the cost to the community?

Strains

As Japanese, American, and European companies intensify their alliances—as they merge, invade one another's territories, and globalize—what happens to the old moorings? Mitsui's internationalization strains its relationship with the Japanese government, Japanese employees, and Japanese ways. Similar strains affect General Motors, the United Auto Workers, and the governments of both Michigan and the United States for which GM's globalization is perceived as a cost.

The sources of authority for the corporation in communitarian countries, at least those such as Japan, Germany, Sweden, and, to a lesser degree, France, have been clear: a well-organized combination of banks, employees, and government. In both the United Kingdom and the United States, there has been a gap between ideology and what seems necessary and practical. In both countries, managers are therefore uncertain, torn by conflict between and among the four sources of authority. The confusion seems likely to spread and intensify in the future as the well-understood principles enunciated by the Mitsui executive and Pickens collide and change—of necessity.

The Structures of Business

Structure tends to follow purpose. Again, the United States and Japan appear to be polar extremes with European countries ranged in between on the spectrum.

Starting with the internal structure of the factory and the firm and extending to the general structure of industries and business in the nation, we see a pattern: the United States individualistic, Japan communitarian; participants—managers and managed, suppliers and supplied, buyers and sellers—tied by contract in the United States, by consensus in Japan; relations among competitors marked by contentiousness in the United States, by a mixture of rivalry and cooperation in Japan. For example, Japan's lead in semiconductors can be attributed to the cooperation as well as the competition among its major computer companies. Furthermore, this cooperation was directed and subsidized by MITI. Such behavior would have been diametrically opposed to American business philosophy at the time, and a clear violation of U.S. antitrust laws. The merchant U.S. semiconductor industry was, for the most part, composed of relatively small, entrepreneurial, fiercely competitive firms, whose driving ambition was to use their relatively thin capital resources to maximize returns to shareholders. Only in 1987, on the brink of disaster, did the industry move to change its structure and relationships.

Clearly, Japanese business is structured in a radically different way from that of the United States.[64] This is true at all levels: the keiretsu, the groups of affiliated companies such as Mitsubishi or Mitsui; the industry associations; and the keidanren, which brings all business together for joint planning with government. Germany, France, Sweden, and even Britain are also characterized by much stronger and more important industry organizations than those in the United States. These European associations work closely and cooperatively with government on hundreds of issues, ranging from occupational health and safety to tax laws and environmental regulation.

There can be no doubt, however, that in recent years some American industries are moving toward a different pattern— around such issues as toxic substances and pharmaceuticals, for example. The pressure of foreign competition is forcing cooperation among domestic competitors in the United States, and the antitrust laws have been loosened to allow some collaboration (the National Cooperative Research Act of 1984). Competitive pressure is also forcing the global alliances we have mentioned. These alliances are profoundly changing the domestic national structures of industries; indeed, when the smoke clears, there may well be very different structures of business the world over. Does this mean convergence toward a common pattern? If so, how much drag will different national traditions present? How will that friction be overcome? Perhaps most interesting, can the structures of business and industries change without their roles and purposes also changing and without changes in their relationships to government?[65] Are we, in fact, dealing not with discreet institutions, but with whole systems?

BUSINESS-GOVERNMENT RELATIONSHIPS

Various relationships between government and business flow from the roles and structures we have described. Broadly speaking, these relationships can be characterized in terms of process and in terms of substance.

Process

At one end of the spectrum in matters regarding process are the widely used and continuing forums of such countries as Japan, Germany, and Sweden. Organized through industry associations as well as through so-called peak organizations, these forums often include formal representation from labor unions, environmentalists, academics, and consumers. The purpose of these networks is to define community priorities and to agree on policies to fulfill them. At the other end of the same spectrum are the more ad hoc, adversarial, litigious procedures characteristic of the United States.[66]

We know, however, that the United States does not always behave according to its founders' most rigid guidelines, as the example of the National Recovery Administration given earlier indicates. Time and again in American history, business—railroads, oil, agriculture—and government have collaborated. Loans and loan guarantees to America's housing industry totalled nearly $160 billion in 1980, and housing and real estate received more tax subsidies than all other industries combined. The nation's 18,000 sugar growers receive about \$2 billion a year, and the defense industry enjoys a more or less symbiotic relationship with government. In 1985, for example, the Department of Defense spent \$35 billion for research and development on new technologies, about one-third of all such expenditures in the United States.[67] Indeed, the ability of those with political influence to secure governmental support prompted Theodore Lowi, professor of American Institutions at Cornell University, to characterize the American system as "socialism for the organized, capitalism for the unorganized."[68] And yet, along with the collaboration has come denial of partnership, protestation of autonomy, and insistence upon noncontamination. Because of the desire to maintain the appearance of business autonomy, the United States lacks the ongoing, formal, and respected mechanisms of cooperation that prevail in other countries. The creation of such mechanisms would suggest an acceptance of business-government cooperation, an ideological taboo.

Substance

Scores of substantive issues lie at the interface between government and business—taxation, public spending, environment, health, safety, tariffs, and many more (see Appendix I). I will focus on two general issues related to substance: (1) the competition among governments to attract foreign investment, and (2) the growing alliance between business and government to foster national competitiveness. These alliances are, of course, strictly speaking a matter of process, but their effects are so substantial as to warrant treatment here.

The Quest for Foreign Investment. Research by Louis T. Wells, Jr., and Dennis Encarnation has established that

> competition among governments for foreign investment appears to be on the rise. Whether the context pits Ohio against Tennessee, Scotland against Ireland, Singapore against Taiwan, the story remains the same: numerous

governments, at all levels and on all continents are actively vying for the opportunity to serve as hosts for foreign firms.[69]

The reasons are straightforward: countries need to earn foreign exchange with which to pay increasingly anxious lenders, they want access to world technology and markets in order to grow and improve their standard of living, and they want to press their business managers into becoming more competitive. The rules of admission of course differ widely. Albania and Burma, for example, exclude virtually all foreign investment.[70] The rest seek it, offering varying terms and conditions, carrots and sticks, in a variety of different ways.

Some conditions for investment relate to the idiosyncrasies of ownership philosophy. The Mexican government has steadfastly opposed foreign investment as a threat to its sovereignty. In recent years, however, its opposition has softened significantly, as the need for foreign exchange overwhelmed traditional ideological precepts. In the 1970s, the Indian government wanted to develop a domestic computer industry. It needed help from foreign firms, but insisted on Indian participation in ownership. IBM was unwilling to alter its policy of 100% ownership of subsidiaries, mindful of the consequences such a precedent would have elsewhere. There were a number of other multinationals to which the Indian government could—and did—turn.[71] (In the 1980s, as we shall see, IBM—like Mexico—was forced to change.)

In negotiations between a host government and a multinational corporation, success depends on the skill with which each organizes itself "to exploit its strengths and defend against its weaknesses."[72] Benjamin Gomes-Casseres notes that high among the skills necessary for the firm is the ability to collaborate with other companies to develop technologies or to integrate manufacturing operations. U.S. antitrust laws, and the practices that they encourage, have caused U.S. firms to be less experienced in cooperative ventures than are their Japanese and European rivals.[73]

Another necessary skill for firms involves coordination of foreign subsidiaries by the headquarters. The nature of foreign governmental policies and regulations and the relative importance of governmental relations in subsidiary management affect the extent to which each subsidiary may be coordinated centrally versus managed locally. In the case of local management, each subsidiary is responsible for its relations with government. IBM has moved in the direction of coordinated management because the "control issue was critical. Optimization of the whole system was not equal to optimization of each of the subparts."[74] Amir Mahini and Louis Wells cite the example of Xerox: "The first steps toward coordination in governmental relations began in a region where a common market had threatened the independence of decisions in different countries. One of the issues that had influenced the change in approach (away from diffusion of focus) involved conflicting positions in different subsidiaries with respect to tariffs."[75] As European governments have cooperated to develop a regional strategy with regard to computers and telecommunications, firms have also had to coordinate their national governmental strategies within a regional context.

Partnerships for National Competitiveness. Government-business collaboration to achieve national competitiveness has reached its most sophisticated form in Japan. The process has four components: government-business forums, administrative guidance, the involvement of government banks, and management personnel with government experience.

In 1987, there were 213 Japanese government-business councils. MITI sponsored twenty, the Ministry of Finance fourteen, other ministries the rest. Some were attached directly to the office of the prime minister, as in the case of the Advisory Group on Economic Structural Adjustment for International Harmony, chaired by Haruo Maekawa. In April 1987, the Maekawa Commission recommended a national goal of "steadily reducing the nation's current account imbalance to one consistent with international harmony." To achieve this goal, the report spoke of the "urgent need" to "seek to transform the Japanese economic structure into one oriented toward international coordination" by enhancing "the quality of the nation's standard of living."

The membership of these councils included scholars, industrial leaders, union leaders, and government officials. They meet about twelve times a year, and each meeting lasts about two hours. Although some councils are more or less permanent, most expire after two years. Each council has many subcommittees composed of junior people who meet often and are responsible for drafting reports.

The purpose of the council reports is, in the words of one participant, "to shape a context for action" by business and government, to define "a vague image," to "establish the basis for consensus."[76]

Although the councils are useful, some observers note their drawbacks. Membership tends to be stagnant and "old-fashioned" thinkers tend to dominate. MITI's council on energy policy, for example, has changed little over the past twenty years.[77]

Administrative guidance means government action, usually by MITI, that encourages companies to achieve an administrative aim. It is rarely, if ever, imposed by law. Indeed, law in Japan is notoriously weak. "It is like an heirloom samurai sword," writes Kawashima Takeyoshi. "It is to be treasured, but not used." In more than thirty years of antitrust enforcement, for example, there have been only six prosecutions and three were begun in 1949.[78] MITI's legal powers are relatively unimportant. Its influence derives from its ability to obtain funds and channel them for research and development in areas deemed critical to national competitiveness; the respect it enjoys in both government and business, which derives partly from its habit of careful consultation with industry leaders before making a decision (arm-twisting is most undesirable); and its skill at securing the cooperation of industry rivals for the achievement of joint projects. In 1980, for example, to promote the use of robots by small and medium-sized firms and to build a large domestic market that would

allow scale economies for its robot manufacturers, MITI encouraged the establishment of the Japan Robot Leasing Company, Ltd. (JAROL), a joint venture between twenty-four
robot manufacturers and ten insurance companies. The Japan
Development Bank provided JAROL with low-interest loans
to allow for easy leasing terms. By 1982, Japan had 31,900
industrial robots in place; the United States had 7,232.[79]

MITI is also useful in limiting excessive competition within
Japan. It acts as a mediator among Japanese firms—sta-
bilizing prices and minimizing price wars—and protects
Japanese firms against pressures from foreign governments.
But its guidelines are sometimes unreliable and inconsistent.
For example, before the Toshiba Machine Company, a member of the Mitsui group, was caught violating regulations of
the Coordinating Committee for Multilateral Export Controls
(COCOM) by selling eight computer-guided milling machines
to the Soviet Union, MITI guidelines had emphasized ways in
which Japanese companies would overcome COCOM rules.*
After the event, MITI guidance became much more strin-
gent.[80]

The Toshiba matter was a *cause célèbre* in the United
States, and even more of one in Japan where in July 1987
television viewers watched nine members of the U.S. Congress smashing a Toshiba radio with sledgehammers during a
press conference on Capitol Hill. The congressmen were ex-
pressing their anger over the fact that the Toshiba equipment
would allow the Soviets to mass-produce a more silent propel-
ler for their submarines and thus avoid detection by the
United States. This was especially galling to those who felt
that Japan was not paying full fare for U.S. military protection. One Pentagon official estimated that it would cost $30
billion for the United States to develop a device sensitive
enough to detect the more quiet-running Soviet subs.[81] (Although Toshiba's chairman resigned after a meeting of the

---

*There is no law against espionage in Japan. Foreigners caught spying are simply
put on a plane home.

Mitsui group chairmen, some Japanese wondered why the congressmen had not smashed any Norwegian products, since a Norwegian state-controlled enterprise, Kongsberg Vaapenfabrikk, was equally guilty of violating COCOM regulations and Norway, moreover, is a member of NATO.)

Furthermore, as Japanese companies have become global in their reach, with many foreign partners and alliances, MITI's guidelines often appear irrelevant or counterproductive. To quote Jitsuro Terashima of Mitsui, "We are always fighting MITI guidelines."[82]

Japanese government banks—the Industrial Bank of Japan, the Japanese Development Bank, and others—have a limited influence on business today compared to the important role they played in the 1960s and early 1970s. Nevertheless, although they are not used to sustain doomed industries, they are still a source of low-cost credit to help promote those vigorous industries important to Japan's future.

In the area of personnel, many big Japanese companies have ex-vice ministers of MITI or MOF in their top management. For example, Eme Yamashita, executive vice president of Mitsui, had been a career vice minister of MITI. This is very helpful in ensuring good relations and understanding between government and business.[83]

In the United States, the Conference Board reports that more than one-third of 185 CEOs it surveyed spent 25% to 50% of their time "dealing with various government agencies (legislative and executive) to influence legislation and policy and to assure their own compliance with government regulation."[84] This movement toward more involvement with government has been exacerbated by the pressures of international competition. Quick action by the Food and Drug Administration is critical to pharmaceutical companies seeking to place their innovations on the market. A respite from Japanese competition was essential to allow Harley-Davidson to regain at least some portion of the U.S. motorcycle business. Retaliatory action against the Brazilian government's protectionist computer strategy was, as we shall see, sought by some U.S. manufacturers.

Andrew S. Grove, president of Intel, one of America's leading semiconductor manufacturers, has decried the deterioration of the U.S. information-processing industry in the face of the Japanese strategy of initial home-market protection, followed by a highly focused attack to acquire market share at whatever cost, followed by the proclamation of free market principles. To remedy the situation, he writes that America needs "a new vision of competitive behavior." He continues, "Even though our preference and value system lean toward the individual, we need to think in terms of national entrepreneurship."[85] He goes on to advocate a manufacturing-development consortium and coordinated action with government.

The obstacles in the way of such an achievement are well exemplified in a study of the worldwide automobile industry made by Davis Dyer, Malcolm S. Salter, and Alan M. Webber. The automobile industry is the world's largest; it is a leading source of jobs and investment; and far from being a stodgy smokestack business, it is at the cutting edge of high technology, "creating not only the car of the future, but the factory of the future."[86] It is an industry, like information processing, in which government policies are strategically critical. "In Germany," says Salter, "the government is financing major automotive R&D programs; in France, the government provides major funding for Renault and a restructuring of the auto end parts industries; and in Japan, the government enacted special depreciation schedules for auto companies and provides . . . R&D assistance and export incentives."[87]

There can be no doubt about the importance of government policy to the auto industry in the United States: loan guarantees to save Chrysler; energy policy in the 1970s that kept gas prices low; federal fuel-economy, pollution, and safety standards; the promise of "deregulation" by President Reagan; voluntary restraint agreements to protect the industry from the Japanese; Federal Trade Commission permission allowing General Motors to enter into a joint venture with Toyota; and a ballooning federal budget deficit that raised interest rates, which in the early 1980s, increased the value of the dollar, cheapened imports, and hurt exports.[88] An observer from Mars might conclude that U.S. government and industry must be in close contact, if not cooperating, with one another, but nothing could be further from the truth. "Instead, both government and management have continued to espouse the philosophy of the past, of separate responsibilities, separate authority, and separate interests, while settling into the practice of business as usual in handling day-to-day regulatory matters and ignoring long-term questions of strategic thinking."[89] This behavior is not a function of a rogue bureaucracy or of a particular political party, but is very much a matter of the system.

Howard Paster, a United Auto Workers lobbyist, said, "The administration is willing to let the marketplace determine whether there is an auto industry and if so, what size and what level."[90] An OMB official in charge of regulation supported Paster's criticism, saying, "In the case of regulation, I almost never know how it will affect the different companies." Furthermore, in spite of the talk of deregulation, the evidence is that virtually none took place. Paster continues, "We have no ongoing auto policy in this country. There is no institutional continuity or capability in the government, no industry-driven consensus, no long-term thinking, and no congressional authority or capacity to look long range at autos."[91] And the industry doesn't want any. Said James Johnston, GM's vice president for industry-government relations, "GM is strongly in favor of the market. We believe we're better off if the government doesn't direct or impede where we're going, but sets a climate where the market can decide."[92] Nevertheless, FTC approval of the joint venture with Toyota (New United Motors Manufacturing, Inc. [NUMMI]) dictated how many cars the venture could make, how the price should be set, how long the venture could last (twelve years), and how the two partners could communicate.[93] Thus the government continued, as it always had, to play a critical role in the industry's development at the same time that both sides vigorously denied it. Ideology and practice were far apart.

In 1988, however, there were some signs of change. Robert J. Eaton, vice president in charge of General Motors technical staffs, spoke of the cooperative research efforts of companies and governments in Japan and Europe in automotive electronics. "If we in the United States are to gain and preserve a technological edge in this area, the time to make the commitment is now. . . . Building government and private sector consensus and cooperation . . . is always difficult, but we know it can be done once we all acknowledge that it should be done."[94]

New models, not too different from those of Japan, were also being created at the state level: investment incentives, special allocations for training and education, linkages among firms and with university research centers, infrastructure development—all to help the state compete against other states and nations.

Whatever the attitude of American corporate executives may be about the role of state and federal governments in the United States and about the most desirable relationships between business and those governments, there has been a dramatic increase in the time, money, and effort that business is investing in managing the relationships. As power in Washington has proliferated and dispersed, moving from the executive branch to several hundred congressional subcommittees, Washington's decisions have affected the lifeblood of companies. As a result, by 1987, 23,011 lobbyists were registered with the secretary of the Senate, forty-three for each member of the House and Senate. This compares with only 365 in 1961. During the same time period, the number of lawyers listed with the District of Columbia Bar Association climbed from 12,564 to 46,000, and journalists accredited to Congress or the White House from 1,522 to 5,250. Thirteen hundred corporations had Washington offices in 1986, compared to only 100 in 1968, and the number of trade association headquarters had tripled to 3,500 with a work force of about 80,000.[95]

At the same time, business, labor, and other interest groups have become more aggressively involved in the funding of political campaigns. In his book *The Power Game,* Hedrick Smith, Pulitzer Prize-winning former reporter for the *New York Times,* records "the skyrocketing growth of corporate political action committees" (PACs) that raise money and contribute to candidates of their choice. In 1974, there were eighty-nine corporate PACs. Ten years later they numbered 1,682. Overall, PAC donations increased from $8.5 million in 1974 to $132.2 million in 1986.[96]

ISSUES FOR MANAGERS

The managers of a corporation that has had a particular pattern of relationships with government may have a difficult time adapting to a different pattern. Even though it may be plainly rational to do so, old mindsets may get in the way.

Take, for example, a hypothetical American telecommunications company intent upon increasing its global market share. For years, its managers have dealt with Washington as a customer, a rate setter, a law enforcer. Government has been either a contractor or a setter of constraints, and always an adversary to be held at a distance in order to allow maneuvering room within which the corporation and its allies can organize to achieve their objectives. Lawyers and political infighters are prominent in the Washington office. Their principal task is to keep government out of the company's way, insulating the decision-making apparatus in headquarters from interference. But the Washington office is only marginally connected to that apparatus. Headquarters sets the firm's strategy, which the government affairs people are supposed to protect from governmental attack.

Now let us assume that the company is trying to sell its

services in areas of the world where government is a major player in determining the shape and purpose of the telecommunications market. The company's competitors have long been intimately tied to their respective governments, sharing purposes, conditioned to working with governmental bureaucracies. The American company may have superior products and services, but if it does not know how to establish appropriate relationships with governments, it will fail. It may need the assistance of the U.S. government in conducting the political and diplomatic negotiations that are often crucial in telecommunications decisions. It will need also to understand the ways in which foreign governments act as partners and players in the telecommunications business. Furthermore, it will need experience in understanding the bureaucratic power game at the heart of all government decision making. Without this understanding and experience, it will find itself at a disadvantage against competitors that have always thought of government as a partner and a player. It might even happen that its friends in foreign governments, respecting its superior products and mindful of its corporate habits, might inform the American company about its shortcomings in, for example, choosing local allies or designing its market offerings. It would be natural for such advisers to approach the company through its Washington office, supposing that to be the appropriate place to speak of governmental affairs. But the Washington office, even if it were understanding and sympathetic, would be poorly positioned in the corporate hierarchy to influence decisions at headquarters.

The foregoing raises a variety of questions for corporate managers: (1) Regarding information and intelligence: What is the best way to collect and analyze global data for making corporate decisions, and how is the product of such analysis best transmitted to corporate decision makers? In this respect, how are old mindsets about government and business reviewed and changed to reflect reality? (2) Regarding transition and transformation: How can firms that originate in individualistic settings reorient themselves to manage government relations in communitarian ones, and vice versa?

In the same vein, how can firms in individualistic countries prevent themselves from being exploited by those from communitarian countries? (3) Regarding organization: What is the most effective way for firms within an industry to organize themselves for governmental relations? Is it better to go it alone or to act jointly and cooperatively with others? (4) Regarding nationalism versus internationalism: In the face of seemingly inevitable global alliances among major corporations, how do firms manage the costs to particular nations? Are new and more vigorous transnational governmental bodies needed to provide more reliable standards of adjustment for those adversely affected by global competition?

These are questions the following chapters will address.

NOTES

1. Michael E. Porter, "Competition in Global Industries: A Conceptual Framework," in Michael E. Porter, ed., *Competition in Global Industries* (Boston: Harvard Business School Press, 1986), pp. 39–42.
2. Interviewed for BBC Television, *Horizon,* March 10, 1986, quoted in Stephen Wilks and Maurice Wright, eds., *Comparative Government-Industry Relations* (New York: Clarendon Press, 1987), p. 10.
3. These models are similar to the "governance" and "politics" model described in Joel D. Averbach, Robert D. Putnam, and Bert A. Rockman, *Bureaucrats and Politicians in Western Democracies* (Cambridge, MA: Harvard University Press, 1981), pp. 141–142.
4. For a more elaborate explanation of these paradigms, see George C. Lodge and Ezra F. Vogel, eds., *Ideology and National Competitiveness* (Boston: Harvard Business School Press, 1987), Chapter 1.
5. Ibid., Chapters 3–10.
6. Mikhail Gorbachev quoted in the *New York Times,* February 19, 1988, p. 1.
7. Chalmers Johnson, *MITI and the Japanese Miracle: The Growth of Industrial Policy, 1925–1975* (Stanford, CA: Stanford University Press, 1982), pp. 17–19.
8. The concept of "inward-looking" and "outward-looking" strategies was developed by Bela Belassa of the World Bank and is explained in Bruce R. Scott, *As If by an Invisible Hand* (preliminary title), Chapter 7, forthcoming. Scott also has a useful description of neo-mercantilism in that chapter.
9. John Zysman, Stephen Cohen, and Laura Tyson at the University of California at Berkeley must be credited with inventing the notion of

"created" comparative advantage. See, for example, Zysman and Tyson, *American Industry in International Competition* (Ithaca: Cornell University Press, 1983), pp. 422–427.

10. Pat Choate and Jayne Linger, "Tailored Trade: Dealing with the World as It Is," *Harvard Business Review* (January–February 1988): 86.

11. Paul R. Krugman, "Is Free Trade Passé?" *Economic Perspectives* 1, no. 2 (Fall 1987): 136.

12. Ibid., p. 139.

13. Ibid., p. 140.

14. Ibid., p. 141.

15. Quoted in Bruce R. Scott, "Japan as Number One?" #387-005. Boston: Harvard Business School, 1988, p. 10.

16. Johnson, *MITI and the Japanese Miracle,* p. 28.

17. Yoshiro Ikeda, former chairman of the board of Mitsui, quoted in Scott, "Japan as Number One?" p. 8. The point was confirmed by the author in an interview with Yotaro Kobayashi, president of Fuji Xerox, in December 1987.

18. Quoted in Scott, ibid., p. 9.

19. Ministry of International Trade and Industry, *Trends and Future Tasks in Industrial Technology—Developing Innovative Technologies to Support the 21st Century and Contributing to the International Community—Summary of the White Paper on Industrial Technology,* Tokyo, September 1988, pp. 3, 18.

20. Johnson, *MITI and the Japanese Miracle,* pp. 16, 18.

21. James McGroddy, speech to participants in the Advanced Management Program, Harvard Business School, October 31, 1987.

22. The Department of Defense Critical Technologies Plan, prepared for the Committee on Armed Services, U.S. Congress, May 1989, pp. ES1, 2.

23. Johnson, *MITI and the Japanese Miracle,* p. 17.

24. For a comparison of the industrial policies of Japan, France, Germany, Brazil, and Taiwan, see Jack N. Behrman, *Industrial Policies: International Restructuring and Transnationals* (Lexington, MA: D.C. Heath, 1984), Chapters 1–3.

25. Quoting the report of the Beveridge Commission, in Bruce R. Scott, "The Beveridge Plan and the Welfare State," #388-032. Boston: Harvard Business School, 1988, p. 6.

26. Andrew Shonfield, *British Economic Policy Since the War* (London: Penguin Books, 1958), p. 89, quoted in Stephen Blank, "Britain: The Politics of Foreign Economic Policy," in Peter J. Katzenstein, ed., *Between Power and Plenty: Foreign Economic Policies of Advanced Industrial States* (Madison: University of Wisconsin Press, 1978), p. 97.

27. Jorge I. Domínguez, "Revolution and Flexibility in Mexico," in Lodge and Vogel, *Ideology and National Competitiveness,* p. 271.

28. Porter, "Competition in Global Industries," p. 39.

29. Ibid., p. 53; and Amir Mahini and Louis T. Wells, Jr., "Government Relations in the Global Firm," in Porter, p. 291.

30. Helen V. Milner and David B. Yoffie, "Between Free Trade and Protectionism: Strategic Trade Policy and a Theory of Corporate Trade Demands," *International Organization* 43, no. 2 (Spring 1989): 240.

31. Michael Kreile, "West Germany: The Dynamics of Expansion," in Katzenstein, ed., *Between Power and Plenty,* p. 199; see Clyde V. Prestowitz, Jr.   *Trading Places* (New York: Basic Books, 1988) for an insightful account of interagency dispute on trade matters in the United States.

32. Thomas K. McCraw, "From Partners to Competitors," in Thomas K. McCraw, ed., *America versus Japan* (Boston: Harvard Business School Press, 1986), p. 25. Karel van Wolferen, a Dutch journalist who has lived most of the past twenty-five years in Japan, argues that the diffusion of power is so great that Japan lacks "anything that can really be called a state." Searching for it, he says, is "like groping in the proverbial bucket of eels." [Karel van Wolferen, *The Enigma of Japanese Power* (New York: Alfred A. Knopf, 1989), pp. 26, 47.]

33. Institute of Politics, John F. Kennedy School of Government, *Proceedings,* Harvard University, 1986–1987.

34. See George C. Lodge, *The New American Ideology* (New York: Alfred A. Knopf, 1976), p. 116.

35. Samuel P. Huntington, *American Politics: The Promise of Disharmony* (Cambridge, MA: Harvard University Press, 1981), p. 39.

36. Steven Kelman, *Regulating America, Regulating Sweden: A Comparative Study of Occupational Safety and Health Policy* (Cambridge, MA: MIT Press, 1981), p. 119.

37. Ibid., p. 115.

38. This is a modification of criteria for a strong government suggested by Stephen D. Krasner in Katzenstein, *Between Power and Plenty,* p. 60.

39. McCraw, "From Partners to Competitors," p. 24.

40. *The Economist,* November 28, 1987, p. 72.

41. Katzenstein, *Between Power and Plenty,* p. 200.

42. John Zysman, *Governments, Markets and Growth* (Oxford: Martin Robertson, 1983), p. 256.

43. K. Dyson, "The Politics of Economic Recession in West Germany," in A. Cox, ed., *Politics, Policy and the European Recession* (London: Macmillan, 1982), p. 39, quoted in Wilks and Wright, *Comparative Government-Industry Relations,* p. 40.

44. See Christopher S. Allen in Lodge and Vogel, *Ideology and National Competitiveness,* p. 80.

45. Katzenstein, *Between Power and Plenty,* p. 17.

46. *The Economist,* December 5, 1987, p. 76.

47. Ibid., p. 77.

48. Janice McCormick, "France: Ideological Divisions and the Global Reality," in Lodge and Vogel, *Ideology and National Competitiveness,* pp. 55–78.

49. Ibid., p. 56.

50. Zysman in Katzenstein, *Between Power and Plenty,* p. 267.

51. Ibid., p. 269.

52. Katzenstein, *Between Power and Plenty,* p. 20.

53. Andrew Shonfield, *Modern Capitalism* (Oxford: Oxford University Press, 1965), p. 88, quoted in Katzenstein, *Between Power and Plenty,* p. 101.

54. Richard Darman, undersecretary of the Treasury, speech at the Harvard Business School, 1987.

55. See Michael S. Dukakis and Rosabeth Moss Kanter, *Creating the Future* (New York: Summit Books, 1988) for additional examples.

56. See Alfred D. Chandler, *Strategy and Structure: Chapters in the History of American Industrial Enterprise* (Cambridge, MA: MIT Press, 1962).

57. David B. Yoffie offers an interesting example of structure restraining strategy in the United States of the late 1980s. Institutional arrangements to make and enforce trade policy were designed to promote free trade. Increasingly, Congress was forcing a departure in the direction of a strategic trade policy—"contingent protectionism"—to promote competitiveness. To be effective, such a departure requires an entirely new and different structure. See Yoffie, "American Trade Policy: An Obsolete Bargain?" in John E. Chubb and Paul E. Peterson, eds., *Can the Government Govern?* (Washington, DC: The Brookings Institution, 1989), p. 137.

58. Bernard Wysocki, Jr., "Manager's Journal," *The Wall Street Journal,* December 14, 1987.

59. See George C. Lodge, *The American Disease* (New York: Alfred A. Knopf, 1984), pp. 283–284, for an elaboration of these questions.

60. See Davis Dyer, Malcolm S. Salter, and Alan M. Webber, *Changing Alliances* (Boston: Harvard Business School Press, 1987), pp. 242–243, for a description of the Toyota-GM plant at Fremont, CA, and its innovative human-resource management practices.

61. Adolf A. Berle, Jr., and Gardiner C. Means, *The Modern Corporation and Private Property* (New York: Macmillan, 1933), pp. 8, 281, 285, 357.

62. J. Hirschmier and T. Yui, *The Development of Japanese Business, 1600–1980,* 2d ed. (London: George Allen and Unwin, 1982), pp. 11, 19, 41, 123.

63. Michael Jensen, "Eclipse of the Public Corporation," *Harvard Business Review* (September–October 1989): 61–74.

64. McCraw, *America versus Japan,* pp. 79–86; and Michael Y. Yoshino and Thomas B. Lifson, *The Invisible Link: Japan's Sogo Shosha and the Organization of Trade* (Cambridge, MA: MIT Press, 1986). See also, Alfred D. Chandler, Jr., and Herman Daems, eds., *Managerial Hierarchies: Comparative Perspectives on the Rise of the Modern Industrial Enterprise* (Cambridge, MA: Harvard University Press, 1980).

65. See Joseph L. Bower, *When Markets Quake* (Boston: Harvard Business School Press, 1987), for an informative discussion of the desirability, if not the necessity, of industry collaboration in the face of worldwide overcapacity such as that faced by chemicals, automobiles, and semiconductors.

66. See Joseph L. Badaracco, Jr., *Loading the Dice: A Five-Country Study of Vinyl Chloride Regulation* (Boston: Harvard Business School Press, 1985).

67. Robert B. Reich, "Why the U.S. Needs an Industrial Policy," *Harvard Business Review* (January–February 1982): 74–81. See also Richard H.K. Vietor, *Energy Policy in America Since 1945: A Study of Business-Government Relations* (New York: Cambridge University Press, 1984),

for an analysis of government-business relations in the energy industry; and David Vogel, "Government-Industry Relations in the United States: An Overview," in Wilks and Wright, *Comparative Government-Industry Relations,* p. 91.

68. Theodore J. Lowi, *The End of Liberalism: The Second Republic of the United States,* 2d ed. (New York: W.W. Norton, 1979), p. 279.
69. Dennis J. Encarnation and Louis T. Wells, Jr., "Sovereignty En Garde: Negotiating with Foreign Investors," *International Organization* 1 (Winter 1985): 47.
70. Ibid., p. 55.
71. Benjamin Gomes-Casseres, "Ownership Negotiations Between MNCs and Host Governments," working paper #88-019. Boston: Harvard Business School, 1987, p. 8.
72. Ibid., p. 3.
73. Benjamin Gomes-Casseres, "Competing Abroad: Jointly or Alone?" working paper #88-018. Boston: Harvard Business School, 1987, p. 4.
74. Ibid., p. 24.
75. Mahini and Wells, "Government Relations in the Global Firm," in Porter, *Competition in Global Industries,* p. 307.
76. Interview with Jitsuro Terashima of Mitsui USA, in New York City, December 9, 1987.
77. Ibid.
78. Quoted in John O. Haley, "Sheathing the Sword of Justice in Japan: An Essay on Law Without Sanctions," *Journal of Japanese Studies* (Summer 1982): 265, 269.
79. George C. Lodge and Richard E. Walton, "The American Corporation and Its New Relationships," *California Management Review* (Spring 1989): 9–24.
80. C. Johnson, "Japanese-Soviet Relations in the Early Gorbachev Era," *Asian Survey* (November 1987): 1159; and Terashima interview.
81. George R. Packard, "The Coming U.S.–Japan Crisis," *Foreign Affairs* (Winter 1987/88): 248.
82. Terashima interview.
83. Ibid.
84. Gordon Donaldson and Jay Lorsch, *Decision-Making at the Top* (New York: Basic Books, 1983), p. 13; see also David B. Yoffie and Sigrid Bergenstein, "Corporate Political Advantage: The Rise of the Corporate Political Entrepreneur," *California Management Review* (Fall 1985): 125, 126.
85. Andrew S. Grove, "Forum," *New York Times,* December 13, 1987. For a persuasive argument in favor of such an approach, see Don E. Kash, *Perpetual Innovations: The New World of Competition* (New York: Basic Books, 1989).
86. Dyer, Salter, and Webber, *Changing Alliances,* p. x.
87. Malcolm S. Salter, "Negotiating Corporate Strategy in Politically Salient Industries," #384-141. Boston: Harvard Business School, 1988, p. 7.
88. Dyer, Salter, and Webber, *Changing Alliances,* pp. 211, 212.
89. Ibid., p. 212.

90. Ibid., p. 213.
91. Ibid., p. 217.
92. Ibid., p. 216.
93. Ibid., p. 221.
94. GM Press Release, May 3, 1988, p. 3.
95. Hedrick Smith, *The Power Game: How Washington Works* (New York: Random House, 1988), pp. 29–31.
96. Ibid., p. 32; and Yoffie and Bergenstein, "Corporate Political Advantage."

CHAPTER 2

Industrial Policy Comes to America

He had campaigned against it. His mentor had condemned it. Nevertheless the new president, George Bush, found himself saddled with it. "Industrial policy,"* that excrescence of Democratic Liberalism, had finally come to America.

Unwanted and unwelcome, it had slipped in during the waning months of the Reagan administration to cope with the deterioration of the country's semiconductor industry. Now here it was again at the heart of the controversy kindled in March 1989 by the $8-billion FSX fighter plane deal. Goaded by Congress as well as his own commerce secretary, President Bush had to decide: Is U.S. competitiveness in aerospace important?

In August 1987, the governments of Japan and the United States had agreed to cooperate in building 130 new fighters to replace Japan's aging F-1. In January 1989, the agreement was affirmed by the contractors, General Dynamics and Mitsubishi Heavy Industries Ltd. (The planes were to be extensively modified versions of General Dynamics' F-16.) Under the agreement, the Japanese would build the planes, buying critical technology and perhaps some engines from the Americans. The deal had been hatched in the Departments of Defense and State. However, the new commerce secretary,

---

*In fact, of course, it was by no means new. As noted in Chapter 1, it had been around since the nation began in agriculture, railroads, housing, shipbuilding, and more, but never in the name of competitive survival in the world economy.

Robert A. Mosbacher, together with many members of Congress were concerned that America was surrendering one of its few remaining high-tech redoubts—aerospace. (The industry employed 860,000 Americans with exports exceeding imports by $17.9 billion in 1988. It was the country's largest exporter.)* Proponents argued that it was the best arrangement possible under the circumstances. Without it Japan would simply go it alone.[1]

The FSX (Fighter Support Experimental) affair seemed at long last to have awakened the White House to what other elements of government and many business leaders had long since realized: in virtually every field it chose—steel, television, autos, integrated circuits, telecommunications—Japan was moving better and faster than America. Furthermore, Europe, which only a few years before had been diagnosed as sclerotic, was showing signs of doing so as well.

Most irritating was that the secret weapon of our competitors turned out to be industrial policy: a set of procedures through which government and business join together to determine community needs, organize and allocate resources to fulfill them, and adopt in particular a wide range of instruments to achieve global competitiveness. Perhaps more irritating was the revelation that the United States, far from being free of such policy, was the victim of what was probably the world's least competitive one, a policy that had subsidized consumption, driven savings and investment to ridiculously low levels, kept industry divided and fragmented, produced high capital costs, and discouraged competitive practices in the workplace.

Finally, it seemed, the issue was clear. Much as traditionalists in the White House argued to the contrary, the issue was not whether America should have an industrial policy. The fact was the country already had a bundle of such policies and taken together they were a competitive disaster.

---

*The 1988 U.S. trade deficit was $129.8 billion, of which $52.1 billion was with Japan. Six years earlier, the U.S.–Japan deficit had been $25 billion.

The issue was: What should U.S. industrial policy be? Who should determine it? And how should it be implemented?

AMERICA'S CHOICES

The choices were implicit in the FSX debate. Simply put, the first choice was to let nature take its course: let America be America, multinationals be multinational, and Japan be Japan. In 1988, this course was in full swing with corporate America spending $42 billion abroad on plants and equipment, a figure that had been rising steadily for three years.[2] The alternative was to reorganize American industrial policy, concentrate resources on critical growth sectors, and rebuild the nation's capacity to compete in world markets, especially in those high-tech, high-value-added industries of tomorrow on which a rising standard of living depended.

The two choices are not, of course, mutually exclusive. In many cases, letting nature take its course was necessary to bring manufacturing closer to the growing consumer markets of Asia and Europe, to circumvent trade and tariff barriers, and to access low-cost labor. It was a question of emphasis and purpose. For some, it was the competitiveness of the company, not the country, that counted. Gilbert Williamson, president of NCR Corporation, for example, said, "I was asked the other day about United States competitiveness, and I replied that I don't think about it at all. We at NCR think of ourselves as a globally competitive company that happens to be headquartered in the United States."[3] But by itself, this course meant shrinkage at home as American firms went abroad through a myriad of global strategic alliances, taking with them jobs, learning, skill development, and incomes. It meant a worsening trade deficit and increased dependence on foreign borrowing. Thus, those who were mindful of the need to nurture a strong U.S. economy were augmenting globalization by moving also in the direction of domestic reorganization. This meant staying home and changing; it meant cooperation among firms in related industries to sustain the "food chain" of customers, manufacturers, and suppliers on which all depended; it meant working closely with government and obtaining from it relief from antitrust strictures, coordination of the food chain, and funds. It amounted to industry-led industrial policy, but it was a policy that depended on government for success.

COLLABORATION AND PARTNERSHIP

In 1989, a number of industries that were under pressure from foreign competition were moving in the direction of this second choice. The movement had two separate but related parts. The first was industry collaboration, consortia to pool resources for more efficient research and development; the second was partnership with government to secure industry competitiveness in the world economy.

The Commerce Department reported that 123 consortia, whose concerns ranged from cement to superconductivity, had registered under the 1984 National Cooperative Research Act, which gave them protection against antitrust prosecution. In the words of Lansing Felker of Commerce, these consortia were "an attempt to compensate for Japan's structural advantages. It's the only way we can compete with Japan's vertical integration."[4]

The 1984 act implied that it was in the national interest for companies to collaborate and thus to violate the original tenets of the antitrust laws. It was, in effect, an endorsement of industrial policy, but it was only an implicit endorsement, because the act was silent about what "national interest" was supposed to be served or who should decide what it was. In Japan, where industrial policy is inseparable from consortia, the definition of the national interest is a function of government acting closely with business. But most of the 123 U.S. consortia had no government participation.

At the same time industry associations, such as the Health Industry Manufacturers Association, the Semiconductor Industry Association, and the American Electronics Association, were becoming increasingly important as industry strategists. They sought governmental policies and relationships that were more conducive to global competition, arguing implicitly, if not explicitly, that the national interest was at stake. But government had not determined what that interest was. Indeed, government's several departments and agencies each had their own, often quite different, interpretation and there was no effort to reconcile them.

The case of high-definition TV (HDTV) is an example. Its sales are projected to be $170 billion by 2010; it will be among the largest consumers of semiconductors and thus a critical segment in that industry's food chain. In 1986, at an international meeting called to determine HDTV standards, the Federal Communications Commission and the State Department, representing U.S. interests, endorsed the Japanese standards. Since those two agencies represented the world's largest television market, their endorsement meant that the Japanese standards became the world standards. All competitors would have to use Japanese designs, giving Japan substantial control of the technology.

State's interests were political and diplomatic. The FCC represented broadcasters who wanted standards set quickly because HDTV would lower programming production costs and improve quality. Where was the Office of the U.S. Trade Representative (USTR) and Commerce? Was no one in government concerned about forfeiting a $170-billion market to foreign manufacturers? The problem lay in the historic relationship between the U.S. television industry and government, a relationship that was premised on broadcast regulation, not on trade or manufacturing or competitiveness.

Recalling the events, an official of the USTR said, "We got a call from the European Commission asking why in the world we were endorsing the Japanese standard. Didn't we see how this would devastate our trade balance and destroy our electronics food chain? At the time we didn't even know what HDTV was. The Europeans already had an industry consortium in place with $200 million of government subsidies, and the Japanese had a working system which had been developed by a consortium started in 1981 backed by $500 million of government money."[5]

In September 1988, the FCC subsequently reversed its position by ruling that the HDTV standard must be compatible with the current television system. Since the Japanese HDTV system was designed to make the previous generation of sets obsolete, the FCC was creating a window of opportunity for the dozen or more other system designs in development, including Europe's MAC system. By the end of the year, the U.S. development effort was still fragmented and uncoordinated. The government held several interagency meetings but did nothing.

In 1989, a number of companies, including IBM, called for a consortium and the new secretary of commerce and several members of Congress sought action. The American Electronics Association asked for $1.35 billion in federal grants, loans, and guarantees from the Pentagon and other agencies, arguing that the national interest was at stake. By summer, the Commerce Department's initiative had hit a snag in the White House where the Office of Management and Budget, the Council of Economic Advisers, and key staff members were opposed to the principle of aiding a single industry. Defense, in particular the Defense Advanced Research Projects Agency (DARPA), took a contrary view. It had no difficulty drawing a distinction among industries in terms of their contribution to the national interest. Advanced electronics was more important than clothes pins. DARPA's dynamic director, Craig Fields, had already committed $30 million for the development of high-resolution flat-screen video display, a key component of HDTV, and was offering more. But this raised questions about Defense's interest. If it was military, the results might well not contribute to commercial competitiveness.

Although the bulk of DOD's research budget—about $37 billion a year—went for strictly military purposes, DARPA's $1.3 billion was divided about evenly between commercial and military projects. This division reflected the agency's mission, which was to ensure the nation's technological supremacy and prevent shocking surprises such as occurred when the USSR launched Sputnik in 1958. DARPA itself undertakes no research; it stimulates, funds, and manages research on projects it considers important. The projects are implemented by others, mostly commercial firms and universities. Frequently, DARPA plays a brokering role between the venture-capital industry and high-tech firms.

The military versus commercialization issue worked in reverse for biotechnology, where the United States commanded 90% of the world market. Defense had less interest in biotech than in electronics. Government regulated the industry, but was not heavily involved in its development. However, both Japan and Europe had targeted biotech as a strategic industry. Earle H. Harbison, Jr., president of Monsanto Company, a leading U.S. biotech firm, felt this put America at a competitive disadvantage:

> The Japanese government is doing all it can to catch and surpass the United States. . . . We cannot assume that solely because we have led in the development of genetic engineering up to now that we in the United States will continue to hold this position and be the ones to profit from this technological revolution. Remember the electronics industry. . . . We need government officials at all levels to implement a regulatory process that is safe and effective but that moves with alacrity. . . . The U.S. biotechnology industry must work together for the commercialization of products or it will be done by other countries and we will be buying their products—and soon.[6]

Harbison was crying out for an improved relationship with government and a mechanism to mobilize the industry. Unfortunately, biotech did not have a military connection and consequently it had little government support apart from DARPA's interest. As Japan and Europe began to make inroads in biotech, how would America respond? Would the industry require a national biotech strategy?

The semiconductor industry, under siege from Japan, took a

giant leap in the direction of a national strategy with the establishment in 1988 of Sematech, a nonprofit consortium of fourteen leading U.S. microelectronics firms, including IBM and AT&T, created to develop the manufacturing knowledge required to regain American leadership in semiconductors. Government pledged $500 million over five years to the enterprise, to be matched by the same amount from its members. The government sponsor was the Defense Advanced Research Projects Agency.

Since Sematech was a first* for America, its origins and evolution provide important insights into the problems of managing consortia and new relationships with government.

THE FOOD CHAIN

In 1947, William B. Shockley and a team of Bell Laboratory engineers invented the solid state transistor. Thus was born the semiconductor—or chip—industry, which by 1988 had worldwide sales of $50 billion. U.S. semiconductor manufacturers were of two kinds: "merchants" that produced chips for sale to other companies, and "captives" that produced them primarily for internal use. U.S. merchants included Motorola, Texas Instruments, Intel, and National/Fairchild. In 1987, there were close to 200 U.S. merchants, employing some 250,000 people; most were very small. Captives included IBM, AT&T, DEC, Hewlett-Packard, and Delco Electronics.

Chipmakers of both kinds were part of an elaborate industrial ecosystem, a food chain upon which all were dependent. Upstream were the makers of equipment for chip manufacturing and testing—Perkin-Elmer, General Signal, and 700 others, most having sales of less than $10 million—and silicon manufacturers, like Monsanto, which in 1988 was the only independent U.S. producer of silicon wafers. (Later, as

---

*It was first in several ways: membership included IBM and AT&T; it had 50% government funding; its focus was on manufacturing technology; and it was nonprofit.

we shall see, Perkin-Elmer announced its withdrawal from the business and Monsanto sold its wafer plant to a German firm.) Equipment makers relied heavily on foreign sales since less than 50% of their market was domestic. Downstream, chipmakers serviced the $400-billion worldwide electronics industry, including manufacturers of computers, telecommunications, electronics in consumer goods, industrial products, and military weaponry.

Unlike its Japanese and European counterparts, the U.S. semiconductor food chain was highly fragmented, composed of many hundreds of mostly small companies. U.S. electronics and computer firms—even those who made their own chips, like IBM and AT&T—bought semiconductors from independent producers in the United States and, increasingly, in Japan. By contrast, Japanese chip users, such as Hitachi and Toshiba, not only made all their own chips but were also major exporters. These Japanese firms had close working relationships with equipment and materials (E&M) suppliers, which allowed them to share proprietary information and to cooperate. In the United States, relations between semiconductor firms and their suppliers were marked by mistrust and antagonism. In Europe, the large electronics companies such as Philips, Siemens, and Thomson were, like their Japanese competitors, also producers of chips for internal use and for export. They, however, depended heavily on U.S. and Japanese E&M suppliers.

There are many varieties of semiconductors, but dynamic random access memory (DRAM) chips set the pace for progress in semiconductor technology because their key components more readily permit feature reduction, which increases the chip's power more easily compared to complex logic chips. Between 1975 and 1988, the U.S. share of the world merchant DRAM business declined from nearly 100% to less than 8%, most having been taken away by Japanese firms. Overall, the U.S. share of the merchant semiconductor market declined from 60% in 1975 to 39% in 1987; during the same period Japan's rose from 20% to 48%. (Europe held steady at 11% of the market and Korea was gaining with 6%; see Figure 2-1.)

Figure 2-1　*World Semiconductor Production by Region*

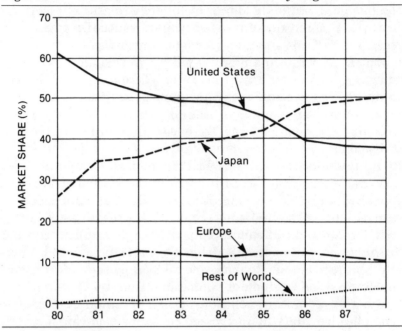

Source: Dataquest, PREL '88.

It was to recover from the withering Japanese attack that the U.S. semiconductor industry developed the idea for Sematech in 1986. To understand Sematech and to evaluate its chances for success, it is necessary to look more closely at Japan's spectacular performance, and especially at the relations between the Japanese government—in particular the Ministry of International Trade and Industry—and business.

COOPERATION FOR COMPETITIVENESS IN JAPAN

In 1965, Japan had virtually no computer industry. MITI and the leaders of the electronics industry decided that to meet Japan's national goals—community needs—for full employment and a rising standard of living Japan had to become a leader in computer manufacturing.[7] As in other key industries such as steel and autos, the nation decided that it had to work up the ladder of technology to attain world leadership in those industries that would eventually produce big financial returns as well as the learning and skills required to keep moving into more advanced sectors. Success in one industry was the building block for success in another; stop building and you slid backward. As was suggested in Chapter 1, the Japanese were unwilling to accept the Western notion of comparative advantage. They were determined to *create* an advantage and to keep doing so.[8]

By the mid-1970s, Japan had developed a computer industry, but it was small—scarcely 5% of the world market—and well behind the world leaders, especially IBM, which still had almost 50% of the Japanese market. Furthermore, IBM was moving ahead fast. MITI planners were particularly alarmed when they read of IBM's hitherto secret plans for a "Future System" of computers to be introduced in the 1980s (generously revealed to them in transcripts from the U.S. antitrust suit against IBM). In addition, Japanese computer users were complaining about being forced to use second-rate Japanese products, and the United States was bringing increasing pressure to lower trade barriers.[9]

It was thus in an atmosphere of mounting crisis that the Japanese computer industry began consultations with MITI about what to do to catch up with IBM. The industry was divided into two groups: the Electronic Industry Promotion Association, composed of seventy to eighty relatively small companies, and the five mainframe manufacturing giants, Hitachi, Fujitsu, Toshiba, NEC, and Mitsubishi. Because the ruling Liberal Democratic Party (LDP) had made it clear that it would not help individual companies, each of the big firms selected partners from the association, resulting in five partnerships.[10]

In April 1976, the Very Large-Scale Integrated Circuit Technology Research Association (VLSI/TRA) was established to produce a better chip. Its members included the five giant companies. MITI's role was crucial: it was to ensure that the major players participate and to force them to cooperate.

Cooperation did not come easily; at heart, the samurai firms were rivals, competing as they had for decades to serve the greater glory of Japan. MITI appealed to their patriotism but also threatened to deny them government funds.

Joseph L. Bower, in his study of the project, notes that one company manager said, "When we looked at the IBM Future System concept, we saw we would not be able to meet the threat without the kind of cooperation MITI wanted."[11]

VLSI/TRA was governed by a board of directors whose chairmanship rotated annually among the company presidents. The executive director who actually ran the board meetings was a widely respected former MITI official. The association consisted of six cooperative labs with a budget set annually, funded 50–50 by MITI and the member firms.

VLSI/TRA was given a four-year lifespan. It was nonprofit; its purpose was solely to help its members compete more effectively and more quickly. Researchers were borrowed from the five member firms and mandated to bring the results of the association's work back to their employers. Would the companies lend their best researchers? One company manager explained, "It was difficult to send our top people so we sent our good people." Project personnel were paid by the parent firm, according to their respective wage scales and standards. They did not know one another's salaries. Personnel evaluations were made by employee committees in the research sections and were then submitted to the employee's company.

There was intense competition among the labs and among teams from the different companies. The executive director had to use this spirit to promote but not inhibit progress. This he was able to do because he was from government and thus not associated with any company, and also because he devoted a great deal of time to the task, including drinking considerable quantities of sake with association personnel in the evening.

When VLSI/TRA closed up shop in 1980, its results stunned the world. It had developed a 256K RAM chip—a giant leap forward from the 64K chip with which it had begun—and it had applied for 1,000 patents in VLSI process technology. At

the second world conference on VLSI in 1982, the number of
Japanese papers equaled those from the United States.

The VLSI/TRA project was successful for the following reasons:

(1) It had clear objectives, which were understood and
shared by all participants.
(2) There was a sense of urgency, if not crisis. The timing
was right.
(3) Deadlines were set.
(4) The key players—the Big Five—were involved.
(5) There was at least a year of advance preparation and
planning.
(6) It attracted competent and strongly motivated personnel.

Although government provided substantial funding ($112
million in direct subsidies and more in tax breaks), perhaps
its most important role was facilitating the achievement of
these success factors. It clearly perceived and defined the national interest at stake. It coerced the key companies to cooperate and facilitated their ability to do so; it mediated and
moderated differences among them; and it kept the project's
standards high. Business alone could not have done these
things.

THE MICROELECTRONICS AND COMPUTER TECHNOLOGY
CORPORATION

For the next act in the drama, let us return to the
United States. In the spring of 1981, William Norris, chairman and CEO of Control Data, alarmed by Japan's strides,
sought to arouse enthusiasm in the computer industry for
cooperative research. "Microelectronics and computer firms in
the United States," he said, "are suffering from a combination
of scarce capital resources, high capital costs, and a rapidly
growing need for capital to develop and exploit appropriate

new technological possibilities. We are also faced with a critical shortage of relevant scientific and engineering talent." Noting the wasteful duplication among company research efforts, he proposed the establishment of a new, for-profit company, the Microelectronic Computer Technology Corporation (MCC), in which members would hold shares. He listed many benefits that would accrue to shareholders: broadening the scope of their research; joint development and availability of tools and services; heightened awareness of technology needs and traps; and optimum utilization of scarce technical talent.[12] MCC's objectives were similarly broad: basic and applied research, instrumentation development, packaging technology, prototype or pilot-plant operation, computer architecture research, and much more.[13]

Industry reactions were similar to those of Japan's Big Five when they were first approached by MITI. "The very essence of our business technology is the chips and microelectronics," said H. Glen Haney, vice president of Sperry Univac. "To willingly put the core of your R&D thrust outside your own control and share it with competitors is basically unattractive."[14]

Nevertheless, sixteen companies met in Orlando, Florida, on February 19, 1982, to explore the possibilities of cooperative research. Norris told them:

> The extent and nature of the Japanese challenge in microelectronics and computer industries has been widely discussed and documented in recent months. We have seen the U.S. semiconductor industry's preeminent position in semiconductor memories eroded in just a few short years, and, just a few months ago . . . the Japanese announced their intent to continue their market momentum in microelectronics while they mount a parallel effort to become the world's leader in computing by the end of the decade.[15]

A few months later, in August 1982, MCC was established with ten members. Neither IBM nor AT&T were among them.

Although the Defense Department had shown an interest in MCC and had sent a representative to the Orlando meeting, there was no government involvement. Expectations were high, however, especially when Admiral Bobby Ray Inman, former director of the National Security Agency and deputy director of the Central Intelligence Agency, agreed to serve as president and CEO. A native of Texas, Inman secured a $23.5-million package of inducements from that state, and MCC was located in Austin. By 1987, there were twenty company members, although before the year ended three of them had left, as had Inman. Grant A. Dove came from Texas Instruments in July 1987 to replace Inman, and he brought with him a commitment to launch MCC into research on superconductivity.[16] With an annual budget of $75 million and 450 employees, most of whom were hired directly by MCC, the company appeared to have defied the skeptics who said it would never work. But only a handful of the member companies have actually put MCC's findings to work. Some said it was too early to expect results. Others argued that it had been very difficult to transfer learning from MCC to the members.

Sanford L. Kane, vice president for IBM and its Sematech board representative, said the tech transfer problem resulted from several structural flaws in MCC. "Companies were allowed to participate on a project basis instead of being full-time members of MCC. This resulted in fragmented funding, consistency problems and recruiting headaches. The lack of a great number of assignees from member companies created two problems: companies didn't send their best people and members had tech transfer problems because assignees are a prime vehicle for information exchange."

Perhaps the most lasting effect of MCC was the legislation that was enacted to amend the antitrust laws in order to allow MCC to exist—the 1984 National Cooperative Research Act. The act was passed by Congress "to promote research and development, encourage innovation, stimulate trade, and make necessary and appropriate modifications in the operations of the antitrust laws." It provided that a joint R&D venture "shall not be deemed illegal per se under the antitrust laws." In 1985, twenty-one companies registered under the act as the MCC consortium.

Whatever history's ultimate evaluation of MCC, it was woefully insufficient to deal with the challenge Norris had clearly seen. Compared to the Japanese VLSI project, to which it was a response, MCC was insignificant. As previously noted, two of the country's major players—IBM and AT&T—were not even members. Indeed, we can imagine the raised eyebrows in the Justice Department had they joined in 1982. Certainly there was no MITI pressing for their inclusion.

MCC's objectives were broad and ill defined, its purpose unclear. Were its profits for itself, the shareholders as a group, or each member company? Was its purpose to engage in basic research that might not show returns for decades, or to disseminate knowledge that could be readily and quickly converted into competitive advantage? Was it concerned with the national interest—restoring America's competitive edge, bolstering our economy, tipping the trade deficit into balance? Its exemption from the rigors of the antitrust laws carried the clear implication that somehow America's community need was at stake. But that need, if it existed, was not precisely defined, so even if corporate members had wanted to serve it, doing so would have been difficult. This meant that they had little choice but to promote and protect their own company interests, which naturally was not conducive to cooperative endeavor. Early on, DOD seemed interested, which implied a military need was being served, and Norris saw a commercial competitive need. But alongside the single-minded, clear-cut, urgent purpose of the VLSI/TRA project—to catch IBM—MCC's mission was vague. It was certainly not the call to arms to which Japan's Big Five had rallied.

SEMATECH: THE PRODUCT OF REASSESSMENT

The year 1985 saw the beginning of a reassessment by the semiconductor industry and government of their roles and relationships—the beginning of industrial policy. Both began to realize the full extent to which America's microelectronics food chain had been ravaged, and what the implications were for the interests of companies and the nation. And although it would still be a few years before each realized that a remedy required a partnership, the germ of that idea was planted in July when the semiconductor industry began to explore an industry-government cooperative venture to meet the Japanese challenge. At first, many industry leaders were highly skeptical. In December, the deputy undersecretary of defense for research and engineering established a task force of the Defense Science Board (DSB), composed of distinguished leaders of business and science, to assess the importance of recent trends in the semiconductor industry. The task force was headed by Norman Augustine, president and CEO of Martin Marietta, a member of MCC. About the same time, Sanford Kane of IBM made a presentation to his company's top management that had an electric effect. "No one was aware of how bad the situation had gotten," he said.[17]

IBM, which had until then thought of itself strictly in global terms, realized that a strong U.S. base was essential to its competition with Japan. "We were one of the largest purchasers of chips in the world," said Kane. "We liked to source locally, and we didn't want to lose the option of buying U.S. chips. Besides, since most Japanese companies were both competitors of ours and suppliers of chips, we didn't want to be in a position where we had no choice but to be dependent on our competitors."

A second reason for IBM's concern was that it was the largest manufacturer of chips in the world. "We produce in-house those chips that give us a technological edge," said Kane. "To stay state-of-the-art, we needed to have sophisticated equipment with which to make semiconductors." IBM could not count on obtaining this equipment from its Japanese competitors. It needed a strong U.S. equipment industry from which to buy, and that depended on a strong U.S. chip industry. Without it, U.S. equipment makers would wither or be drawn abroad. "Thus, when we analyzed the numbers and saw that the U.S. semiconductor industry was dying, we knew we had to do something about it."[18]

In June 1985, Charles Sporck, chairman of National

Semiconductor, agreed at a meeting of the Semiconductor Industry Association (SIA) to forge a consensus among equipment makers, chip manufacturers, end users, and government officials. Sporck said at the time, "Our system creates design excellence, but nothing in regards to manufacturing." So the idea of Sematech was born, a cooperative venture to concentrate on manufacturing process know-how.

Government was not part of the original plan. "We thought the industry could do it alone and we were concerned about the strings that would be attached to government money," said Kane. "But I soon discovered industry was in no position to fund it alone." So the industry passed reluctantly from wanting no government involvement to accepting funds, and these only hesitantly. Later, as we shall see, this conception of government's role changed significantly.

The chances of government support were given a big boost in February 1987 when Augustine's DSB task force concluded that U.S. military forces depended heavily on technological superiority in electronics; that semiconductors were the key to such leadership; that competitive, high-volume production was the key to semiconductor advancement; and that this depended on strength in commercial markets. The report went on to state that U.S. leadership in commercial-volume production was in jeopardy, and warned that U.S. defense industries would soon depend on foreign sources for state-of-the-art technology in semiconductors. Since "the existence of a healthy U.S. semiconductor industry was critical to the national defense," the task force recommended that "DoD . . . encourage and actively support with contract funding [approximately $200 million per year] the establishment of a U.S. Semiconductor Manufacturing Institute formed as a consortium of U.S. manufacturers."[19]

Although industry support for Sematech was growing, there were still strong doubts. One small company president saw it as "a patriotic subsidy for large companies," reflecting concern about IBM's dominant role in Sematech and fear of other giants like AT&T, Digital Equipment Corporation, and National Semiconductor that were among the fourteen founders.

The SIA formally proposed Sematech immediately following the DSB report. Sporck became chairman of the SIA's steering committee on Sematech and directed the lobbying effort in Washington to secure government funds. In testimony before congressional committees, industry leaders offered a variety of reasons why the cooperative was in the national interest: "National economic well-being," said Robert Noyce, "to ensure the viability of the U.S. electronics industry," to maintain "a domestic source for the critical microelectronic products that are vital for our national defense."[20]

Duality of purpose—commercial and military—marked the passage of Sematech legislation through Congress. Introduced in the House in March 1987 as part of what was to become the 1988 trade bill, it was advocated as a means of enhancing commercial competitiveness in an important high-tech area, a purpose that was very much in vogue at the time. A few months later, it was introduced in the Senate as part of the defense bill. By October, both branches agreed on the defense route: DOD had the money, the supervisory personnel, and the votes. The Department of Commerce, which would have had to sponsor a purely commercial Sematech, did not.

The executive branch was, to say the least, lukewarm. Secretary of Commerce Malcolm Baldrige liked the idea but thought the program was too big—the final figure proposed was $100 million in government funds annually for five years. Also, he told the SIA, he was fighting too many other battles and just could not "carry the ball on this one."[21] The Office of Management and Budget was vehemently opposed, but acquiesced in the face of the defense interest. Said OMB's Dr. Tom Dorsey: "The total aggregate R&D budget for these [fourteen] semiconductor firms is over $4.5 billion. They claim Sematech is critical to their success; yet unless government puts in $100 million a year, it won't fly. Where are their priorities?"

There is a real danger of politicization here, a risk that this won't be done for scientific reasons, but instead will evolve into a giant entitlement program. Government shouldn't be allocating resources and making priorities, the market should.

Treasury and the President's Council of Economic Advisers supported Dorsey's views. The office of the USTR was divided, and President Reagan was silent. In the end, government opponents of Sematech concluded that it was not justified for economic or commercial reasons. As Dorsey noted, however, "If DoD says there is a national security problem, we can't argue with them."[22]

In February 1988, Sematech was assigned to DARPA. Craig Fields, then DARPA's deputy director (he became director in 1989), was made point man. Industry leaders were of two minds about DARPA's role. Some feared that the government would interfere in Sematech's management, while others valued the participation because DARPA employed some of the nation's best microelectronics scientists and engineers, and Fields himself was highly regarded. It was thought that the DARPA people might help evaluate Sematech's work, be useful in coordinating and integrating the rival members of the cooperative, help work out relationships between Sematech and the 200 small semiconductor firms who were not members but who stood to gain from its work, coordinate and mediate relations between the all-important equipment makers and Sematech, and help strengthen the connection between the chipmakers and the chip users in the electronics industry.

The press had a field day with the initial friction between DARPA and the industry. Fields had rejected Sematech's first operating plan, and Kane, who by then was chairman of Sematech's Executive Committee, admitted that they had not handled DARPA's expectations well. Fields said it was "really no big deal. I kick back all operating plans; that's the way this business works. It's an iterative process."[23]

Fields was, however, concerned about the level of cooperation among the Sematech members. He told Kane, "As companies, you have submitted advanced research projects for

DARPA funding that you haven't shared with each other. You've told us more than you have told each other."

By the summer of 1988, Fields had gained influence over Sematech's research agenda, but had no operational authority. However, Fields and Congress did have annual review of Sematech plans and government funding, so in fact, the Defense Department wielded quite a bit of power in the relationship. According to Sanford Kane of IBM, "Sematech's leaders are not only glad of DARPA's presence but anxious lest Fields's concerns for other matters, such as high resolution video display, divert his attention from Sematech." This was a sharp reversal in the industry's attitude toward the role of government.

BUT IS IT ENOUGH?

Early in 1989, the Department of Commerce issued its report on Sematech's first year of operation, applauding the progress that Robert Noyce (Sematech's first CEO) and his associates had made. They seemed well on the way to developing high-yield, factory-scale application of 0.35 micron production technology by 1993, which would put the United States ahead of the Japanese chipmakers by six to twelve months, and ahead of most U.S. merchant firms by three years. "The resulting advantage for Sematech's members could be substantial," said the report. (See Figure 2-2 for some thoughts about what it takes to make a consortium successful.)

The report identified some issues for future concern, including the strength of member commitment to the project; the extent and vitality of relationships between Sematech and its suppliers, the equipment makers; the willingness of firms to make the long-run investments required to translate leadership in technology into market share; and the impending threat of Europe's industry-government microelectronics consortium, the Joint Submicron Silicon Initiative (JESSI).[24] In addition, the report might have speculated about the future

Figure 2-2   *Elements for a Successful Consortium*

Industry-led: It's the only way to keep the venture market-focused, and leverage those with the competence; government can't do it. This requires strong industry associations like the SIA.

Timing: It must be right. The semiconductor industry talked about a Sematech type venture as early as 1982. Four years later, a downturn in sales and a nosedive in profits caused the industry to get serious. Perhaps they waited too long.

Top-management involvement: The worse thing to do is to send a bunch of technical people off to do their thing. You'll get back a lot of interesting science, but it will have little relevance to the market.

Membership: The right players have to join; e.g., IBM and AT&T in Sematech.

Entry fee: Membership must be priced according to its value. If it doesn't cost participants very much, it won't be a high priority.

Objectives: They must be clear and measurable. Deadlines are essential.

CEO: The venture must have a leader who is credible across the food chain and in Washington.

Career tracking: Sematech struggled to find a CEO. Many qualified candidates didn't want to leave the corporate ladder for fear of dropping out of sight. Companies must respect and reward such a position and should view it as a viable route to the top.

Employees: There must be a balance between assignees and permanent staff; assignees serve as a conduit to member companies (two-way information flow) and permanent staff provide continuity. Screening of assignees is essential in order to ensure a high-quality staff.

Culture: Bob Noyce claimed this was his toughest challenge. He had to bring together employees whose approaches varied greatly and who considered each other the enemy.

deployment of chip users. Consumer electronics firms had largely left the United States, and Japan was well ahead in the race for high-definition TV, which would be perhaps the biggest chip user of all. Since Japan and Europe were both determined to strengthen chip-making within their borders, they would presumably encourage their users to buy domestically, and might feel doubly justified in doing so since they were excluded from membership in Sematech, a U.S.-only club. (In June 1989, IBM and six other U.S. computer and chip manufacturers announced that they were forming U.S. Memory, a $1-billion consortium to manufacture four-megabit DRAMs with Sanford Kane as CEO. Legislation was before Congress to safeguard the new consortium from antitrusters, but the consortium fell apart early in 1990.)

No sooner was Commerce's report off the press than the fears it expressed began to materialize. In April 1989, Perkin-Elmer, the world's leading producer of chip-making equipment in the 1980s, announced it would abandon the business because of Japanese competition (Nikon Corporation of Japan was later reported to be interested in the plant).[25] For the first time, Japanese companies had captured the top three spots in the equipment business. Perkin-Elmer had slid from number two to number eight and was losing money on the business despite having only recently announced a new world-class generation of machines for transferring the pattern for a computer chip to silicon.[26]

Earlier, Sematech member Texas Instruments had announced plans to team up with Hitachi to share the costs of developing a sixteen-megabit memory chip to be used in high-definition TV and video cassette recorders, neither of which were made in the United States and in both of which Hitachi was a world leader.[27] Monsanto, the last remaining merchant producer of silicon wafers (the base on which integrated circuits are etched to form a chip) and a key supplier to Sematech, announced it was selling its wafer plant to a German firm, Heuls AG. Acting under a provision of the 1988 Trade Act, the president ordered the Committee on Foreign Investment in the United States (CFIUS), chaired by Trea-

sury, to investigate the impact of the deal on "national security." Ultimately it was approved.[28]

Reaction to the Perkin-Elmer announcement reflected the
two choices with which this chapter opened. To those who
favored letting nature take its course, it was a sensible decision in the best interests of the company's shareholders. Those
who favored industry collaboration and government partnership regarded it as an unfortunate continuation of the country's competitive erosion. Said Robert Noyce: "It is the continued saga that there is investment money available in
Japan but not in America. With the dismal saving rate we
have, much of the American manufacturing base is being de-
stroyed, and it doesn't bode well for the future." Similarly,
looking at the implications for the U.S. semiconductor effort,
Jerry Hutcheson, chief executive of VLSI Research Inc., a San
Jose market research firm, said: "I can't imagine that the
government would allow a foreign buyer to buy it [the Perkin-
Elmer equipment business]."[29]

On the other hand, Wall Street was delighted and filled
with praise for Perkin-Elmer's "intestinal fortitude." Said
Stephen J. Balog of Shearson Lehman Hutton, "I gained a
quantum leap in respect for [their] management. They've
done the right thing, given the reality of the 1980s and 1990s.
You'd better do just what you do really, really well, focus on
that and protect it."

Could Craig Fields and DARPA assume in the United
States at least part of the role played by MITI in Japan and
coordinate efforts to bolster the decrepit electronic food chain?
To improve the U.S. position, an integrative government
strategy was required, one that synthesized the military,
trade, diplomatic, and commercial interests of the country.
Furthermore, such a strategy would need to assess the
strengths of other countries and design an appropriate fit between them and the United States. In an age of interdependence, the United States could not go it alone; it required
foreign investments and alliances. Some, however, were better than others. Some contributed to the country's technological competitiveness; others detracted from it. A defense-

sponsored industrial policy might lack that perspective despite DARPA's duality of purpose. Sematech's nationalistic exclusivity was, after all, a result of defense involvement. Would this cause retaliation by angry foreigners? Would it close markets to the United States? Would it cut Americans off from vital innovations abroad?

An argument can be made that the United States had no other option. The semiconductor industry faced increasing R&D costs, tremendous scale requirements, and barriers to global markets. With only limited access to the Japanese market, for example, U.S. chipmakers were at a severe competitive disadvantage. The U.S. industry pressed its government to threaten Japan with closure of the domestic markets unless Japanese firms bought more American microchips.[30] The industry then created a U.S.-only consortium, Sematech, to improve manufacturing capability and strengthen the U.S. food chain. A buy-American-whenever-possible policy was required if the chain was to recover.

These actions prompted a similar response from the Europeans. JESSI was the brainchild of Philips, Siemens, Thomson, and thirty other smaller European companies. With a budget of about $4.5 billion over eight years, about four times that of Sematech, JESSI's aim was to invigorate the entire microelectronics food chain in Europe, from E&M suppliers to chipmakers to end users.

JESSI was part of Europe's drive for unity and global competitiveness, but deciding who would fund JESSI and what governing body would control it was proving more formidable than the technological agenda. Questions such as why Greece should support it when Germany stood to gain much more from the project, or how many Dutch jobs would be guaranteed for direct Dutch funding were slowing JESSI's progress. Clearly, in the long run, all of Europe stood to benefit from JESSI, but in the short run some countries would prosper more than others. JESSI's success, therefore, depended primarily on how effectively its business and governmental partners managed their relationship. Unfortunately, Brussels lacked the authority of a MITI. There was no historical heritage, no successful track record, no ideological commitment to bond the participants. Could JESSI create a forum that could substitute for MITI?

If JESSI got going, it seemed likely that Europeans would have a propensity—governmentally supported or not—to buy from Europeans to the fullest extent possible, and to discourage sales by Japanese and American firms. Again, Sematech's nationalism caused some to worry. Why should JESSI and the Europeans not be equally nationalistic?

Perhaps a strategic trade policy involving bilateral arrangements based on strict reciprocity was close at hand. Similar trends could be found in the commercial aircraft, machine tools, and telecommunications industries.[31] Trade policy was one tool that could be used to accomplish national objectives. But under a defense-centered industrial policy, DOD would assume trade responsibilities, among others, in order to improve our competitiveness. Would this begin to challenge the boundaries of DOD's charter? Certainly, it could mean a sharp change in defense procurement, which in 1989 clearly gave more weight to cost-cutting than to considerations of national competitiveness. One estimate was that $30 billion or roughly 15% of the defense budget flowed directly or indirectly to foreign companies. A report by the Center for Strategic and International Studies found that between 1980 and 1986 import penetration had increased in 104 of the 122 military-related categories for which data were available. Pentagon officials saw the trend as inevitable given the nation's commitment to free trade and budget constraints, and the strategies of other countries, especially Japan and Korea, to gain technological supremacy. The CSIS report questioned whether the "drive for greater efficiency through cost-saving may be counterproductive to the goal of reducing dependence on foreign sources," and, it might be added, the goal of recovering U.S. high-tech competitiveness.[32]

Clearly, there were problems with a defense-sponsored industrial policy. Sematech on its own was not enough; more was required to achieve its aims of a greater degree of integration of suppliers, producers, and users; a coordinated strategic trade policy; more funds; a lower cost of capital generally; and more concern over the dwindling supplies of highly educated engineers. Perhaps the way for the United States to go was to join with the Europeans in order to catch up to Japan, as was suggested by West Germany's minister of post and telecommunications regarding the development of high-definition television.[33] In any case, the need for an American economic strategy seemed essential. The issues were where it should be made, by whom, and according to what criteria.

AN AMERICAN MITI?

At the end of 1988, the Defense Science Board (DSB) urged the secretary of defense to take a more assertive role in setting economic policy to head off "an increasing loss of technological leadership to both our allies and adversaries." The board recommended an Industrial Policy Council, to be headed by the president's national security adviser, that would propose policies to strengthen industries that were militarily important. Others felt that the Council on Competitiveness established in the 1988 Trade Bill could be made into a strategy maker for American recovery. Another option was to enhance the office of the United States Trade Representative. When it took office in January 1989, the Bush administration wanted none of these. Industrial policy was anathema to the new team; national competitiveness was left to a task force of government officials headed by Vice President Dan Quayle.

Left unresolved at Sematech's creation was the issue of whether the purposes of such ventures were to be military or commercial. Perhaps, as the DSB's 1988 recommendation suggested, commercial competitiveness was a prerequisite for economic strength, which in turn was essential for national security. In that case, of course, there would be scarcely any constraint on the purview of the Department of Defense. Inasmuch as DARPA appeared to have highly respected talent, might it not be the most logical candidate for an American version of MITI? This idea had particular appeal because although it was ideologically troubling to grant government a planning role in industrial competitiveness, Americans had no such hang-up when it came to defense. So it might make sense for political reasons to construe economic competitiveness as a security problem, which of course it surely was. On the other hand, this course might give short shrift to other industries, such as biotechnology, in which the defense connection was more tenuous. If DARPA was to be a MITI of some sort, perhaps it would be best placed outside the defense orbit. But where could DARPA be safely placed? Its $1.3-billion annual spending was well screened by DOD's $300-billion budget, whereas it would be both overwhelming and vulnerable in a department like Commerce, for example. Furthermore, DARPA, a wild card in Defense, was supposed to safeguard the nation's technological capability, which gave it a military *and* a commercial purview.

By the end of 1989, the role of DARPA and the surrounding issues of a high-technology strategy to recover U.S. competitiveness had become a matter of intense controversy in Washington. With unexpected speed, the Cold War had faded and the struggle for power in the world had become economic rather than military. The greatest danger to the security of the United States was the erosion of its industrial base, and the United States was alone among the world's industrial nations in having no strategy to ensure its economic position in the world. It was falling behind in critical technologies of the future on which its standard of living and economic strength would depend.

DARPA and Sematech were in place but in jeopardy. President Gorbachev had done much to destroy military security as a politically satisfying justification for anything, including DARPA's programs. The White House budget-cutters were demanding reductions in DOD expenditures. The old ideologues were reiterating their familiar dogmas about the invisible hand and free markets. At the same time, however, two eminent groups of economists, industry leaders, and government officials warned that the nation faced dire economic con-

Figure 2-3   *World Production of DRAMS by Region*

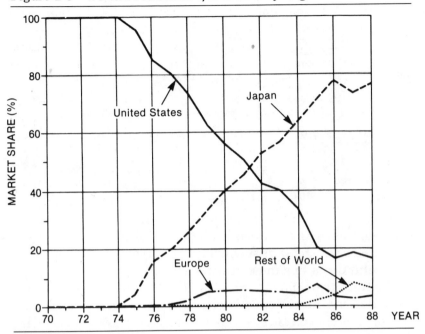

Source: Dataquest, PREL '88.

sequences unless the government adopted a far larger and more extensive strategy to save the electronics industry. The Economic Policy Institute reported that the failure of American industry to participate in high-definition television and the related industries of semiconductors, computers, and video displays would result in a trade deficit of $225 billion for those industries alone in the year 2010, as well as the loss of two million jobs. The National Advisory Committee on Semiconductors recommended an immediate increase of $100 million a year in financing for Sematech and extensive efforts to bolster the battered electronics food chain, lower the cost of capital, and reestablish a consumer electronics industry in the United States. The committee's chairman, Ian Ross, president of AT&T's Bell Laboratories, said, "Every trend you look at . . . is in the wrong direction." (See Figures 2-3 and 2-4.) Especially serious was the decline of the companies who make

Figure 2-4   *Leading Chip Producers' Revenues ($ millions)*

1973		1978		1983		1988	
Texas Inst.	65	Intel	283	*NEC*	786	*NEC*	3,114
AMI	56	Texas Inst.	238	Intel	720	*Toshiba*	2,546
Intel	41	*NEC*	183	Motorola	697	Intel	2,328
Rockwell	40	Motorola	143	*Hitachi*	638	*Hitachi*	1,885
Mostek	39	*Hitachi*	139	Texas Inst.	572	*Fujitsu*	1,437
NEC	37	Mostek	125	*Toshiba*	458	*Mitsubishi*	1,399
Hitachi	35	National	95	*Fujitsu*	406	Motorola	1,399
RCA	35	*Toshiba*	88	Mostek	315	Texas Inst.	1,271
National	21	AMD	71	National	280	*Matsushita*	882
Mil	20	AMI	71	*Mitsubishi*	247	*Oki*	841
Total Market	591		2,332		7,951		26,964

(Japanese Firms *Italicized*)

Source: Intel Corporation.

the equipment and materials used to produce chips. Dr. Ross predicted that the industry would be a technological generation behind the Japanese unless corrective action was taken in the next two years.[34]

So despite much opposition, especially from the White House, the United States was moving in the direction of industrial policy—a national strategy for competitiveness—because the alternative was so disastrous. But it had a long way to go before it had in place a procedure as effective as that of Japan. The habit of consultation between MITI and the major companies regarding the long-run future of the country had not been established in the United States. There was still the suspicion that government could not pick winners and losers, and there was no understanding that this was *not* what the Japanese did. Japan had asked itself: Given the expanding technologies of tomorrow on which future industries will be built—microelectronics, biotechnology, telecommunications—where do we Japanese want to excel? And what is required for success? How do we build a climate that will allow us to achieve our goals? In the semiconductor example, the United States moved in the Japanese direction. It said, "Yes, we want to preserve our capability in this all-important field. We are not prepared to let nature take its course. If other nations have strategies, so must we."

Figure 2-5   *Government Role in a Consortium*

Legitimizer: Has the authority to give it credibility.

Power broker: Can offset industry giants like IBM so that smaller companies feel safe.

Provider of supplemental funds: Can offset other national subsidies.

Coordinator: Is the only player that can bring coherence to trade, monetary, fiscal, regulatory, and education policies. Also can reduce duplication and inefficiencies in government's basic R&D efforts. Can improve links among industry and national labs, defense research, universities, and venture capital providers.

Socializer: Can spread benefits throughout the community.

Overseer: Can ensure that the project stays on track.

Definer of national interest: Consortia and government assistance are only justified if they serve a well-defined national interest. The definition must be precise, reliable, and widely shared.

The role of government vis-à-vis Sematech had evolved from the MCC experience. (See Figures 2-5 and 2-6.) After several meetings with the Justice Department, Sematech leaders concluded that under the antitrust laws the consortium was possible if it was set up as a nonprofit corporation, sold no products on the open market, gave U.S. firms first opportunity to supply its products, did not have any foreign-based members, was not dominated by a few large companies, and treated all U.S. suppliers equally and fairly. Underlying these criteria was the notion that Sematech served a community need or the national interest. Likewise, congressional endorsement was based on that notion. The role of government had become—inadvertently, to be sure—to define community need and to ensure that Sematech complied with it. Most important, government was a legitimizer of Sematech. It also protected Sematech against domination by IBM and AT&T, and served as a guarantor of fairness and equity among the fourteen members and the suppliers of equipment and materials. Further, DARPA's interest in HDTV implied

Figure 2-6 *Some Thoughts for Government*

---

(1) Use the competitiveness task force, the Council on Competitiveness, and DARPA to bring coherence and consistency to government action on industry.

>   Set the vision of America. What do we want our industries to look like in ten or twenty years? What are our priorities?

>   Bring in government, business, and academic leaders to set a national strategy.

(2) Implement the strategy through industry-led initiatives.

(3) Consider policy changes to:

>   Coordinate trade, fiscal, monetary, and regulatory policies. Don't implement in a vacuum.

>   Ensure that U.S. firms have equitable access to foreign markets. The playing field will never be level, but that does not mean we cannot control our destiny. Use access to our market as leverage.

>   Improve science and math in the schools. Reduce illiteracy. Improve links among academia, national labs, and industry.

>   Address the short-term mentality of Wall Street and the high cost of capital. Reduce the budget deficits and change tax policy accordingly.

>   Knit up the ravaged food chains through discrete protection and tax breaks for buying U.S. products.

>   Relax antitrust laws in certain cases for *production* consortia as they are now relaxed for *research* consortia.

---

that it might become a coordinator if not a manager of the electronics food chain on which Sematech's success would depend, although the uncertainty surrounding Perkin-Elmer's equipment business was not a good sign. DARPA might also be a useful goad, a setter of deadlines.

These functions may well turn out to be as significant as DARPA's funding role, and perhaps more so. They resemble the functions that the Japanese government performed in the VLSI project. What remains to be seen is whether the functions will mature and flourish or atrophy and wither. Will Craig Fields be inclined—or allowed—to spend the time required to produce cooperation among rivals? Will he drink enough sake or whatever with the players? Or will Noyce, Sematech's talented CEO, be able to do it alone?

The answers to these questions depend in large part on how conscious all those involved are of what they are doing. A radical shift in the roles and relationships of government and business in the United States is under way. Sematech has certain pragmatic virtues. To succeed it must be accompanied by ideological renovation; otherwise it will fall victim to incoherence and illegitimacy.

CONCLUSIONS: SUPERCONDUCTIVITY AND THE FSX REVISITED

Specifically, ideological refurbishing is required concerning:

(1) The role of business in industries that are essential to the needs of the community and that cannot survive in world markets without internal cooperation and external help from government;

(2) The role of government with respect to the definition of community needs, especially the delineation of the relationship between commercial competitiveness and the national security; and

(3) The relationship between business and government.

As the Sematech-related episodes involving Perkin-Elmer, Monsanto, and Texas Instruments suggest, the long-run health of the microelectronics industry in the United States and indeed the health of the American economy as a whole may require managers to define corporate purpose in terms broader than the satisfaction of Wall Street traders or takeover entrepreneurs. Even the long-run interests of shareholders may be incompatible with the short-run concerns of the traders and LBOers. This is especially true when industry survival and competitiveness require government assistance and the contribution of taxpayers. In such circumstances, the purpose of the firm becomes the satisfaction of community needs.

It therefore becomes urgent that managers have a reliable definition of those needs, for without it they are bound to flounder. Only government, preferably with the assistance of business, has the authority to provide such a definition. At the same time, only business has the competence to implement it, to see that the needs are truly fulfilled. Therefore, government must be structured to provide timely and reliable definitions of community need and must be related as efficiently as possible to business so that the need may be met.

This is the ideological justification for the experimental changes I have described. Since it is elusive, let me tie it to two cases—superconductivity and the FSX deal—with which I began this chapter.

In 1986, two IBM scientists announced the discovery of new materials that carry an electric current without resistance at relatively high temperatures—288 degrees below zero Fahrenheit. This announcement set off a drive in Japan, Europe, and the United States to find superconducting materials that would work at room temperature. In 1988, the U.S. government channelled $95 million into high-temperature superconductivity (HTS), about $25 million more than the Japanese government did. And yet, according to Congress's Office of Technology Assessment, Japan appeared to be ahead in the race for commercial success.[35]

The U.S. difficulty stemmed from two factors. First, government money, 70% of which went through DARPA, emphasized specialized military applications and has had little impact on commercial applications of HTS. Other funds have passed through the Department of Energy's laboratories, which have little experience in working closely with industry or the inclination to do so. Second, an OTA investigation revealed that "Japanese firms have assigned considerably more people and funds to superconductivity than have their U.S. counterparts."[36] The investigators found that "Japanese industry has made heavy (and often risky) investments in new technology on the basis of its ultimate promise, whereas U.S. firms have held back, waiting for it to be proven cost-effective."[37]

Thus, as with machine tools and semiconductors, there is tension and ambivalence regarding whether the community need is commercial competitiveness or military requirements. DARPA is under bureaucratic pressure to link those funds to military goals, even though it is trying to help companies like IBM and AT&T develop commercial applications. Small amounts of federal money have been allocated to the National Science Foundation, which works closely with universities on basic research. But here again the interface with industry is distant.

On the business side, as the OTA study discovered, conventional financial considerations and traditional conceptions of purpose have impeded U.S. efforts.

Success requires a fundamental change on both sides: a clear definition by government that the community need—including national security—is commercial competitiveness, the formation of industrial consortia with federal cost-sharing focused on those areas that business thinks will have the most commercial payoff, and a long-term commitment by business and government to persevere until successful results are achieved.

Returning to the FSX debate, there was a failure on the part of the administration and Congress to be clear about community needs. What had been conceived of as a purely military transaction, backed by Defense and State for national security and foreign policy reasons, suddenly became a matter of economic interest concerning U.S. employment, the trade balance, and the commercial competitiveness of the aerospace industry. Caught by surprise and unprepared with facts or analysis, decision makers were angry and confused.

Mitsubishi and the Japanese were vilified for what was unquestionably an American failure.

George Packard, dean of the Johns Hopkins School of Advanced International Studies and a former defense official, said "a new wind is blowing" through American foreign policy with the "acceptance of the idea that economic security is as important as national defense."[38] There was, perhaps, reason to believe that a lesson had been learned, that industrial policy was an undeniable reality. The choices were ones of definition and implementation.

NOTES

1. Bruce Stokes, "Beat 'Em or Join 'Em," *National Journal,* February 25, 1989, pp. 459–464. For a Japanese perspective, see Akio Morita and Shintaro Ishihara, *The Japan That Can Say "No"* (Toyko: Kobunsha Kappa-Holmes, 1989). In an unofficial translation of this work, Ishihara, a candidate for prime minister in 1989 and former minister of transportation, writes:

   The FSX is a marvelous and formidable fighter. No existing fighter, including the F-15 and the F-16, can match it in a dog fight. I [Ishihara] recall when then Secretary Weinberger became serious about quashing the FSX Japanese development plan, strictly out of fear. Unfortunately, Japan has not yet developed a powerful enough jet engine, although I advocated such a development when I was a member of the Upper House. Japan must still purchase jet engines, which are mounted on the F-15 and F-16. If America gets really nasty, Japan can buy engines from France. . . . If France is reluctant to sell what we need, I would not mind going to the Soviet Union. . . . New Mitsubishi jet fighters equipped with Russian engines may only have a top speed of 95% of existing F-15 and 16 class fighters . . . [but] their combat capability is far superior in a dog fight situation. It can make a 380 degree turn with a third of the diameter needed by other top fighters. . . . The FSX was a surprise to Americans, as were the Zero fighters at the beginning of the Second World War. . . . That such a formidable weapon as the FSX is in production today outside the United States came as a shock to Americans. . . . Such a marvelous idea probably is not the monopoly of Japan, but it was a Japanese manufacturer who developed the idea to reality, thanks to Japanese advanced high technology. . . . Russian fighters are also equipped using Japanese know-how, especially in the area of ceramics and carbon fibers. Special paints on American reconnaisance planes which assist in avoiding radar detection are also made in Japan. . . . [Nakasone's] submission to American pressure eventually caused the mothballing of the FSX.

2. *New York Times,* March 26, 1989, pp. 1, 23. Robert Lipsey and Irving B. Kravis reported that between 1957 and 1983 the world market share of U.S.-based firms went from 21.3% to 13.9% while the world share of U.S. multinational companies held steady at about 17.7% between 1966 and 1983 (National Bureau of Economic Research, 1986: "U.S. Multinationals and World Trade").
3. Ibid., p. 23.
4. R. Williams interview, April 1989.
5. R. Williams interview, August 1988.
6. Excerpt from Earle H. Harbison, Jr., speech at Biotechnology Strategic Management Conference, March 11, 1987.
7. Marie Anchordoguy, "Mastering the Market: Japanese Government Targeting of the Computer Industry," #389-016. Boston: Harvard Business School, 1988.
8. See works of Bruce Scott, John Zysman, Stephen Cohen, and Laura Tyson cited in Chapter 1.
9. Joseph L. Bower and Kosei Furkawa, and Research Assistant William J. Murphy, "Cooperation for Competition: U.S. and Japan," #386-181. Boston: Harvard Business School, 1986, rev. 1988, p. 10.
10. Ibid., p. 11.
11. Ibid.
12. Ibid, p. 32.
13. Ibid., p. 33.
14. *Electronic News,* June 15, 1981, quoted in Bower et al., "Cooperation for Competition: U.S. and Japan," p. 3.
15. Ibid.
16. Thomas C. Hayes, *New York Times,* June 24, 1987, p. D6.
17. Associates Fellow Robert Williams and Professor George C. Lodge, "Sematech," #389-057. Boston: Harvard Business School, 1989, p. 8.
18. Ibid.
19. Ibid., p. 7.
20. Ibid., p. 10.
21. Ibid., p. 14.
22. Ibid., p. 15.
23. Ibid., p. 18.
24. "SEMATECH: Progress and Prospects," Report of the Advisory Council on Federal Participation in Sematech. Washington, DC: Department of Commerce, 1989.
25. *New York Times,* November 27, 1989, p. 1.
26. *New York Times,* April 22, 1989, p. 37.
27. *New York Times,* December 23, 1988, pp. D1–D2.
28. *New York Times,* December 27, 1988, pp. D1, D6.
29. *New York Times,* April 22, 1989, p. 37.

30. Helen V. Milner and David B. Yoffie, "Strategic Trade Policy and Corporate Trade Demands," *International Organization* (Spring 1989): 272.
31. Ibid.
32. *New York Times,* October 23, 1989, pp. 1, D14.
33. *Financial Times,* May 16, 1989, p. 1.
34. Andrew Pollack, *New York Times,* November 21, 1989, pp. D1, D11.
35. Dorothy Robyn, W. Wendell Fletcher, and John A. Alic, "Bringing Superconductivity to Market," *Issues in Science and Technology* 5, no. 2 (1988): 6.
36. Ibid., pp. 40, 41.
37. Ibid., p. 42.
38. *Washington Post,* March 15, 1989, p. D1.

CHAPTER 3

Power and Control: Who's in Charge?

As we saw in the previous chapter, two contradictory activities were at work in microelectronics. U.S. multinationals were entering into an increasing number of global alliances to enhance their competitiveness as *companies;* at the same time, they were securing governmental support to bolster the competitiveness of their *country.* The company and the country, of course, do not necessarily have the same objectives. If the company's highest priority is short-run shareholder satisfaction, the company's behavior will almost certainly not be in line with long-run community need as perceived by government. The question of control thus arises: If there is a conflict between the two interests, who will resolve it, government or business? What criteria will be used? Some nations answer these questions through tested mechanisms backed by a widely shared consensus about the roles and relationships of government and business. They use criteria of national or—in the case of Europe—regional competitiveness, which are well known and well accepted. Other nations are uncertain. Not surprisingly, economic power drifts to the former, and so, eventually, does political power.

The purposes, relationships, and structures of Japanese business and government sketched in Chapter 1 suggest that Japan is accomplished at deciding questions of control about its own community. Although there are doubtless tensions between the interests of Japan's great multinationals and MITI, there is a long tradition of mutual respect and dedication to the national interest that will not unravel quickly.

Japan knows itself well and knows what it wants. It is hard to imagine that Japan will not use its global competitiveness to exert economic control in its own national interest. It is likely that such control will inevitably extend into the political arena.

Indeed, such was the forecast of Shintaro Ishihara, former minister of transportation and candidate for prime minister in Japan's politically stormy summer of 1989. Discussing the critical importance of accuracy in ballistic missilery and the United States' dependence on Japanese semiconductors to assure that accuracy, he wrote: "If, for example, Japan sold chips to the Soviet Union and stopped selling them to the United States, this would upset the entire military balance." He went on to cite a secret U.S. Defense Department report that, he said, states "that if Japan is left to go as it is, it will be impossible to get the lead back."[1] Perhaps such a reallocation of global power is unimportant to the U.S. government and U.S.-based companies. Those hooked on the myths of the free market, free trade, and free enterprise would likely argue that the United States should not contaminate its economic thinking by even contemplating such political realism. But strategic thinkers, those conditioned by years of scheming to retain power vis-à-vis the Soviet Union, will surely have concerns. As these concerns rise, we can predict that the evolution of policies designed to promote the economic interests of the country, of which Sematech is but a small example, will proceed apace.

Such an evolution has been under way in Europe for years. It is further advanced than in the United States—and far more complicated. To beef up their ability to catch up and compete in high-tech markets, European companies have been cooperating with one another, with national governments, and with the European Commission since the early 1980s. Under the banner of ESPRIT and EUREKA, literally hundreds of joint ventures have been consummated, mostly in the microelectronics field. By far, the most elaborate and expensive is the Joint European Submicron Silicon Initiative (JESSI), which took shape in 1989 with a budget of some $4.5

billion over eight years. (One-half of this amount was to come
from national governments and the European Commission;
the rest from the thirty-odd member firms.) JESSI's leaders,
primarily Philips and Siemens, were motivated by several
factors. First, they and their U.S. subsidiaries were excluded
from Sematech; second, they observed the shocking slippage
of U.S. competitiveness in electronics against Japan. They
reasoned that Europe had better strengthen itself or become a
Japanese vassal, because the United States was not going to
be of much help.

It is not too much to say that JESSI's success depends primarily on how effectively its business and governmental partners manage their relationships. This capability may well
turn out to be an important European competitive advantage—at least against the United States—because it is a field
of management in which both the private and public sectors
have gained considerable experience and skill over the past
decade. Europe's industrial giants, such as Philips, played
leading roles in both the political decisions to go for European
unity in 1992 and the economic actions to make it work.

The lack of such experience and skill in the United States
represents a serious deficiency, and threatens the country's
ability to retain what economic and political control it has
left. The United States must learn, and learn fast, if it is to
hold its own against Japan and Europe. An object lesson is the
fate of America's commercial venture into sensing the earth
from space. This case demonstrates poignantly the importance of business-government relations to a company's fortunes and to a country's capacity to control itself. It is a par-
able for our times, in which the French, not the Japanese,
teach the lesson.

REMOTE SATELLITE SENSING (RSS)

Satellites orbit through space gathering increasingly
valuable information about what is on or beneath the earth's
surface. Data are recorded by electronic sensors for such pur-

poses as mapping, weather prediction, water and crop management, oil and mineral exploration, urban planning, and, of course, the detection of military activities. Although governments, especially defense and intelligence agencies, had dominated the field, by 1988 satellite technology was a blossoming commercial industry with annual sales of $90 million and estimates that within a decade commercial sales would grow to as much as $600 million a year.[2] As an industry in which profits were perhaps decades away, however, government assistance was essential.

By 1988, the U.S. government had spent more than $1.5 billion to promote the development of what has come to be termed "remote sensing from space" (RSS) for civil purposes. (This does not include the billions spent for satellite imaging by defense and intelligence agencies.) During the 1970s and early 1980s, civil RSS was in the hands of the National Aeronautics and Space Administration (NASA), which designed, developed, and operated the Landsat program, which consisted of a series of satellites, Landsats 1–5, and a network of fifteen ground stations around the world that receive data from the satellites. The data were processed and sold to governmental and commercial users—primarily the Departments of Defense, Agriculture, and Interior, other governments, some oil and mineral companies, and a host of private companies that refined the data for specialized use.

In 1979, the Carter administration decided to move Landsat from NASA to the National Oceanic and Atmospheric Administration (NOAA) in the Department of Commerce, which already had responsibility for operating weather satellites. It was also decided to gradually turn the program over to private companies. President Reagan sought to hasten privatization. In 1985, an NOAA contract granted the right to exploit the commercial potentialities of the Landsat system to EOSAT, a new company that had been created for that purpose by Hughes Aircraft and the space division of RCA. Both companies had long been government satellite contractors; they were later acquired by General Motors and General Electric, respectively.

In 1981, the French space agency, CNES, entered the field, starting from scratch with the world's first strictly commercial remote-sensing venture. It established a quasi-private company, SPOT (Satellite Pour l'Observation de la Terre) Image, to distribute and market earth images. SPOT Image was a collaborative venture of the French, Swedish, and Belgian governments and several big private companies, most notably Matra, the French defense giant. The first SPOT satellite was launched in 1986 with a government investment of $500 million (about one-third that of the U.S. government). By 1989, the French were gaining momentum, if not assuming the lead, in the field because of more effective government-business relations coupled with a coherent strategy.

While SPOT was taking more than 30% of the world market and growing fast, EOSAT was struggling for its life. Moreover, the Japanese were entering the business with promising new technology, and a number of other countries had announced plans to launch remote-sensing systems. There was considerable fear among developing countries that with the decline of U.S. capacity in remote sensing, they would be denied access to data, which had been assured by the U.S. commitment to the UN's policy of "open skies" (the United States had been a staunch defender of nondiscriminatory access to images from space).

Leonard Spector of the Carnegie Endowment for International Peace suggested some serious foreign policy implications flowing from EOSAT's decline and SPOT's success:

> The timing in delivery of an image is a key issue in the nondiscriminatory access policy, especially for governments using these images for intelligence and other military purposes. A country with a Landsat or SPOT ground station—like India or South Africa—can get its images, including the images of neighboring states, almost instantaneously. In contrast, a rival state that lacks a ground station may have to wait weeks for images of the ground station country to be sent out from EOSAT or SPOT headquarters. What's more, in targeting the SPOT

satellite, SPOT Image is starting to give preference to its larger customers, which can spell big delays for disfavored clients. With this discretionary power, SPOT Image could all too easily begin giving preference to foreign governments on political grounds.[3]

In effect, U.S. capacity in remote sensing had been a protective umbrella that tended to guarantee fair play for those who had no easy access to the data obtained from space. Without such protection, many feared exploitation. A poor African country, for example, was not only vulnerable to South African spying but also to mining companies' discovering and keeping secret valuable ore deposits within its borders.

The Defense Department was also concerned about EOSAT's flagging performance. As DOD Assistant Secretary Donald C. Latham told Congress: "Landsat (EOSAT) has great value in being able to search very large areas very rapidly. . . . For example, it helps us tell whether there's an airfield being constructed in some part of the world, or if highways have been changed."[4]

To fully appreciate the fears of Latham, Spector, and others who were alarmed by EOSAT's plight, a bit of background about how the system works is required. Remote sensing has two main components: the space and ground system, and the data collection and interpretation system. The space and ground system consists of the satellite and its corresponding ground stations. The satellite provides a platform for sensors, communications, and operational support equipment. Sensors record the images in the form of digitized bits of information that reveal specific characteristics of sensed objects. Depending on the type of sensor used, the characteristics vary according to two broad categories: the smallness of the object to be viewed ("spatial resolution"), and the "spectral band," which determines the area to be covered and the attributes to be sensed (heat, moisture, or particular substances, for example). U.S. defense and intelligence satellites have two-inch spatial resolution, which is so powerful that a car's license plate can be read from space. Commercial resolution capability, on the other hand, is more limited: EOSAT sensors have thirty-meter resolution, and SPOT has ten-meter resolution. Spectral bands enabled forest service officials in Yellowstone National Park to determine where the hot spots were in the summer blaze of 1988. Farmers use them to determine crop growth and mining companies to analyze areas for development. Utility companies purchase images to determine growth patterns and changes in land use to help with planning; local governments monitor urban sprawl; Ducks Unlimited, a conservation group, keeps track of wetland habitats in the world; and progressive farmers use the data to monitor the growth of competitors' crops.

In 1984, when Congress passed the Land Remote Sensing Commercialization Act, making EOSAT possible, it declared that the government's Landsat system "has established the United States as the world leader in land remote-sensing technology"; that "the national interest . . . lies in maintaining [such] leadership"; and that the best way to do that was through "private-sector involvement" because the use of remote-sensing data had been "inhibited by slow market development and by the lack of assurance of data continuity." Congress recognized that the private sector could not do the job alone because of "the high risk and large capital expenditure involved," and therefore proposed a cooperative effort between government and private industry to assure U.S. leadership and fulfill the national interest.[5]

Scarcely three years later, in 1987, Cong. James H. Scheuer (D-NY), chairman of a subcommittee of the House Committee on Science, Space and Technology, warned that unless action was taken "the U.S. earth remote sensing satellite program, with all of its benefits to our government and to the private sector, will simply cease to exist and we will have abandoned the field . . . to our international competitors, the French and the Japanese."[6] In February 1988, President Reagan issued a directive on National Space Policy and Commercial Space Initiatives that called for a program that would be "competitive with or superior to foreign-operated . . . systems."[7]

Nevertheless, by 1989, the situation had become worse.

Landsat satellites 4 and 5, the source of EOSAT's data, were about to expire, and even though they might be kept operating for a short time, the funds to keep them going were exhausted. Landsat 6, which was supposed to have been orbiting in time to replace them, was delayed until 1991, and the fate of Landsat 7 was uncertain. EOSAT faced the real possibility of dissolution.

In February 1989, Vice President Dan Quayle was put in charge of a Space Council, composed of representatives of interested departments and agencies of government, to deal with the situation. His office contacted U.S. government users of Landsat data and scraped together enough funds to keep Landsats 4 and 5 aloft for a few months. He also promised funds for Landsat 6.

EOSAT customers around the world, however, wondered about the reliability of the United States and of the flow of data on which they had come to depend. The French were forging ahead with higher resolution capability and a far more energetic and extensive marketing effort, which EOSAT could not match because of the uncertainty it faced. The Japanese, having developed a new radar technology to record images during cloudy conditions, indicated that they intended to have a major part of the market by the end of the 1990s.

What had gone wrong?

In spite of pledges and promises from Congress and President Reagan, the U.S. government had failed to adopt a long-term, reliable, coherent strategy. Torn by conflicting priorities, pressed by budget constraints, and rent by interdepartmental wrangling, it was about to waste the billions it had invested to attain leadership. EOSAT and its parents, GM and GE, reacted to government's wavering policies by cutting back, slowing down, and complaining to Congress about the repeated failure of the Commerce Department and NOAA to provide the promised funds EOSAT needed to survive.

There was thus a failure of leadership. Reagan's style and conception of government's role precluded a long-term plan. The immense power of the Office of Management and Budget and its charge to cut spending meant that the commercial space program, lacking any grass-roots constituency, was a sitting duck for the budget cutters. NOAA and Commerce had enough worries without going out on a limb for EOSAT. Similarly, Defense, Agriculture, Interior, and the other users were not going to volunteer their resources.

Deeper down was an ambivalence about the propriety of government's responsibility for commercial competitiveness. Part of the appeal of privatization was that it unleashed the competitive capabilities of private enterprise, relieving government of responsibility and allowing it to save money. In the remote-sensing industry, however, as Congress itself recognized in 1984, private enterprise alone was helpless in a world of big government-business partnerships. The risks were too great, the profits too distant, and the capital required too much.

If present trends continue, the United States will not only lose its $1.5-billion investment in commercial space sensing, it will also lose the 100 or more firms that have emerged to process and add value to the raw EOSAT data, and with them will go learning and skills that could have unimaginable importance for the future. In addition, the United States will lose international standing. In the 1950s, President Eisenhower led the world in pushing for a policy of equal access to data procured from space—"open skies." Although the policy was never accepted by military and intelligence agencies in the United States or elsewhere, it continues to have force in the civil field. If the United States abdicates its place in the field, it will not be able to keep its forty-year-old pledge. It will also have to renege on commitments to the countries in which Landsat's fifteen ground stations are located.

At this writing, NOAA is discussing a joint venture between Landsat and SPOT for future development. A consultant has recommended an international consortium. Donald Latham of Defense, however, has opposed such an alliance: "I'd rather go it alone. We have to continue our leadership in space. . . . Third World nations look to the United States for imagery. We generate a lot of intangibles—political good will and international relations."[8]

If the vice president can pull the government and private players together, establish a long-term strategy, and obtain congressional support, U.S. leadership in remote sensing may survive. If not, an international consortium with the French and probably the Japanese will be the best alternative. Then the question will be: Who will control the consortium? The answer depends on what each of the players brings to the table: Funds? Technology? Know-how? Carelessly, inadvertently, without counting the cost, the United States has allowed its supply of all three to dissipate.

SPOT's Rise; EOSAT's Decline

SPOT's success and EOSAT's difficulties reflect two quite different patterns of relationships between government and business.

David Julyan, executive vice president of SPOT Imaging Corporation, the U.S. subsidiary of the Toulouse-based SPOT Image, is responsible for marketing and distributing images in the United States. "France wanted to step up to the world space table," he said. "The French government wanted the international prestige and saw remote sensing as a complement to its space efforts." These efforts included the successful Ariane launch vehicles, which benefited from a launch site in Kourou, French Guyana. Satellites launched from this site entered a particularly favorable orbit, extending their lives by as many as eighteen months over their Landsat counterparts. In addition to the $500 million that the French government invested in SPOT, it subsidized its insurance system. Ironically, in its early years NOAA provided key technological assistance to the SPOT program without which it would have been substantially delayed.

According to Julyan:

> We have been successful for many reasons, but the most important has been defining up-front what role the commercial entity, SPOT Image, would play, and what CNES [the French government] would be responsible for.

SPOT Image is completely responsible for the marketing and distribution of the data. We decide what images are taken and as soon as those images hit the ground, we take over. The operation and launch of the satellites is CNES' responsibility. By keeping the lines divided clearly, we keep politics out and allow business to thrive.[9]

SPOT's ten-meter resolution, compared to EOSAT's thirty-meter resolution, and its rapid revisits to an area, stereo imaging, and continuity of data flows were its major advantages. In 1988, it had fifty distributors worldwide, compared to EOSAT's twenty-five. "We expect this network, in conjunction with our image database to be a formidable barrier to entry."[10]

The saga of EOSAT reflects none of the clarity of roles between it and government to which Julyan attributed the French success. The out-going Carter administration left a 1981 plan for commercializing Landsat in phases, but it recognized a large role for government. There was $743 million in NOAA's 1981–1986 budget plan to complete satellites 4 and 5 and to design and construct satellites 6 and 7. President Reagan came into office with what he advertised as a "revolutionary" approach, and Budget Director David Stockman suggested cutting satellites 6 and 7 from the budget, saving $597 million. He also advocated turning the program over to the private sector immediately, although the president had stated in a February 1983 memorandum that the federal government might provide $150 million a year for several years. Three months later, in May 1983, Secretary of Commerce Malcolm Baldrige appointed a task force to study how to effect commercialization.

Dr. Cary Gravatt, director of commercial space programs at Commerce and one of the leaders of Baldrige's task force, recalled the ambivalence in the government's thinking about funding. The president had said there might be some funds available; Stockman felt the program was a waste. Reagan disagreed with Stockman but refused to be specific. Twenty companies eagerly followed the proceedings. In January 1984,

Commerce issued a request for proposals (RFP), and received solid bids from Kodak/Fairchild, EOSAT, and Space America, an entrepreneurial venture led by former astronaut Deke Slayton.

"It came down to Kodak or EOSAT," said Gravatt. "Kodak was stronger on the marketing side; EOSAT was stronger on the technology. But both bids were submitted expecting a total of about $500 million in government support over ten years. They had both come up with this number independently."

EOSAT's proposal was to cover marketing of data from Landsats 1–5, which were up and going at the time, and the design, construction, launch, and operation of four more satellites, Landsats 6 and 7 and a backup for each. Charles Williams, president of EOSAT, added: "In addition, we intended to automate the ground stations to improve response times and cut operating costs."[11]

"Other Programs Seemed More Important." Baldrige went to the OMB with the two bids. "When Stockman heard about the $500 million, he blew his stack," said Gravatt. Negotiations continued throughout the spring of 1984. Baldrige insisted that a minimum of $425 million was needed to construct satellites 6 and 7, $175 million more than Stockman was willing to give. According to a former OMB official: "Baldrige was putting in requests for other Commerce programs at the same time, and Stockman wanted Baldrige to set priorities. Baldrige claimed that everything was important."

By July 1984, the two men were at an impasse. The next step was to go before the Budget Review Board, composed of Stockman, Edwin Meese, and White House chief of staff James Baker. The board considered three options: $425 million, $250 million, or $0. The board's vote was unanimous: $0. Baldrige, infuriated, went to the president. Within a week Stockman and Baldrige had agreed: $250 million for two satellites, numbers 6 and 7.

Baldrige took the deal to the two bidders and Kodak backed out. EOSAT said that with modifications it could do it. "It meant higher operating costs," Williams said, "because we wouldn't be able to automate the ground stations. And without backup satellites, one catastrophe would wipe us out. But since the space program hadn't had many problems, we thought we could do it for $250 million." Congress passed the Landsat Act in July 1984 to allow the deal to go forward.

Because of the 1984 elections, nothing much happened until early 1985. EOSAT unsuccessfully attempted to increase the $250-million government pledge. Williams said, "We had spent about $12 million before the contract was signed. We changed our proposal 19 times in 15 months." Gravatt said, "Already in late 1984 the relationship was souring. EOSAT was acting like a government contractor, not an entrepreneur. We had screwed them. We had asked them how much government support they would need and now we were cutting back their number."

Although EOSAT had verbally agreed to satellites 6 and 7 in the summer of 1984, the responsibility for launching them had never been explicitly defined. When its formal proposal came to Commerce early in 1985, it included only one satellite (6) and its launch. Stockman again tried to wipe out the deal. The feud with Baldrige was renewed.

At this point, four senators intervened to try to resolve the impasse and produced what became known as the Laxalt Letter, named after Sen. Paul Laxalt (R-UT). It smoothed the way for congressional authorization of $297 million. The difference from $250 million was the cost of two launches. Congress actually appropriated $125 million for fiscal 1986. Of this $125 million, $90 million was to go to EOSAT via NOAA in its FY1986 budget for development costs. The remaining $35 million was to go to NASA as a down payment for shuttle launches. Actually, an Air Force Titan II launch would have been far cheaper, but Congress wanted to subsidize the shuttle.

The contract between EOSAT and Commerce was signed in September 1985. The government agreed to support two new satellites and their launches. EOSAT would receive the revenue from data marketed from Landsats 1–5 and would design,

construct, and operate Landsats 6 and 7. Additional investments beyond 6 and 7 would be EOSAT's responsibility.

About this time, Stockman left OMB. He was replaced by
an equally enthusiastic trimmer, Jim Miller, who felt the
added pressure of the Gramm-Rudman-Hollings legislation.
In October 1985, when NOAA's FY1986 budget request came
before him, he "zeroed out" the second round of EOSAT funding—$62.5 million.

Gravatt recalled: "Baldrige tried everything, but nothing
happened. I had pleaded with OMB in August. I said we are
about to sign a contract. If you're going to say no, say it now
before the train starts down the track. What they did was to
say no two months after the contract had been signed."

An OMB official recalled: "It was a difficult time. We had a
new director. Gramm-Rudman had just passed. Budgets were
tight. Landsat was relooked at and it was determined that we
couldn't afford it. Neither OMB nor Commerce saw Landsat
as a high priority. Other programs seemed more important."

Donald Latham echoed this sentiment during congressional
hearings in 1987: "It was Commerce's responsibility to fund.
. . . Defense will do all it can to support it, short of funding it."

Commerce, however, had other constituencies to serve.
NOAA, especially, had its own interests, which did not include Landsat's commercialization. In fact, NOAA was a com-
petitor with EOSAT for commercial sales of its own satellites'
data! It agreed to manage the EOSAT contract but not with
great enthusiasm and certainly with no intention of giving up
its own budget resources.

Similarly, EOSAT had no real following in Congress.
Robert Palmer of the House Space Subcommittee staff said:
"Landsat never had a broad-based constituency and EOSAT
has done nothing to expand it on the Hill. No agency has
enough interest in it to put up the money, so it just slips
through the cracks."

Countdown for EOSAT. In January 1986, a totally unexpected event struck EOSAT: the Challenger space shuttle ex-
ploded. Now EOSAT lacked not only funds but a launch vehi-

cle. (It was forbidden, incidentally, to buy a ride on the French Ariane.) In addition, an important relay satellite that would have expanded Landsat 5's global reach went down with Challenger.

In January 1987, EOSAT ran out of operating funds. It terminated hardware development and laid off most of its work force. "We were at the point of completely shutting down six times in 1987," said Williams. Finally, in October 1987, a new agreement between Congress and the administration was reached:

(1) EOSAT would receive $209 million to cover expenditures already made and additional work required to complete Landsat 6. The company said it required an additional $11 million to complete 6, and the government agreed to loan EOSAT the money, to be paid back over four years. In the meantime, projected operating costs for 6 had risen from $6 million to $12 million a year. And EOSAT had lost legal rights to Landsat 7.

(2) The Air Force would get $50 million for one Titan II launch for Landsat 6.

(3) A $2-million study would be made about what to do beyond 6.

A few months later, in February 1988, President Reagan made his pronouncement about encouraging "the development of commercial systems, which image the Earth from space, competitive with or superior to foreign-operated civil or commercial systems." A Senate staffer commented: "Reagan was famous for policy declarations. The public remembers the directive, but forgets about the implementation."

In the spring of 1988, NOAA was experiencing serious cost overruns. It told EOSAT that Landsat activity would have to be curtailed. Williams went to the Hill, pleading for the company's life. In March, NOAA agreed to provide $62.5 million and work began again on Landsat 6. Because of delays, however, it could not be launched until 1991. Meanwhile, operating funds for Landsats 4 and 5 would dry up in March 1989. A two-year data gap loomed. And NOAA was talking with the French about Landsat 7.

Waste

Looking back, Williams commented on the waste of the process:

> Over 25% of my top executives' time is spent dealing with Congress and the administration. We are understaffed at the moment, but we are afraid to staff up again, because of inconsistent funding. The government has already defaulted on our contract five times. The original deal would have cost taxpayers $297 million. They'd have gotten a fully integrated system, two satellites, 6 and 7, and two launches. Now they're going to get a limited data system, one satellite and a launch for $256 million.[12]

More serious perhaps than the waste of money was the waste of national power demonstrated by the EOSAT saga— the waste of effort, innovation, technology, leadership, influence, and authority; the loss of the nation's ability to control itself, to marshall its resources, to determine its future. And this example is but one of many, although it is particularly telling because of the precision with which it identifies the roles and relationships of business and government as the villain in the piece.

Harvey Brooks states the case more generally:

> Since the end of World War II the science and technology policy of the U.S. has been predicated on the assumption that leadership in the creation of new technology was the key to competitive success in the utilization of technology both for commercial and public purposes. It has been taken for granted that if the U.S. was the first to demonstrate the viability of a radical new technology it would almost automatically retain the lead in its ex-

ploitation and diffusion through its own economy and society. . . . However, the experience of the last 20 years seems to have demonstrated in field after field, and increasingly even in the highest technology fields, that superiority in the capacity to create new technology is not enough to ensure superiority in realizating the benefits of technology in either the private or the public sector.[13]

Sensing the earth from space is an extreme example of a commercial endeavor whose success depends on a reliable and purposeful relåtionship between government and business. There are others: superconductivity, high-definition television, microelectronics, maybe biotechnology, and perhaps even banking. In these areas, the industries of other countries benefit from concerted long-run government policies and in some cases government funds. U.S. companies cannot go it alone, and although Paul Krugman's warnings against such targeting, cited in Chapter 1, are well taken, since interest groups could conspire to prop up the weak at the expense of the strong with results that are anything but competitive, the alternative is national decline, not only economically but also in political influence. Unable to rely on our commercial institutions or economic commitments, other countries will doubt our political promises. So the question is how we change our system to make targeting work. A look at the health equipment industry will shed light on the issue.

NOTES

1. Akio Morita and Shintaro Ishihara, *The Japan That Can Say "No"* (Tokyo: Kobunsha, Kappa-Holmes, 1989), unofficial translation, p. 4.
2. See Robert A. Williams and George C. Lodge, "Sensing the Earth from Space," #389-154. Boston: Harvard Business School, 1989; also "The Future of the Landsat System," *Hearings* before the Subcommittee on Natural Resources, Agriculture Research and Environment, and the Subcommittee on International Scientific Cooperation of the House Committee on Science, Space, and Technology, March 31 and April 2, 1987; Washington, DC: U.S. Government Printing Office, 1987.

3. Williams and Lodge, "Sensing the Earth from Space," p. 18.
4. *Hearings;* and Williams and Lodge, "Sensing the Earth from Space," p. 20.
5. See Section 101 of the Land Remote Sensing Commercialization Act.
6. *Hearings,* p. 2; and Williams and Lodge, "Sensing the Earth from Space," p. 1.
7. Williams and Lodge, "Sensing the Earth from Space," p. 13.
8. *Hearings,* pp. 94, 95.
9. Williams and Lodge, "Sensing the Earth from Space," p. 16.
10. Ibid., p. 17.
11. Ibid., p. 8.
12. Ibid., p. 14.
13. Harvey Brooks, "Government Policy: Technology Demonstration or Service Delivery?" *Technology in Society* 11 (1989): 55.

CHAPTER 4

Organizing the Interface

The story of EOSAT and the faltering efforts of the United States in commercial earth sensing from space raise a question about the role of business in managing the interface with government more effectively. Where were General Motors and General Electric while EOSAT, the luckless offspring of their subsidiaries, Hughes and RCA's space division, was floundering? Hardly neophytes in the affairs of Washington, why did they not intervene and force the government councils to face reality? Commercialization was impossible without long-term, reliable government support. If GM and GE had regarded themselves as partners with government in fulfilling the national interest, they could have used their power and influence to drive this truth home.

The evidence suggests, first, that they had different priorities and, second, that their conception of their roles and relationship to government precluded such intervention. EOSAT was a remote nonentity in their vast empires, representing only one among scores of government contracts. The idea of EOSAT implicit in the 1984 Act—an entrepreneur ready to take up world leadership in space commercialization in partnership with government—was not their conception of things at all. As we saw in Chapter 1, General Motors has not seen its role as helping government formulate a national strategy for competitiveness. Nor has General Electric. Government business they will seek and take, of course. Government policy, when it directly affects them, they will attempt to shape. But their purpose is the satisfaction of their share-

121

holders, not the competitiveness of the nation. The EOSAT story, like that of semiconductors in Chapter 2, suggests that without the latter the former will suffer.

And where were the 100 or more value-added firms that depend on Landsat data? Were they prepared to shift their dependency to France and Japan? Had they thought about the implications of the shift? Apparently not, for they too were silent as U.S. fortunes deteriorated. Unlike the semiconductor industry, which in the face of catastrophe had organized itself through the Semiconductor Industry Association and exerted leadership in Congress and the executive branch, the space-imaging industry was leaderless, unorganized, and passive. In short, there was no leadership anywhere.

One wonders why the Reagan administration did not use the charter route to fulfill the community need for the development of commercial remote sensing, an approach that had been extremely successful twenty years earlier in the case of communications satellites. In 1962, a new corporation, Comsat, was created by an act of Congress to become "the custodian and promoter of communications satellite technology." Comsat was authorized to sell shares to the American public, and proceeded to work with a number of American companies, including Hughes, to revolutionize global communications. Even though its road since then has been rocky, it serves as a dramatic example of how business and government can work together if the aims are clear and the proper mechanism for cooperation is used.[1]

THE CRITICAL ROLE OF INDUSTRY ASSOCIATIONS

The costs of apathy are telling and crisis is rousing some industries to the new reality. The issue seems to be: How much crisis will it take? Or, putting it in a more managerial way: How does a manager make maximum use of minimum crisis for maximum change? Crisis is expensive; it should not be wasted. The costs of playing catch-up in remote-sensing electronics, and elsewhere, exceed those of staying ahead in the first place.

In this chapter, I shall examine a leader and an organization in the health equipment industry that have attempted to reduce the expense by redefining the roles and relationships of business and government in that area. Like the SIA in semiconductors, the Health Industry Manufacturers Association (HIMA) has sought for the past five years or so to develop a more cooperative relationship with government. As in semiconductors, the task has included prodding government to define community need more precisely and reliably, and to identify the relationship of industry to the fulfillment of that need. Health equipment, however, differs substantially from semiconductors in that, like many other industries, it is heavily constrained and controlled by government regulations, which set the standards that products must conform to: standards of safety, effectiveness, and, increasingly, economic value. Both the contents of those standards and the processes through which they are adopted greatly affect the competitiveness of the U.S. health equipment industry in the world economy. And that competitiveness is eroding. The $1-billion trade surplus that the industry enjoyed in 1981 had been cut in half by 1987, and 1988 brought continued and substantial deficits with Germany and Japan in spite of the lowered value of the dollar.[2] So the fortunes of the industry are directly tied to the government's definition of community need and the speed and reliability with which that need is determined.

The same is true of the biotechnology industry, which, as we saw in Chapter 2, may be on the way to the same competitive fate as electronics. Indeed, in 1987, MITI had announced its intention to seek world leadership in biotechnology, consolidating the industry structure, promoting research and development, establishing standards, and providing tax incentives. (See Appendix II.) So in the following discussion of HIMA we shall look from time to time at the Industrial Biotechnology Association (IBA), which represents some ninety companies.[3]

HIMA

The Health Industry Manufacturers Association (HIMA) represents a wide range of companies that develops and manufactures more than 90% of the medical devices, diagnostics, and health care information systems in the United States.[4] The products range from Band-Aids and tongue depressors to dialysis machines and artificial hearts—in short, from bedpans to brainscans. Member companies include billion-dollar giants like Johnson & Johnson, Pfizer, IBM, and General Electric. Eighty percent of the membership, however, consists of smaller companies with less than $20 million in domestic sales. Most of the large companies had their own Washington offices, but for its smaller members HIMA was the only conduit to the federal government. Membership dues were structured by sales and large companies essentially controlled HIMA's board of directors.

HIMA consistently sought cooperative relationships with government, especially with the Food and Drug Administration (FDA), the Health Care Financing Administration (HCFA), and the House and Senate committees on health. The association was formed in 1976, when the Food, Drug, and Cosmetic Act was amended to extend FDA regulation in the medical area beyond drugs to "devices." (The former metabolize in the body while the latter do not.) The FDA determined what was safe and effective; the HCFA decided what would be paid for under Medicare, the government's $80-billion-a-year health plan for elderly and disabled Americans. These two government agencies thus played a central role in the health industry's development. HIMA was concerned that its membership's ability to compete effectively in the world economy might be threatened unless the agencies' actions were carefully coordinated and managed and unless both agencies were fully aware of and sensitive to the problems and capabilities of the industry.

Organizational Purpose. In 1984, HIMA's board of directors chose Frank E. Samuel, Jr., to serve as president. A 1965 graduate of Harvard Law School, Samuel worked for the Agency for International Development in the Kennedy administration, part of a new generation committed to the ideals of more effective government. In 1968, he moved to a private law firm and then to a four-year stint at the Department of Health, Education and Welfare. He joined HIMA as general counsel in 1975.

As president, Samuel increased HIMA's staff from thirty-nine to fifty-one, recruiting some highly skilled and experienced talent from government, including Ted R. Mannen, senior vice president for policy, who had been legislative assistant to Sen. Adlai Stevenson (D-IL). Samuel was given high marks by many government officials with whom he worked. One House aide said: "He's put together a top-notch staff . . . not just competent, but free from the 'obnoxiousities' typical of most trade groups." Another added: "He is effective because he is honest and straightforward and presents information for my use that is helpful."

Samuel believed that the U.S. regulatory system needed "retooling to meet certain agreed-upon national objectives. One goal of the regulatory framework should be to get new medical technology products to patients as quickly as possible consistent with public safety. Second, the medical device and diagnostics industry contributes to U.S. international competitiveness and should be encouraged."

Acknowledging the necessity of the FDA imprimatur for public confidence in a product, he felt that the time that the agency took to approve new products could be greatly shortened. (In 1988, it was nine months, four months shorter than in 1986.) "But what's really needed," he said,

> is a basic change in the philosophical concept of the regulatory relationship between device manufacturers and the FDA. The FDA has to get off its high horse; it's not morally or scientifically superior to industry. Congress needs to act responsibly; headlines do not improve health unless they reward innovation. And the industry has to give up its dolls and needles and do a better job

of working closely with the FDA regulators. Industry should be prepared from the CEO level down to cooperate and initiate, not just react and complain.[5]

John A. Gilmartin, CEO of Millipore and another HIMA board member, endorsed Samuel's approach to government relations but was pessimistic about its chances of prevailing.

> It's the only sensible way to go, but look at what he's up against. First there is the diversity of HIMA's membership. The big pharmaceutical companies have long had adversarial relations with FDA over drugs, and that extends into devices even though the two are very different. A drug doesn't change. New ones come along but the old ones remain. Devices change all the time; they evolve. The pacemaker of today is very different from the one 10 years ago. So with devices ongoing cooperation is essential. But old habits change slowly and the big companies have their own Washington offices—lobbyists. These company representatives are kind of a Bedouin tribe in Washington. They are pros trying to get done what the boss wants. They may have some influence back at headquarters but not much. They are generally not in on the strategy making. They are implementers. They may have good relations with HIMA's staff but they still have to obey headquarters where the old assumptions are often still very much intact. So they run around HIMA anytime they want.[6]

B. Kristine Johnson, vice president for public affairs, public relations, and corporate planning of Medtronic, had this to say:

> What Frank has really brought to HIMA is the realization that the industry must be involved in a broad array of issues which go well beyond—but eventually affect—short-term, narrow interests of particular companies. If the industry is going to have a place at the policy table,

we have to be interested in and knowledgeable about the big picture—reducing the federal deficit, health policy generally, United States competitiveness. Company interests, after all, are but a subset of these larger questions.[7]

Leah Schroeder, HIMA vice president for government affairs and a former congressional administrative assistant, added: "Our goal is to ensure that any time a health policy issue is being considered in the White House, the Office of Management and Budget, the Department of Health and Human Services, or the Congress, we will get a call at HIMA to come and help."[8]

On the other hand, people like Robert M. Moliter, manager of government programs for GE's Medical Systems group, felt that Samuel "fails to recognize the inherent tensions between the regulators and regulated which are quite proper and which are designed into the system." He also questioned whether HIMA was "really as macro as it should be. Take Medicare, for example, I think we should be out there with the hospitals lobbying against excessive cuts." Moliter was chairman of HIMA's government and public affairs section, composed of representatives of twenty-four association members.

Samuel estimated that about 30% of his membership agreed with his call for a more cooperative approach, some because they were genuinely enthusiastic and others because "you attract flies with honey." About 20%, he thought, were negative, "feeling that things are fine as they are, don't rock the boat. If we were more forthcoming, we would give the government new ideas about how to regulate us and would be forced to disclose our secrets. Let sleeping dogs lie. We also have antitrust fears, and believe that in general government equals grief—the less we have to do with it the better." The remaining 50% were, he felt, essentially indifferent.

Among the enthusiasts was HIMA's long-time board member Ben L. Holmes, vice president/general manager, Hewlett-Packard Medical Products Group, which had 4,000 employees manufacturing electromedical devices such as monitors, ul-

trasound imaging equipment, electrocardiographs, and advanced computer systems for medical use. HP had an exem-
plary record with the FDA. Holmes explained why his
company needed HIMA:

> First it imposes discipline on us. It's sort of like school.
> You have to read the studies HIMA prepares. You have
> to prepare for the meetings, seminars and conferences.
> That keeps us on our toes and up to date.
> Second, Hewlett-Packard benefits when the industry
> standards are high—the higher the better for us. HIMA
> membership includes all the major players. It imposes
> pressure on all its members to do their very best. That's
> good for us. It protects us from fly-by-nights.[9]

The critical role of an industry association in a rapidly
evolving high-technology sector like health equipment begins
to emerge. We also see the impressive difficulties it must overcome.

Mission. An industry association's mission can be described
as follows:

- It is an economical mechanism for collecting and analyzing information concerning government rules, regulations, and policies; it presses its membership to understand the needs of government.
- Conversely, it is a credible and authoritative channel
  through which the needs and capabilities of the industry can be made known to government regulators and
  policymakers.
- Through the power of its governing board, it can discipline members so that delinquent firms do not taint the
  industry.
- It provides special services to the many small companies that are often the source of invention and innovation but that lack the resources to staff a Washington
  office.
- More controversially, it serves as a strategist for the

industry, shaping industry policy and objectives and perfecting their fit with those of government.

- When big issues come before the Congress or the executive branch, it can bring the full power of the industry to bear; it is an instrument for collective action. In the words of Richard Godown, president of the Industrial Biotechnology Association (IBA), HIMA's counterpart in the bio-tech area: "We can influence Congress and the regulators much more effectively than an individual company because we represent the industry. It's much easier for a legislator to do something for an industry as opposed to an individual company."[10]
- Finally, there is the subtle role industry associations can play in encouraging the disparate agencies, departments, and branches of government to overcome their inherent separateness and attain a greater measure of coherence.

Obstacles. But consider the obstacles an aggressive association confronts in executing these functions:

- First is the diversity of its membership. HIMA represents some 300 firms. Some are very large and have been around a long time. They have well-ensconced Washington offices with entrenched habits of behavior. As Gilmartin said: "They run around HIMA anytime they want." The small companies, for their part, have their own needs and concerns. For example, as Godown of IBA said: "We had talked about creating an R&D consortium for biotechnology but the small companies—that represent the majority of our membership—were against it. They're afraid they'll come up with a breakthrough that must be shared."[11] Furthermore, the small firms may not want or feel they need the "discipline" to which Holmes of HP referred above.
- There is also the traditional fear of antitrust action against any kind of industry cooperation, as well as the basic mistrust of government, especially one that does any kind of planning.

- On the government side, as we shall see, cooperators like Samuel face skepticism and anxiety. Government regulators do not see the international competitiveness of industry as their mission. (Indeed, we shall see that in the case of HCFA's director, it is not even considered a problem.) This means that when priorities are being set for position on the wait list for approval, global competitiveness is irrelevant. An AIDS cure, for example, will get quick review, but a product like Bovine Somatotropin (BST), a protein hormone that increases the milk production of cows, will linger for years before getting the approvals required to go to the market. America is already awash in milk, it is argued, so why rush? What is ignored is the world market for the product.
- And, of course, there is the natural resistance among governmental players to the coherence industry would like. We shall see, for example, that cooperation between the industry and the FDA runs contrary to what many in Congress view as proper and desirable.

So Samuel at HIMA and his counterparts at other associations such as the IBA are important to the improved management of business-government relations. They are bridge-builders, or perhaps gap-closers. But by many in both government and business they are mistrusted, unwanted, and, when they talk of international competitiveness, irrelevant. Nevertheless, their mission is bound to become more essential as the fortunes of the two sides become inexorably more interdependent.

Let us, therefore, look more closely at the gaps they try to manage: at the regulators, the Congress, and the health equipment industry leaders.

The Food and Drug Administration

The FDA regulates safety standards for all drugs, most of the food that is eaten, cosmetics, health equipment, and devices and materials ranging from gauze bandages to pacemakers. Products under FDA regulation come from 90,000 companies and represent $550 billion, or one-quarter of the U.S. gross national product. FDA spends $550 million a year—$2 per American—and has 7,000 employees. Like HCFA, it is part of the Department of Health and Human Services (HHS) and has two functions mandated by Congress: product approval and ensuring good manufacturing practices.

Medical device regulation was first authorized in the Federal Food, Drug, and Cosmetic Act of 1938, but was greatly strengthened by amendments to that act passed in 1976. The amendments were the result of numerous injuries reported in the early 1970s as a result of fraudulent and hazardous use of medical devices. The amendments required medical device manufacturers to register and list their products annually, to submit to regular inspections of manufacturing practices, to make periodic reports on product experience, and to submit new devices for premarket approval (PMA). According to Section 510(k) of the amendments, "new" devices could not be marketed until they had received a PMA or had been classified as Class I or Class II products, meaning that they were less risky than those in the Class III category. There was considerable controversy over the meaning of the word "new" in Section 510(k), as we shall see later. Firms were required to notify the FDA ninety days in advance of marketing a device that had not been sold prior to the enactment of the 1976 amendments.

In order to obtain a PMA, a manufacturer has to satisfy the FDA that its product is both safe and effective. [In 1986, 5,153 PMA and 510(k) submissions were filed with FDA, double the number filed in 1977.] The manufacturer can contend and the FDA can agree that a product is not new, that it is substantially the same as a product manufactured before the amendments were passed. In such a case, FDA approval is not required. (Original PMAs were reviewed in an average of 337 days during 1987, down from 395 days in 1986.)

HIMA worked hard to help the FDA be more effective, and especially to shorten approval time. In 1986, for example, the association lobbied Congress to provide the FDA with an additional $800,000 that the Office of Management and Budget had not allowed it to request. The funds were earmarked for product approval. Again, in 1987, HIMA was instrumental in Congress' appropriating an extra $2 million above the OMB-imposed FDA limit. The following year, it supported an FDA request for an additional $1.3 million, and also sought to recover regulatory authority, which had slipped from FDA to the states during the Reagan years.

In 1988, James Benson was acting deputy commissioner of FDA. Before that, he had been deputy director of FDA's Center for Devices and Radiological Health, HIMA's interface with the agency. He said:

> Samuel is a good man and I'm in favor of the concept he is advocating [emphasizing the word concept]. Take, for example, home blood-glucose monitors which allow diabetics to regulate the flow of insulin they are taking. This device required the most intimate cooperation between our people and the industry. Its safety and effectiveness depend not only on the device itself, but also on how well the patients using the device are educated. We have to be concerned and involved in both areas.
>
> But there are serious problems. Right now we're being investigated by Cong. John Dingell's Oversight Committee[12] and by the inspector general of HHS for the alleged misbehavior of an employee in the generic drug area. The employee is suspected of arranging for a company to be moved up on the waiting list for approval in return for a gift. This is a serious offense. It's taken half my time for the past two weeks. If Dingell holds hearings on this, the whole agency will tend to increase its distance from companies. Our integrity is absolutely critical; we cherish our reputations. We must.
>
> There are 3,000 FDA inspectors in the field. They see themselves as cops. They are concerned that cooperation with industry might taint their integrity. I believe much more can be accomplished by working with business as

partners but it takes a while to change the old practices. If we don't do better, frankly I'm worried that our industry will go down the tubes in the face of competition from countries such as Japan where industry and government work much more closely together. Their approval times are much shorter than ours and their products are often better. I don't know how they do it but it sure works well.[13]

Benson accused the industry—including HIMA—of sometimes being excessively rigid and legalistic. "One-half of the product recalls we find are due to bad design, not manufacture. So we put out guidelines—just guidelines, nothing more—on product design. HIMA complained that there had been no due process, no industry participation in drafting the guidelines, no hearings and so on."

On the other hand, he spoke approvingly of HIMA's educational programs for its membership and the numerous workshops, seminars, and conferences that bring FDA regulators and industry people together to discuss common problems. "They have been very helpful. They serve as a useful clearinghouse for information. HIMA has also helped us a great deal on the Hill with our appropriations. They realize that if we are to give them timely PMAs, we need the staff to do the work."

Regarding FDA's relationships with HCFA, the other government agency critical to the health industry's future, Benson admitted that they did not work closely together. "It's a turf problem. We should be much more involved in each other's decision making. I wish industry would help us here but I find that particularly the big companies are unwilling to use their clout for such bureaucratic purposes. I guess they fear a backlash."

Dr. Kshitij Mohan, director of the Office of Device Evaluation, said:

Samuel is reaching for a team approach. There's nothing wrong with that but it's kind of nebulous. Do we have a common goal with industry? If so, what is it? Our goal is public health. What's industry's? It's profits and often quick profits. Let's face it, we have different roles.

The United States is not like Japan. The medical device regulatory group in the Japanese government has fewer than a dozen people; we have 800. But in Japan government and industry are synergistic. Business respects government, looks to government for standards and even leadership, helps government, and government respects business. They are extensions of one another. Here we believe in a separation of roles, due process, adversary proceedings and the rest. Our society is distrustful of collaboration between government and business. Congress would never allow close collaboration, neither would consumer groups. So we must maintain an essential tension between the FDA and the industry. But having said that I think there is substantial room for more cooperation and interaction. Here I agree with Samuel.

He cited a number of steps he thought should be taken:

We should get together with the company earlier. As soon as a company starts to think about a new product, they should involve us. When they are designing prototypes, they should know our requirements. Quality should be built in. And we can learn from them as well.

Companies, especially the small ones, are so eager to hit the market that they don't pay enough attention to quality. Here again the Japanese are impressive.

If a company has a failed device, they should admit it straightaway and get it off the market. They shouldn't pretend and try to squeak by. That wastes everybody's time and erodes trust.[14]

Walter E. Gundaker, director of the Office of Compliance, Center for Devices and Radiological Health, oversaw seventy-five field investigators whose task was to ensure good manufacturing practices among HIMA members. "We see three kinds of companies," he said. "Those who are way out of line, those who are always good, and then a middle group that may swing one way or the other. Our job is to get the violators. We are cops, let's face it. How close do you want us to get to those whom we are supposed to police?"

He continued:

> We want companies to monitor their failures and to analyze the trends which the data show. They argue that that's not part of the regulations and we can't force them to do it. Some companies are, of course, outstanding. They do what they're supposed to do and we have good relations, but many fight us every inch.
>
> HIMA has been very helpful, but there's lots of room for more cooperation. Take defibrillators, those pads used to shock heart attack victims. Often they malfunction because of bad batteries. They lie around the fire house or somewhere and nobody checks the batteries. It's not the manufacturer's fault, but they often get the blame. Here we need an education program for users which should involve the manufacturers as well as us.[15]

The Health Care Financing Administration (HCFA)

At the same time that federal regulation of medical devices was increasing, the government became more actively involved in deciding which health services would be paid for by Medicare and Medicaid.[16] For HIMA, "these programs symbolized a national commitment to assuring quality health care for all Americans. And they encouraged investment in research that led to advances in medical technology and practice virtually unimaginable two decades ago."[17]

In the 1980s, however, this commitment was threatened by rising costs[18] and federal budget constraints. By 1987, health care costs had reached an estimated $496.6 billion per year, or about $5 a day for each American. The most dramatic cost containment effort was Medicare's 1983 shift to a prospective payment system (PPS), setting the payment rates for hospitals before treatment was provided instead of paying for the actual costs afterward. The payment system was administered by HCFA, which placed all medical problems into diagnosis-related groups (DRGs) and established a fixed payment for each group. The payment covered *all* services and supplies provided to Medicare patients.

HCFA decided what medical devices could be paid for by Medicare, and HCFA's policies were being followed by an increasing number of other Medicare contractors, such as Blue Cross/Blue Shield and commercial insurers. As a consequence, those policies were a significant factor in decisions by hospitals concerning expensive medical equipment. Recent HCFA review and approval times varied from about nine months for an implantable automatic defibrillator to five and a half years for a phrenic nerve stimulator.

Robert Streimer, HCFA associate administrator, explained some of the complexities:

> Adjustment to the PPS rates went well beyond HCFA just saying "yes" or "no" to a particular device. HCFA could say, for example, "Yes, this new artificial hip is covered. It goes to the DRG 210, but the payment rate for that DRG will not change." It might take anywhere from 18 to 24 months before the PPS rate formulas would recognize that a new and presumably more expensive hip was being routinely used in DRG 210. In some cases, a service or device might be so unique that it didn't fit into a DRG, in which case a separate pricing judgment would have to be made. Cochlear implants or heart transplants for example.[19]

HIMA was concerned that budget pressures on Medicare might discourage or delay innovation in medical technology. In 1986, Medicare consumed about 7% of the federal budget; in 1988, that figure rose to 8%, and by 1993, it would be more than 10% even if no new benefits were added.[20] (See Figure 4-1.)

HIMA negotiated with HCFA on whether and how to incor-

Figure 4-1

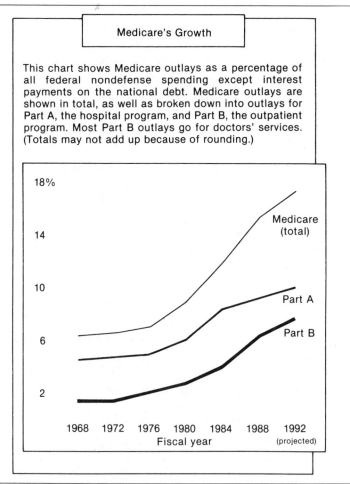

Medicare's Growth

This chart shows Medicare outlays as a percentage of all federal nondefense spending except interest payments on the national debt. Medicare outlays are shown in total, as well as broken down into outlays for Part A, the hospital program, and Part B, the outpatient program. Most Part B outlays go for doctors' services. (Totals may not add up because of rounding.)

Medicare (total)

Part A

Part B

18%

14

10

6

2

1968   1972   1976   1980   1984   1988   1992
Fiscal year   (projected)

porate new technologies into the payments system. This was a complex and subtle process that had to take into account the range of possible technologies, and balance their short- and long-run costs and benefits, their social and economic value, and the interests of patients, taxpayers, and the economy in general.

Dr. William Roper, administrator of HCFA, said, "We have to ask how cost effective a particular device is." HCFA would not, for example, cover an experimental device. Consider a therapeutic implantable pump for cancer patients, which was installed surgically and injected drugs regularly, and obviated the need for chemotherapy. In the short run it was expensive but over the long run it saved money. Under HCFA rules, a hospital would have to pay for this product initially. If the pump became accepted as a proven form of treatment, hospitals would report that they were using the pump and that their costs were greater. "We would then increase the DRG payment accordingly," said Dr. Roper. "Generally it takes from 18 to 24 months for the billing information for a new device to be reflected in the DRG rates."

Dr. Roper's response to HIMA's contention that this procedure discourages innovation was that it "encourages innovation in cost saving." He added, however,

> I am concerned at the margins. We look at things as they come along. It is hard for us to take a long view. Our accounting practices don't work that way. We need to have a better way of looking at long-run costs. Take bone growth stimulators, for example, which are costly to begin with but which speed up the healing of broken bones. We don't have a very good way of thinking about these kinds of things. We also need to think more about which technology works best for which kinds of patients. What works in one case may not in another.[21]

Dr. Roper was generally not concerned about the competitiveness of the U.S. industry. "I've just come back from Europe. We are still the premier developer in health equipment. We devote 11% of our GNP to health care. That's more than any other country. So I think we're doing pretty well." (Dr. Roper, whose leadership at HCFA earned him promotion to the Bush White House staff in 1989, apparently assumed that because U.S. health care costs were the world's highest, its health industry was maintaining its competitiveness in the world economy.)

Dr. Roper spoke enthusiastically about Samuel's work:

> He wants to deal in public policy issues instead of only those matters which directly affect his industry. He tries to help us do our job better. For example, the other day he was in here with executives from four of his member companies which make software for health information systems. He wasn't trying to sell us anything. He pointed out that these companies provide hospitals with information systems which are able to collect a lot of information that would be helpful to us in measuring the clinical outcomes of various technologies. He was suggesting that we talk to the hospital information systems people about getting data to help us contain costs better. In some instances, of course, this might alert us to inefficiencies— instances, for example, where some product might be overutilized—and this in turn might actually adversely affect one of HIMA's members.

Dr. Roper saw many areas where more cooperation would be desirable:

> We have a major problem with decubitus ulcers [bed sores]. These are very common among old people who are bedridden. They are painful, dangerous, and, when they get infected, expensive. They are a primary reason for old people being forced into nursing homes, and thus account for a huge cost to us. But neither the government nor the industry had addressed the problem. Some companies I suppose make money out of bed sores. Then HIMA put together a coordinated industry approach. New products were developed, including beds which continually move the patient, and special pads. Samuel looks at health problems systemically, from our point of view. He's helped us to find common ground with the industry.[22]

The interactive approach with Samuel described by Dr. Roper was less well accepted by the lower levels of the HCFA bureaucracy where analysts and rulemakers tended to regard themselves as the enemies of business, which they perceived as reaping huge profits at the taxpayers' expense. Furthermore, the company people with whom the bureaucrats dealt were invariably rigid and legalistic, often reporting to the general counsel in the firm, who had little technical knowledge or concern.

Other Government Agencies

Historically, U.S. medical device and diagnostic products were strong competitors in the world marketplace; in fact, the United States exported more medical technology than any other nation. But as we have seen, the large trade surplus that the industry enjoyed in 1981 had been halved in less than a decade.

Japan presented a special problem to HIMA. Although Japanese imports into the United States in 1987 were only 3.1% of the market, they were double what they had been six years earlier. At the same time, a web of regulation effectively prevented access for U.S. medical equipment makers to Japanese markets. For example, until 1985 and partially even thereafter, Japan required that all test data submitted in support of product approval applications be generated from clinical trials in Japan on Japanese citizens. HIMA sought and received help from the United States Trade Representative's office in pressing Japan to open up.

HIMA staff were also increasingly involved in Europe. In Germany, most health equipment was purchased by cities and towns for their hospitals. "They are loyal to Mother Siemens," said Bob Moliter of GE. "It would be unpatriotic to be otherwise." Similarly, the French government was extremely reluctant to buy health equipment not made in France. And as Europe headed toward unity in 1992, the harmonization of health regulations was important to HIMA.

Association staff also worked closely with the Department

of Commerce to gain relief from crippling export controls imposed by the United States for security reasons on many electronically sophisticated products such as ultrasound fetal monitors, blood flow detectors, heart monitors, blood analyzers, and computerized tomography (CT) scanners. Although most applications for relief eventually received approval, the industry's foreign competitors used the delay to establish a substantial competitive edge.

THE MEDICAL DEVICE IMPROVEMENT ACT OF 1988

In 1989, there was reason to believe that the close and cooperative relationships Samuel had sought to create, especially with the Congress, were in jeopardy. Following months of negotiations with HIMA staff, the House passed a bill tightening and expanding FDA regulation of the medical equipment industry and sent it to the Senate for approval. It was endorsed in a letter from Samuel to Sen. Edward M. Kennedy (D-MA), chairman of the Committee on Labor and Human Resources, which handled health matters in the Senate, and Sen. Orrin Hatch (R-UT), ranking Republican on the committee. At the same time, however, three of HIMA's most powerful members—Pfizer, Eli Lilly, and Bristol-Myers—lobbied against the bill, and it was defeated. Some key House members and particularly their staff assistants felt betrayed.

The bill, called the Medical Device Improvement Act of 1988, was introduced in 1987 by Cong. John B. Dingell (D-MI), chairman of the House Committee on Energy and Commerce, and Cong. Henry A. Waxman (D-CA), chairman of the committee's Subcommittee on Health and the Environment. It grew out of long-standing congressional dissatisfaction with the FDA's regulation of the health equipment industry, in particular its enforcement of the Medical Device Amendments of 1976.

In a 1983 report on the FDA's implementation of the 1976 amendments, Congressman Dingell's Subcommittee on Oversight and Investigations found "a picture of bureaucratic neglect for public health and safety that shocks the conscience."[23] The report went on: "Reflecting what the subcommittee can only regard as a cavalier disregard for the potential consequences, the FDA has barely begun to implement the provisions of the law."

The report was particularly critical of what it called the 510(k) "loophole" under which risk-laden Class III products were exempted from a full premarket review because they were not held to be new under the language of the act or were substantially equivalent to products that existed before the 1976 amendments were enacted. The result, said the report, was that many of the riskiest devices, such as pacemakers, were essentially unregulated.

"Perhaps the agency's most disturbing default of all," the report continued, "is its failure to move forward with a requirement that manufacturers inform FDA when their devices kill, injure or lead to some other adverse experience. As a result, neither the FDA nor the public knows today how dangerous medical devices are, and we as legislators lack an adequate basis to decide whether the device amendments . . . are adequate."[24]

"We really beat up on the agency in that report," said Patrick M. McLain, oversight committee counsel.

The 1988 act was designed to tighten up industry reporting and expand regulation. The 1976 bill required firms to report equipment failures to the FDA. The 1988 bill would have required that hospitals report on any serious problems with equipment. It also mandated "an orderly timetable under which FDA either reviews old and new devices for safety and effectiveness or reclassifies them so that they no longer require such approvals." It would also give new authority to the FDA "to take action against products that pose an unreasonable risk of harm to the public health."[25] The bill followed hearings held in 1987 before Congressman Waxman's subcommittee.

"We found that more than 90% of the 5,000 or so new products going on to the market each year employ the 510(k) loophole," said Dr. Peter Budetti, counsel to the subcommittee. "That is, they are found to be 'substantially equivalent' to old products. They are reviewed by FDA but they do not get the thorough treatment which they should get."

Dr. Budetti continued:

> Manufacturers are required to report device failures but they don't always know about them because hospitals don't tell them. Some companies never report. Others report everything.
>
> We spent a year and a half negotiating this bill with HIMA. In June [1988] we finally had agreement. We bent over backwards to be cooperative. And it wasn't easy because we have many groups watching us; we have to be fair to everyone.

The Waxman committee staff had a reputation in Washington for being particularly hostile to business. "Staff members compete with each other to see whose witnesses attract the most TV cameras," said one observer. Indeed, in the 1987 hearings, one witness testified he had received five defective artificial knees, which made a special impact on the committee members who suffered from arthritis. A couple told of how their baby had been "roasted to death" in a defective incubator. The media crowded the hearing room.

"We agreed to call off more hearings we had planned at HIMA's request in return for their promise to cooperate," said Budetti. "Next time we're going to give it all we've got." Budetti was clearly angry that "HIMA's efforts to counteract lobbying by its maverick members against the bill in the Senate were ineffectual."[26]

At its March 1988 board meeting, all agreed that HIMA should support the House bill if some changes were made in it. The changes were negotiated to the satisfaction of all except the three firms that opposed the bill in the Senate.

Gerald R. Conner, vice president, legislation, of HIMA, pointed out, however,

It was only three out of 300 after all. When we started
with the 1988 bill our people were all over the map. We
pulled things together and limited the dissenters. We
convinced our members that there was going to be a bill,
if not in 1988, then in 1989, and we would get a better
bill if we cooperated. But you can't get everybody to agree
on something this close to their hearts.

There were three camps among our members: those
who said no way, those who said we've got to take it but if
nothing happens that's O.K., and the vast majority who
didn't care.[27]

According to congressional insiders, the bill's failure in the
Senate was apparently due to a variety of factors. The three
maverick companies persuaded Senator Hatch to put a hold
on it. This alerted the Senate leadership that the bill's passage would be difficult and time-consuming, so it went to the
bottom of their list.

Senator Kennedy's Labor Committee staff were not enthusiastic about the bill. It did not arrive from the House until
July, which was late in a busy session. For Dr. Steven Keith of
that staff, the bill did not go far enough. Furthermore, if there
was to be a bill, they wanted it to be a Kennedy bill not a
Waxman one.

By the second week of October, it was clear the bill was
dead in the Senate. Said one observer, "Hatch refused to negotiate with Waxman and Dingell. He wouldn't even return
their phone calls."

"There's no doubt at all that the 1989 bill will be much
worse for the industry," said Gerry Connor. "I'd be very surprised if next time the TV cameras don't focus on products of
Pfizer, Lilly, and Bristol-Myers," added Bob Moliter of GE.

As it happened, Chairman Dingell of the House Energy
and Commerce Oversight Subcommittee did not wait long
to retaliate. In February 1989, he threatened hearings on
Pfizer's conduct with regard to sales of its Bjork-Shiley heart
valve.[28]

Pfizer Hospital Products Group was generally regarded as

among the HIMA members that have been most active in presenting their viewpoints on recent congressional proposals to modify the FDA's regulation on medical devices. For Pfizer, a key sticking point in the Waxman bill was a provision that would allow FDA to use the innovator's scientific data as a basis for approving an imitator's device as safe and effective. Pfizer and other research-oriented sponsors of new devices spend millions of dollars and years of time to develop such data, and treat them as proprietary. Edward C. Bessey, HIMA director and president of Pfizer Hospital Products Group, observed, "The proposed legislation posed an unacceptable risk to the innovator, and amounts to appropriation of intellectual property."[29]

Apparently Waxman wanted to lower barriers to the introduction of new products and thus increase competition and lower prices for consumers. Clearly some HIMA members would benefit from the waiver provisions, but other companies found it unfair.

Ben Holmes of HP was with the majority of the board who felt that HIMA should have endorsed the Waxman bill. He valued close relations with FDA:

> We train FDA inspectors—15 or 20 a year—in our plant. Our quality managers work closely with them. It's a dangerous game to be at loggerheads with government. Generally they win. We're better off working with them, trying to understand their problems rather than trying to overpower them. In a political process you can never get the whole hog. You have to compromise. The House bill as it finally emerged was the best we could get.
>
> I know that the pharmaceutical companies [which also make devices] were concerned about the PMA waiver business. They felt it would genericize equipment, but I don't think that's a real problem in practical terms. We had a big debate about it in the board. Indeed, we were still trying to get unanimity in August and we almost got it. There were only three hold-outs. Feelings ran high. This was the first time that the HIMA board was divided

on an issue. I've been wondering since then whether we should reorganize our committees in some way to assure continuing consensus.

Our committees now are set up around issues areas. Perhaps we should think about issues as they affect different kinds of companies: those who make equipment, for example, or implantables, or hospital supplies.[30]

IMPLICATIONS

In the high-tech industries of tomorrow—semiconductors, electronics, biotechnology, commercial uses of space, and more—collective industry action is becoming essential. The nation's standard of living depends on it because it is a prerequisite for competitiveness. We have seen the reasons for this in what has gone before, and they are amply demonstrated in the case of health equipment.

Collective action is necessary because the investment required to develop new technologies and manufacturing processes is often too large for one company, and the degree of knowledge and experience required to beat the competition to innovation in the marketplaces of the world is often greater than that possessed by a single company.

Government policies—those that promote and those that constrain industry—are critical to competitive success. To the extent that the policies affect all the players in an industry, collective action is required in order to encourage and assist government decision makers to make a clear and consistent definition of community need in a timely way. The conflicting priorities of different constituencies must be balanced. This only government can do; it alone has the authority. Industry must understand and respect that fact, making its competence and judgment available to government decision makers in every possible way.

The power of collective action is needed to bring together government agencies—FDA and HCFA, for example—as well as the subcommittees of Congress and their staffs so that the executive and legislative branches of government can achieve a continuing consensus about community need. Cooperative relations between the health equipment industry and the FDA, for example, are marred by the lack of such relations with Congress. In the case of HIMA, we saw that the Waxman Committee staff relish attacking the FDA for being too cozy with the industry. To change this situation requires broad public awareness of the importance of industrial competitiveness to the American people. Collective action is necessary to achieve this new mindset.

And government must be a partner with a strategy, a vision of where it wants the country to go. In 1989, there was no such vision. Speaking of biotechnology, Monsanto's president, Earle Harbison said, "The industry, and those who regulate it, operate largely in a political vacuum. There is no clear signal from our political leaders to go for it. Much effort is being expended to see that nothing goes wrong, but little effort is being expended to see that things go right. . . . We need proactive leadership from government. . . . Government should be the agent of change, and catalyst for the development of this technology."[31]

In order for collective action to succeed through an association such as HIMA there are a number of conditions to be met:

First, the members of the association must know their separate interests and be clear about how their interests fit with those of others. For example, small companies derive benefits from HIMA that large companies do not and vice versa. This is inevitable and acceptable if the rules are clear.

Second, all members must understand and accept the mission of the association: to design and manage a strategy for the industry as a whole that will enhance its global competitiveness without unfairly aiding or hurting individual members. In order to do this it must use the power, influence, and competence of the members to assist the full range of relevant government policymakers to do their work effectively, mindful of their relationships to one another. Oddly, perhaps, it is also the mission of the association to help government become more coherent. Government has difficulty pulling itself together because the conceptions of separation and fragmentation are deep-rooted in American law and practice. Industry must lead if perestroika is to come to Washington. Government cannot and should not impose it.

Third, trust among the association's members is essential to success. It can only grow out of collective debate about the industry's interests and the relation of each company's interest to them.

Fourth, the association (including all its members) and government are not and cannot be adversaries; they are partners. Although there will and should be vigorous disagreement, both are concerned with promoting community need and having it defined well and soon. If this is not accepted, the interests of both business and government will suffer. At the same time, business and government have distinct roles that must be respected. FDA inspectors are and must be cops. It is in the interests of all that they, like their counterparts on the street, do their job diligently. But industry competence is also essential and worthy of respect. If it is eroded, all suffer.

So the functions of an association are to be a clearinghouse for information and an educator of government and business; to bridge the gaps separating different parts of government and different parts of the industry from each other and to keep before all the parts a coherent vision and sense of direction for the whole; to discipline its members by setting standards and requiring acceptance of agreed-upon norms and positions; to negotiate and represent the industry viewpoint in the councils of government and to bring the concerns of government to the attention of its membership; to shape an ongoing consensus.

For collective action to be effective, its management must have very special qualities. First, the CEOs of the member companies must be personally involved and committed to the principles stated above. Second, the association management must have the strength, skill, and courage to take what often will be lonely stands between many conflicting interests. It is no job for a wimp!

One thought needs elaboration. It concerns the relationship

between bureaucrats and politicians, which appears to be changing in the United States as well as in other countries, including Japan. This relationship is crucial to effective collective action, to the management of an industry association, and to the management of business-government relations generally.

There was a time when the tasks of executive bureaucrats, such as those of the FDA, and elected politicians, such as Congressmen Dingell and Waxman, were more separate and distinct than they are today. The politicians made laws, and the bureaucrats carried them out. Today, it is by no means that simple. As Robert Putnam, dean of Harvard's Kennedy School of Government, and his colleagues point out in a classic study of senior civil servants made in 1981, bureaucrats, especially in the United States, have been taking on increasingly political functions and politicians through their burgeoning staffs have been assuming more technical ones. There is thus a "clash between the dual and conflicting imperatives of technical effectiveness and democratic responsiveness."[32]

The merging of functions, Putnam found, contributed to a "fragmentation of authority," a blurring of the line between political and administrative leadership with politics reaching down into the upper layers of the civil service and administrative concerns moving into the staffs of the congressional subcommittees.[33] This "bureaucratization of politics and . . . politicization of bureaucracy" has meant that Congress plays a more "powerful and independent role in formulating policy and overseeing implementation than for its sister legislatures in Europe."[34] (The number of Capitol Hill aides has risen from 5,600 in 1957 to some 15,000 in 1989.)[35] Indeed, congressional oversight is so effective that "many administrative officials . . . receive a good deal more day-to-day guidance from Congressmen than they get from the President."[36] When the two are from different political parties, with different aims and objectives, administrators are naturally torn. Recall from the HIMA story the conflicting pressures on the FDA caused by the antiregulatory disposition of President Reagan's Office of Management and Budget, the demands of the law, and the expectations of Dr. Peter Budetti and Patrick McLain. HIMA sided with the FDA against OMB, helping it to obtain additional funds for review and inspection and recognizing its interests as being nearer those of the Democratic Congress than the Republican administration.

Putnam offers a neat conclusion: "The moral dilemma posed by bureaucratic policymaking is power without responsibility; the dilemma of policymaking by politicians is power without competence. Excessively bureaucratic policymaking may lead to a crisis of legitimacy, but excessively political policymaking threatens a crisis of effectiveness."[37]

What Samuel seems to be saying and what HIMA reflects is that policymakers must make the competitiveness of American industry a legitimate and high-priority community need; and that bureaucrats and industry, often acting collectively and in cooperation, must reshape their thinking to meet that need.

NOTES

1. Albert D. Wheelon, "Von Karman Lecture: The Rocky Road to Communication Satellites," American Institute of Aeronautics and Astronautics, 1986, New York, NY.
2. Michael C. Fuchs, medical equipment industry analyst, "Economics of U.S. Trade in Medical Technology," unpublished report for the International Trade Administration, U.S. Department of Commerce.
3. See MITI document, "General Regulatory Aspects for Biotechnology in Japan," 1987.
4. Much of what follows is drawn from George C. Lodge, "The Health Industry Manufacturers Association," #398-085. Boston: Harvard Business School, 1989.
5. Address to Food and Drug Law Institute Conference, Washington, DC, December 15, 1987.
6. Lodge, "The Health Industry Manufacturers Association," p. 4.
7. Ibid.
8. Ibid.
9. Ibid., p. 5.
10. Interview, July 1989, Washington, DC.
11. Ibid.

12. The function of oversight committees is set forth in Rule X2(b)(1) of the Rules of the House of Representatives: "Each standing committee . . . shall review and study, on a continuing basis, the application, administration, execution, and effectiveness of those laws . . . the subject matter of which is within the jurisdiction of that committee, and the organization and operation of the federal agencies and entities having responsibilities in or for the administration and execution thereof, in order to determine whether such laws and the programs thereunder are being implemented . . . in accordance with the intent of Congress and whether such programs should be continued, curtailed, or eliminated."

13. Lodge, "The Health Industry Manufacturers Association," p. 6.

14. Ibid., pp. 7, 8.

15. Ibid., p. 8.

16. Medicare was the federal health insurance program that in 1988 served 30 million elderly Americans and some disabled persons; Medicaid was a federal-state health program for 22 million poor people. It cost $55.2 billion in 1988, 50% of which came from the federal government.

17. HIMA brochure, 1989, p. 2.

18. Experts expected medical costs to increase 21.5% in 1989 with 11.2% of that increase being due to "pressure on hospitals to purchase current technology." Hewitt Associates, in *Medical Benefits,* November 30, 1988, p. 5.

19. Lodge, "The Health Industry Manufacturers Association," p. 9.

20. Office of Management and Budget, Social Security Trustee estimates, 1988.

21. Lodge, "The Health Industry Manufacturers Association," pp. 10, 11.

22. Ibid., p. 11.

23. *Medical Device Regulation: The FDA's Neglected Child,* Washington, DC, U.S. Government Printing Office, 1983, p. *iii.*

24. Ibid., p. 59. Since 1983, the FDA has required reporting by manufacturers of alleged device failures.

25. U.S. House of Representatives, Report 100-782, p. 10.

26. Lodge, "The Health Industry Manufacturers Association," p. 14.

27. Before coming to HIMA, Connor was special assistant to the assistant secretary for legislation, Department of Health and Human Services.

28. *Medical Devices, Diagnostics, and Instrumentation Reports* ("The Gray Sheet"), February 1987, p. 3.

29. Lodge, "The Health Industry Manufacturers Association," p. 16.

30. Ibid.

31. Excerpt from Earle H. Harbison, Jr., speech at the Biotechnology Strategic Management Conference, March 11, 1987.

32. Joel D. Aberbach, Robert D. Putnam, and Bert A. Rockman, *Bureaucrats and Politicians in Western Democracies* (Cambridge, MA: Harvard University Press, 1981), p. 3.

33. Ibid., pp. 9, 19.

34. Ibid., p. 22.

35. *Newsweek,* April 24, 1989, p. 30.

36. Ibid., p. 27.

37. Ibid., p. 25.

CHAPTER 5

Governmental Affairs Managers: Masters of the Fine Line

Corporations and government are separated by a turbulent sea, stirred by currents of power and influence, rippled with suspicion, and swept occasionally with gales of corruption—Rose Mary's list* of the Watergate era, Wedtech, the Defense procurement scandal, the Recruit Company influence-peddling scandal in Japan. It is hard to imagine a time or a place where capitals have not known bribery, kickbacks, payoffs, fraud, and blackmail. No country, no system has a clear lead in the morality race.

For this reason alone, those who manage relations between a corporation and the several governments it must contend with have a difficult assignment. They are suspected by government of slavish devotion to the narrow objectives of the corporation. At headquarters, their superiors tend to assume that they have "gone native" and joined "the enemy," or have been corrupted, or both. They live in a twilight world between those they represent and those with whom they must deal.

In America, the governmental affairs (GA) manager has special problems that stem from traditional ideological assumptions about the roles and relationships of government and business. If one believes that government is a necessary evil, the least government being the best, and that business is endowed by God and nature with inalienable rights of own-

---

*This was a list of major U.S. corporations that had made substantial—and illegal—contributions to President Nixon's 1972 campaign for reelection. It was kept by the president's personal secretary, Rose Mary Woods.

ership, the relations between the two have consequent characteristics: business is inherently the more legitimate of the
two; constraints imposed on it by other than the marketplace
are highly suspect and never accepted without a fight; and
although government has few, if any, rights to tamper with
business activity, business has every right to demand and
expect help from government. This may seem farfetched, but
consider, for example, the big American banks and their
travails with Latin American debt. They got themselves into
the mess and yet expected government to help get them out of
it, apparently without any change in government's influence
over bank policy. That is "free enterprise"!

As unrealistic as these beliefs are, they are held—explicitly
or implicitly—by many top executives. Thus, the GA manager is frequently torn between realism and effectiveness on
the one hand, and catering to the ideological biases of his or
her boss on the other. The manager is at the center of the
storm surrounding perestroika in America. The role is thus
spectacularly important, equalling at least and perhaps sur-
passing that of the chieftains of finance, marketing, production, and control. But invariably GA managers are unap-
preciated and underpaid; they are regarded as order-takers or
appendages to the general counsel. Their creativity and imagination, which should be encouraged, are stifled. Everyone
suffers as a result: the corporation, the government, and the
larger community.

The GA office is peculiarly vulnerable to cost-cutting, because its role is inherently controversial and because it is not
a profit center, at least not obviously so. To the extent that it
is measured by results, these tend to be short term and negative—defeating this or that bill, for example. Achieving long-
run improvement in important relationships may be hardly
noticed, even though it is quite possibly a significantly
greater contribution to the corporation's competitiveness.

Given these difficulties, government affairs managers in
Washington are hard-pressed. Those who are effective are
wisely and understandably secretive. They do not talk much,
and never, if they can help it, for attribution. Scholarly re-

search of their activities, therefore, is scarce. The best of them are satisfied with little credit for their achievements, since their power and authority come from helping others in government or in their firm to benefit, to look good, to seem farsighted. They keep a low profile, and run hard and lean: no chauffeured limosines, fancy parties, big offices, nothing to give their adversaries a target or lure government officials from the path of virtue. Like a good newspaper editor, they know something about most everything, are widely read and broadly educated. They are humble in the face of the powerful with whom they constantly mingle, but supremely confident of their course and independent in perceiving and describing reality as they see it. At the same time, they are sensitive to the ideological blinders worn by those around them so that their presentation of reality will be shaped so as to be received and understood. They are skilled at inspecting their own assumptions about prevailing conditions, values, and beliefs, never allowing wishful thinking or concerns with what ought to be to color their insight about what in fact is. Their loyalty to their firm is only matched by the persistence and honesty with which they tell the CEO the truth. They—that is, the best of them—are masters of the fine line. To appreciate the complexity of governmental affairs management, let us examine the office in several companies, beginning with IBM's Washington office, which, according to many in business and government, is among the most effective.

IBM'S OFFICE OF GOVERNMENTAL PROGRAMS

Until the 1960s, IBM did not regard governmental relations as a separate function.[1] It took the view that the corporation was little affected by government policies and that it could live with whatever policies there were. When government policies did occasionally impinge on corporate interests, it was the job of top management in the United States and country managers abroad to respond.

Two events, one in Europe and the other in the United

States, prompted change and resulted in the establishment by IBM of a new function called Governmental Programs in the United States and External Programs abroad. The first event occurred in the mid-1960s, when a serious controversy arose in Europe over the U.S. government's denial, on national security grounds, of a license to export a non-IBM computer. In the ensuing debate over "extraterritoriality," IBM World Trade management recognized that European governments could well regard U.S.-based companies, including IBM, as unreliable suppliers. Management concluded that a problem of this magnitude could not be handled by individual country managers. It would require extensive analysis and continuing relationships with staff in the departments of State, Defense, and Commerce who were responsible for export control policy. It would also require coordinated management of relations with other governments.

Shortly thereafter, in the United States, the second event occurred. Legislation to repeal the credit that the United States allowed on taxes paid in other countries was working its way through Congress. Its passage would have been a serious blow to the ability of U.S. companies to compete in world markets. The proposed legislation also contained provisions that would have restricted foreign imports into the United States, thus provoking retaliation against U.S. exports. IBM, along with many other companies that were deeply involved in international trade and investment, believed that the bill would change its environment disastrously.

So it was that in the early 1970s IBM's corporate office of Governmental Programs (GP) was established. The first question was who should head it. Should it be someone whose experience and knowledge was primarily in government, or someone who knew the company, its business, and its culture? Top management leaned toward the latter option and appointed Charles E. McKittrick, Jr., as vice president, Governmental Programs. At the time, McKittrick was a vice president of IBM's Data Processing Division, with twenty-five years of experience in marketing, much of it to government.

Other equally important questions to be decided were

whether to locate the head of Governmental Programs in Washington or at headquarters; whether to unite or separate those who would interact with government and those who would be responsible for studying public policy trends and determining corporate positions on them; and whether to staff the new organization with experienced Washington hands or with employees from within the corporation. IBM decided to locate the office in Washington, to combine government relations and public affairs staff, and for the most part to hire internally.

Staffing from within IBM enabled the office to identify and establish close links with its "clients" at headquarters, those whose work was significantly affected by public policies, who were interested in certain issues and outcomes in Washington and other national capitals. The Washington location was necessary so that the office could understand and forecast governmental policies and decisions as well as influence them. "You need to live with the government people if you are to know their requirements and to make your policy story successful," said McKittrick. "Our value-added to IBM is our knowledge of the government for IBM's information, advice, and advocacy."

McKittrick regards as most important the decision to put together in one office the government relations or lobbying function and the management of policy issues. Although the two departments are quite separate and employ different personnel, their relationship is "almost seamless." The governmental relations manager registers as a lobbyist, focuses on the legislative process, and develops IBM's relationships with legislators. The issue manager, on the other hand, is a cool professional whose task is to become an objective expert in an assigned substantive area such as trade, taxation, technology, or health and safety. Issue managers should be part of the inner circle of Washington decision makers in their area. They should be called on for help by government officials as well as corporate clients. They should be ahead of the game, helping to resolve conflicts before they harden into problems or crises. The issue manager's knowledge informs and is amplified by the lobbyist's efforts, and together they are a bridge between IBM and government. They influence IBM so that the interests of government and the likely trends of public policy will be taken into account when the company formulates its policies, and they also influence government so that it is fully aware of IBM's interests when it shapes its policies. Thus they seek to align and conform IBM with the community needs of the United States and the scores of other countries where IBM does business.

IBM Governmental Programs is responsible for coordinating government relations activities with professionals in country affiliates around the world. These professionals manage governmental problems at the national and regional level, each day exchanging among themselves a flow of information through IBM's international computer and communications network. McKittrick's office participates both as a recipient and originator of information and is ultimately responsible for ensuring that the policies followed by the countries and regions are consistent with corporate strategy.

Country external programs managers handle issues unique to the country, but increasingly issues cut across national boundaries. "Trade policy actions in the United States—to take only the most obvious example—reverberate not only in Japan, Europe, and Canada but among the newly industrialized countries (Brazil, Hong Kong, Korea, Mexico, Singapore, Taiwan), and less developed countries including China and even the COMECON (Eastern European) countries."

"In general," says McKittrick, "IBM's experience is that success in the public policy arena depends on ensuring that what IBM wants to achieve is generally compatible with the government's priorities. To that end, we make a conscientious effort, in shaping our policies and strategies, to understand what each government is seeking to achieve. . . . We try very hard to have a consistent philosophy. That means that we seek to advocate policies in one country that are related, or at least not diametrically opposed, to the policies we are advocating in other countries."

He offered IBM's approach to telecommunications as an example:

> The connecting policy thread is our firm belief that a
> private, deregulated, transparent network, allowing easy
> and relatively inexpensive access to value-added systems,
> serves the best interests of users [as well as equipment
> and service providers]. . . . To be sure, we are serving
> IBM's interest; but we think these policies also serve the
> best interests of the regions and countries that imple-
> ment them.

The objectives of McKittrick and his colleagues abroad may
be said to be to align the interests of IBM with those of the
governments that it affects, and to prepare the corporation for
the shock of future events. Achieving these ends requires
credibility with IBM clients and with government officials.
Government affairs managers must be believed by all. Both
sides must trust that their confidence will not be betrayed.
Finally, McKittrick and his associates must have authority.

How do GA managers achieve the three attributes of credibility, trust, and authority? First, they must have knowledge;
this is crucial. IBM's global network, connected by computer,
must provide the governmental relations organization with
quick, reliable, and relevant information that issue managers are able to digest, analyze, and interpret so that it becomes useful and usable. The network provides virtually in-
stantaneous communication between terminals anywhere in
the system, allowing those in charge of the issues to ask questions and receive quick answers. "Those responsible for strategy," says McKittrick, "who are often the same people asking
and answering the questions, are able to talk more frequently, and, in some cases more interactively, than they
could if they depended exclusively on the telephone."

Second, they must have access to the decision-making apparatus in IBM and in government. To ensure this access,
McKittrick relies on a combination of his issue managers and

government relations staff. Both are needed to maintain close relations with IBM clients and government officials. Their access and authority in government depend on their access and authority in IBM, for if government officials believe that no one listens to McKittrick at corporate headquarters, they will not be attentive either. A deputy U.S. trade representative spoke about the importance he attached to being able to obtain company views on trade matters quickly and reliably: "You call IBM and you get an answer back the same day." Referring to another U.S. multinational, which was having trouble breaking into foreign markets, he said: "That company is terrible at using government for its purposes. I call them up and ask them for their position on something and it takes them a week to call back. When they do, they often say that there is disagreement within the company."

Third, there is a continuous effort to educate IBM and government people in an honest and objective fashion. IBM must be aware of government's concerns fully as much as government must be of IBM's.

Finally, there is a mindset that does not consider IBM and government as adversaries. McKittrick knows that IBM operates at the sufferance of many governments. His task is to define and make manifest their mutual interests.

There are, of course, many obstacles and hazards in his path. His office must guard against distortions, biases, blinders, and blind spots, which McKittrick seeks to minimize by rotating his staff regularly so that non-American IBM personnel serve tours of duty as issue managers in Washington and Americans serve abroad. "While this system exacts a price in learning time, the benefit is a far more sophisticated understanding of the global environment." The office is also vulnerable to blockages in the lines of communication to headquarters as well as to government officialdom. McKittrick attempts to keep the lines free through constant and careful attention to the needs of each. Equally careful attention is paid to the often fine lines separating the interests of different governments and those of IBM, which we shall see dramatically displayed in the case of Brazil's targeting of minicomputers, and separating IBM and other computer companies.

In all of this, McKittrick is out on the point. His network, backed by the economic strength of IBM, has important political influence throughout the world. His office can make a significant contribution to public policymaking in the United States and around the world. Thus, he can affect the welfare of many people. He realizes, however, that his legitimacy and that of his corporation come directly from the communities they serve. This realization is at the heart of his effectiveness.

Obviously, one could not expect IBM to reveal the details of its government relations activities, and so we must use our imagination to grasp more fully the art of managing those relations. We can infer from two situations, one centered in Brazil and the other in Japan, the challenges that each posed to government affairs managers at IBM. Fortunately, both cases have been carefully analyzed by eminent political scientists, Emanuel Adler and Peter B. Evans (Brazil) and Chalmers Johnson (Japan); I shall draw on their work.[2]

The first situation concerns Brazil's adoption of restrictive trade policies in the 1970s and 1980s to promote and protect its domestic computer industry. The second involves Japan's development of a telecommunications policy in the 1980s and impediments to the Japanese market encountered by foreign firms. In both cases, the U.S. government and IBM were active players, and for both the stakes were high. The United States was concerned with free trade and with bolstering its declining competitiveness in the world economy. Although it shared these objectives, IBM's interest was to expand the sales of its products as well as ensure the long-run political and economic interests of its venerable subsidiaries in Brazil and Japan.

In each situation, there were many conflicting interests: those of the governments of Brazil, Japan, and the United States, and particularly of various departments, agencies, groups, and individuals within those governments; those of domestic companies in each country, including IBM, that were by no means of one mind; and those of U.S. companies seeking to export to the two countries, again including IBM, that were themselves divided.

In each case, some tasks for an IBM government affairs manager become immediately obvious. She would have to start with history, probably 100 or more years of it, to get a sense of the long-term trends leading up to the present time. In particular, she would need to know the historical development of the legislative bodies and administrative bureaucracies involved: how and from where they obtained their power, whether it was waxing or waning, the nature of their constituencies, and what pressures and impulses lay behind the current policies and initiatives. Her mapping of the players would also include the relevant business associations and individual companies and their interests and sources of power. She would want to examine key personalities and get a sense of their motivations and concerns. Then she would doubtless ask what all these facts taken together indicate about the prevailing ideology: the role of government, the role of business, both foreign and domestic, the relationships of government and business, and the prevailing definition of community need and how and why it might be changing.

With this information as background, the GA manager could then start to fill in the details of the picture, eventually isolating with some precision the points of tension, the sticking points in need of resolution. From an analysis of these points would come an awareness—again precision would be crucial—of trends. Which way might things evolve? What is most likely to happen? Then and only then would she consider IBM and its long- and short-run interests. With her best picture of reality and IBM's concerns before her, she could begin to identify choices for the company. These would depend on the company's resources, its friends and enemies, its bargaining power with other players, the risks it was prepared to take, and its long-term view of itself. If she had done her work well, if all elements of the system had been charted accurately and realistically, if the data were reliable and correct, the wise choice would fall out rather easily. Implementation might not be simple, but the direction would be clear.

Throughout this process, she would have been questioning her clients at headquarters, checking her views, exchanging insights, so that when the time came for decision, those who would make it would have shaped it.

BRAZIL'S INFORMATICS POLICY AND THE U.S. RESPONSE: 1970–1988

On March 15, 1985, José Sarney became Brazil's first civilian president since the military had seized power twenty years earlier to prevent what was perceived to be a leftist takeover. At the time Sarney assumed the presidency, inflation was running at an annual rate of 250% and rising, unemployment was at an all-time high, and the country was in the deepest recession of its history. Even though the Brazilian economy had boomed at times during the previous two decades, many Brazilians had not shared in the prosperity—the richest 1% owned as much as the poorest 50%. And foreign bankers were clamoring for interest payments on Brazil's $100-billion external debt.

Sarney recalled: "The greatest optimist thought I might last 90 days at most, as Brazil slid back into institutional instability. The question was whether we would return to a harsh military regime and total dictatorship, or whether we were on the road to civil war."[3]

By November 1985, the threat of instability had eased after direct elections were held for national and state offices and work had begun on a new constitution—the eighth in Brazil's 163 years of independence. New presidential elections were set for November 1989.

Shortly before Sarney took office, the Brazilian Congress had ratified by enacting into law a number of actions the government had taken to encourage the development of an indigenous computer industry. Starting in 1975, government policies prohibited any company that was not 100% Brazilian owned from doing business in small-sized computers as well as in a wide range of related products: software, terminals, and semiconductors.

The Informatics Law and the policies preceding it were highly controversial inside and outside Brazil. Proponents included some of Brazil's most brilliant intellectuals, scientists, and political leaders. They believed that only by reserving a share of the computer market for domestic firms could Brazil gain the technological capability to compete successfully in the world economy and raise its standard of living. They were determined to liberate Brazil from what they termed "the colonialism of the multinationals (MNCs)."[4] Indeed, since 1979 the multinationals' share of Brazil's computer market, worth an overall $1.5 billion, had dropped from 77% to 54%. Since then also, the national small-computer manufacturing industry had grown 30% a year. By 1985, all the computer companies in Brazil, including IBM, were generating revenues of nearly $2 billion, of which half was produced by the Brazilian national, small-computer sector under market reserve. Nearly 40,000 workers were employed in that sector in 1987, of which 12,000 were high-level professionals.[5]

Opponents saw the market reserve policy as an expensive way to enrich a handful of Brazilian entrepreneurs and widen the technological gap between Brazil and the rest of the world. Sen. Roberto Campos claimed that Brazil was "seriously behind in terms of computer production," and would never catch up without the benefit of foreign multinationals at all levels of the industry.[6] Robeli Libero, president of IBM do Brasil (established in 1924), said that his company's exports from Brazil in the four years following the introduction of market reserve would be only $1 billion, half of what they might have been without the government's policies.[7] Also, IBM's investment in Brazil was falling, from $176 million in 1982 to $80 million in 1983. IBM's worldwide policies prohibited shared ownership of foreign subsidiaries. Other U.S. companies in Brazil, such as Burroughs, were also cutting back. U.S. economist William Cline estimated that "the informatic strategy in Brazil is probably costing user-firms and the public as much as $500 million annually." He calculated that "if the crucial goal of informatics policy is to create scientific and technological infrastructure . . . it may be said that Brazil is paying approximately $42,000 annually per job for scientists and technicians."[8]

Externally, the U.S. government was bitterly opposed, claiming that the Brazilian strategy violated the principles of free trade, was unfair, unreasonable, and bad for Brazil. And many U.S. companies not in Brazil, such as Data General, were incensed at being cut off from a lucrative market. Indeed, in the late 1970s and early 1980s, Data General had beseeched the Office of the United States Trade Representative to take action against Brazil in order to open the market, but to no avail.

Ricardo Saur was among the small group of Brazilian technocrats responsible for planning and implementing Brazil's informatics policies. Emanuel Adler called them "ideological guerrillas," because of the tactics they used to mobilize diverse groups behind their goals—the military, the banks, intellectuals, and key governmental leaders. Furthermore, the language of their speeches and writings was cast in a tone of nationalism, liberation, and independence. In the 1970s, when the guerrillas began their efforts, IBM controlled 60% of Brazil's computer market, which was the world's fastest growing. Manufacturing large- and medium-sized computers, IBM had not yet begun to manufacture the mini- and microcomputers, which had been pioneered in the 1960s by Digital Equipment and Data General. In fact, no small-sized computers were manufactured in Brazil, which gave Saur and his group what they perceived to be a technological window, one that might not remain open for long. So they moved fast to acquire the power required to become the "guardian of the gates" (their phrase).[9]

Let us pause here in the story to ask: How might an issue manager at IBM have known in 1974, when Saur and his group began their efforts, that they would be able to overcome many powerful elites in Brazil—ranking members of the Senate; industry, which wanted the best and the cheapest computers as soon as possible; the multinational corporations, especially IBM, who over seventy years had gained many friends; the U.S. government; and others?

First, it was clear that the group had considerable *authority* behind its claims. It was sustained by ever-present feelings of nationalism and by the needs of the Navy for technological know-how and equipment. This produced an odd coupling of university intellectuals and military people. Then too the timing was right; Brazil was burdened by ever-increasing trade deficits. In addition, the group never went too far in its rhetoric; it avoided any hint of autarky, stressing independence instead.

Second, it had *access to power* provided by key cabinet ministers, leaders of the state banks, and military officers in what was still a military regime. It was kept in place by that regime, which had been successful in producing high growth over several years and had thus accumulated substantial surpluses for investment in the new computer industry and for the establishment of a state-owned computer company, COBRA. In these circumstances, the guerrillas could use the power of IBM, the foreign giant, against itself: the more it struggled, the more powerful its opponents became.

The third factor in their favor was *competence*. They had lots of it and the right kind. The technology of microelectronics was changing fast, becoming simpler and less expensive, and a growing number of Brazilian graduate students were capable of handling it. The institutional resources were present in government and a rapidly growing private sector. And Saur and his colleagues had an ideological pitch that united disparate elements.

Fourth, they had exceptional *communications* abilities. They spoke the right language, used the right words. They were clever phrase makers, these "guardians of the gates."

In a 1988 interview, Saur recalled those early days:

> We were young and impatient; we were also very
> lucky. The timing was right. It was clear that computers
> would change the way we lived. They would shape our

country socially as well as economically. We had to develop knowledge and capabilities among a critical mass of people—in engineering, production, marketing and distribution—or else we would lose our independence. We would be always in somebody else's hand.

We were concerned about very bright Brazilians who came out of the university and couldn't use what they had learned creatively. When I graduated in 1964, my best opportunity was to work as an IBM salesman.[10]

What would have prevented our hypothetical issue manager from predicting what was to come? First, there would have been the natural confidence in the status quo and the complacent conviction that IBM's enormous contribution to the Brazilian community would preserve its interests. A close second would have been the acceptance of the economists' argument, voiced above, that the policy was irrational in economic terms. To have foreseen the "success" of the Brazilian policy, one would have had to look at Brazil as a total system. Then it would have been clear that Informatics—"The Model," as Saur called it—was almost an ideological imperative. Its economic efficiency was relatively unimportant.

Returning to Sarney's early days as president, it must have been with some shock that he learned of the speech made by President Reagan on September 7, 1985, Brazil's independence day—the equivalent of the Fourth of July in the United States. Reagan said: "I am directing the U.S. Trade Representative to start proceedings . . . against a Brazilian law that has restricted U.S. exports of computers and related products and squeezed out some American computer firms operating there."[11]

Thus began three years of political battles between the governments of the United States and Brazil. Oddly enough, there was little if any support for the president's action among U.S. multinationals.[12] Even Data General, which had been so eager for government action to force Brazil to change its policy in the early 1980s, had by 1985 made a deal to market its machines through a joint venture with the state-owned Brazilian computer manufacturer (COBRA). IBM, still the largest computer firm in Brazil and about six times the size of its nearest local rival, was also finding an increasingly cooperative spirit on the Brazilian side, and over the years had changed its policies on joint ventures. In February 1986, the Brazilian Secretariat of Informatics (SEI) approved a joint venture between IBM and Gerdau, a powerful local electronics group, and designated the venture a "national firm" eligible for government contracts. SEI also authorized IBM to construct a new hard-disk plant and approved company plans to build more advanced models of its 4381 (a small mainframe) in Brazil.[13] Thus, although the ban on minis and micros was still in place, there appeared to be some softening around the edges, at least enough so that MNCs wanted to avoid embarrassing Sarney in his time of troubles. Nevertheless, President Reagan persevered, and the United States Trade Representative, Clayton Yeutter, became the point man.

The USTR and Section 301

The USTR is a part of the executive office and reports directly to the president. In this sense, it is similar to the Office of Management and Budget (OMB) or the Council of Economic Advisers (CEA). The USTR was created by Congress in 1962, and its role and influence were expanded in the Trade Act of 1974. Under Section 301 of the act, whenever the president suspected that a foreign country might be violating the precepts of fair trade, he could authorize an investigation into that nation's trade practices and, if they were found to be "unreasonable," authorize economic sanctions.

A separate investigating body, the 301 Committee, was formed for each suspected trade violation. Each committee consisted of subcabinet-level representatives from State, Treasury, Commerce, Justice, Agriculture, Labor, CEA, and OMB. A member of the USTR's office chaired the 301 Committee, and all hearings and negotiations for the investigations were conducted by USTR personnel.

Investigations were lengthy, ranging from two to six years.

The committee had to quantify the extent to which a U.S. industry was being damaged by the targeted trade restriction, and it had to determine whether the trade restrictions were unreasonable, which was rarely easy given the conflicting goals among the departments and the ever-changing foreign trade policies of the international community. Hence, 301 investigations were usually tightly focused. The broader in scope an investigation was, the harder it was to quantify results and the more difficult it was to develop an interagency consensus.

Typically, 301 actions were initiated by U.S. exporters who felt that they were being victimized by restrictive trade policies. The USTR benefited from this procedure. First, by requesting a 301 investigation, industry associations signalled when they had a serious trade problem; this spared the USTR from investing the time and resources needed to track and identify foreign trade barriers. Second, in requesting a 301 action, the associations normally provided valuable background data. Finally, an industry push for 301 action assured the USTR's office of strong lobbying support if retaliatory action were recommended to the administration and Congress. (The 301 action against Brazil, along with cases against two other countries mentioned in the same presidential speech, was the first such action initiated by the U.S. government.)

If a trade practice was found to be unreasonable and economic sanctions were imposed, the retaliation had to be roughly equal in value to the damages caused by the unreasonable practice. The 301 Committee tried to ensure that possible sanctions would not hurt U.S. companies located in the targeted nation. The trade representative would recommend options to the president, who had the authority to impose any form of retaliation that was deemed appropriate.

Responding to 301 Actions

Let us pause here and consider the role of IBM's GP office in a 301 proceeding. Clearly the work of the committee and its ultimate decision were important to IBM, its Brazilian subsidiary, and, indeed, the interests of the company wherever 301 proceedings were likely. The Washington office, through its international communications network, was an important source of data. Knowing the interests and viewpoints of the 301 Committee's members, the office was in a good position not only to advise them but also to promote some consistency in the attitudes of Washington and Brasilia.

Within the USTR and the White House, "decisions to retaliate are taken with great reluctance," according to a USTR negotiator. She likened sanctions to a blunt instrument whose effects were difficult to calibrate with precision. Apart from Brazil, the United States had imposed sanctions on only one other country. In 1985, the United States determined that Japanese manufacturers were illegally dumping semiconductors on the market, and two years later the Reagan administration had responded by limiting certain Japanese imports.

Foreign trade issues were normally politically neutral in the United States, but in 1985 they became highly controversial. The United States had recovered from the worldwide recession of 1981–1982 more quickly than other nations. Domestic demand increased rapidly, while at the same time the value of the dollar climbed. Consequently, imports flooded the U.S. market and exports declined as U.S. manufacturers were burdened with overpriced products and sluggish markets. Record trade deficits resulted. Between 1979 and 1985, total U.S. exports to Brazil, for example, fell by 10%. In the same period, Brazil's exports to the United States more than doubled, causing its trade balance to shift from a deficit to a surplus of more than $5 billion.

Trade worries set the stage for a partisan clash. The Congress, controlled by Democrats, wanted U.S. companies and jobs protected. "Japan-bashing" and "Buy American" became popular themes among business and labor groups. The textile industry introduced an advertising campaign with the slogan "It matters to me—Made in the U.S.A.," which featured celebrities such as Bob Hope and Don Johnson. Rep. Richard Gephart (D-MO) first entered the national spotlight by proposing legislation that would mandate U.S. retaliation whenever the balance of trade with another nation dropped below certain levels. Both Republicans and Democrats decried the loss of 600,000 manufacturing jobs since the beginning of the Reagan administration.

The White House was committed to free trade and sought to reduce trade barriers through the GATT and bilateral talks. Reagan officials feared that new protectionist legislation would undercut these efforts and provoke a trade war.

In the first week of September 1985, the president received a trade bill from Congress. He objected to several protectionist measures in the bill, but protectionist sentiment was mounting in Congress—over 300 proposals for restricting trade were pending—and there was no guarantee that a presidential veto would be sustained. He also rejected a congressional request to ban Brazilian shoes from the U.S. market. Then came the president's September 7 announcement that the USTR would investigate unfair trade practices in Japan, the European Economic Community, and Brazil in accordance with Section 301 of the Trade Act of 1974.

There was much speculation about the reasons for the president's action. Was it concern about America's trade deficit, especially with Brazil? Was he angered by the threat posed by Brazil's policy for American companies operating in Brazil, or was he merely defending free trade principles?

Some suggested that President Reagan was trying to impress Congress. As one U.S. computer industry executive put it:

> The president was trying to prove to key members of Congress that the U.S. did in fact have a viable trade policy—it self-initiated a series of unfair trade practices cases—and since everyone thought that a Latin American country was necessary and since Brazil was known to have very restrictive import policies, Brazil was chosen as a test case.[14]

Here again, IBM's Washington office was well prepared to appreciate the range of pressures being exerted on President Reagan and to explain events to its people in Brazil.

The USTR invited briefs from all interested parties. In response, the two major U.S. computer industry associations submitted short letters that offered lukewarm support for the 301 action. According to the American Electronics Association (AEA):

> We support efforts to negotiate mutually acceptable changes to the Brazilian informatics policies. Our member companies welcome the opportunity to work closely with you in negotiations with Brazil. We are also exploring the possibility of initiating industry-to-industry discussions with our Brazilian counterparts on these questions. Our hope is that these efforts will lead to expanded, rather than contracted, trade relations between our two nations.[15]

The Computer and Business Equipment Manufacturers Association (CBEMA) wrote:

> The overwhelming margin by which the Informatics Law passed in Brazil attests to the strong political support for this law. For this reason CBEMA feels that the fundamental objective of U.S. negotiations should be to improve the way the law is implemented and to assure the timely phase-out of its provisions.[16]

Do we perhaps see here the work of IBM, working with other computer companies through the industry associations, trying to conciliate, to move toward an amicable solution, to develop a reliable and acceptable consensus among industry players?

Several corporate members of the two associations pushed for stronger support of the 301 action. However, companies with ongoing business in Brazil, such as IBM, Burroughs, and now Data General, resisted a harsh line. According to an AEA officer, "Before the administration unveiled the 301, the USTR approached the industry for our support. Almost unanimously we advised against it."[17]

The 301 action evoked a strong response in Brazil. One

Brazilian businessman said that "it probably elected 40 leftist congressmen and if retaliation ensues it will be 80."[18] On September 23, President Sarney defended the Informatics Law in a speech before the United Nations.

The Reagan administration had difficulty developing a consensus in Washington. State and Treasury opposed putting pressure on Brazil when delicate negotiations on Brazil's repayment of its debt to U.S. banks were under way. (Indeed, a year later the U.S. ambassador to Brazil was to denounce the 301 action as "a stupid policy.")[19]

By March 1986, the U.S. computer industry finally reached a consensus. According to an industry executive:

> Most of the activity concerning trying to define an industry position occurred in the association and industry groups. Eventually, everyone realized that none of us were going to get what each of us individually would have liked. . . . In the end, although the issue of copyright protection was not the ideal one to choose, given domestic concerns and the present U.S. international trade agenda, intellectual property rights became the key issue in the Brazil 301 case.[20]

A USTR negotiator called the agreement to concentrate on copyright protection and move away from opposition to the market reserve policy "the lowest common denominator." Software copyright protection was chosen because all the U.S. hardware and software manufacturers were concerned about the possible loss of their proprietary technology. It was also important to the Reagan administration, which had recently persuaded Japan and other countries to adopt strict intellectual property rights laws and was trying to get these protections included in the GATT.

In October 1986, the Brazilian Computer Industry Association (ABICOMP) filed a brief with the USTR defending the Informatics policy and summarizing supporters' rationale for the restrictions. The ABICOMP statement argued that the Informatics Law was justified under the terms of two GATT articles that allowed import restrictions to accomplish balance-of-payment objectives and protect infant industries (Article XVIII), and because of national security considerations (Article XXI). Similar grounds had been cited by the U.S. government in rejecting Fujitsu's application to acquire Fairchild, a U.S. semiconductor manufacturer.

No progress was made in the 1986 meetings between U.S. negotiators and their Brazilian counterparts. Consequently, the United States decided to "up the ante," in the words of one official. In October, only months since the proceedings had begun, the Section 301 Committee concluded its investigation and found that the Informatics Law unreasonably "burdens and restricts U.S. commerce."[21] The estimated annual damages to U.S. manufacturers from loss of sales was placed at $105 million.

Because the Brazilians had begun direct negotiations, the United States suspended any retaliatory action until December 1986. Reluctantly, the Brazilians bent under U.S. and internal pressure. Less than twenty-four hours before the U.S. deadline was to expire, President Sarney proposed legislation that would provide copyright protection for software. (Let us again speculate: Might not the government affairs offices of IBM and the other major computer companies in Brazil have been especially helpful to President Sarney in drafting this legislation? Their offices, through their corporate clients, had access to highly sophisticated expert judgment about the technologies involved, they knew the interests of other concerned companies through their participation in industry associations, and they were well aware of the interests and viewpoints of the U.S. government players.) Sarney also offered guarantees that the market reserve policy would not be renewed when it expired in 1992, and that the market reserve would not be extended to other areas of U.S. concern, such as pharmaceuticals. The Brazilians refused the U.S. request to define the area encompassed by the Informatics Laws on the grounds that it was a rapidly changing, high-technology field. Administratively, the Sarney regime restructured SEI, established a formal appeals process to a new

National Council on Informatics and Automation (CONIN), and proposed an ad hoc group of Brazilian and U.S. government representatives that would meet to discuss the problems that U.S. companies might have with SEI or the market reserve policy.

The 301 Committee was not completely satisfied with the provisions of the copyright protection bill or Sarney's response to objections about the market reserve. Moreover, the issue of investment restrictions had not yet been addressed. Nonetheless, Yeutter was pleased with the progress of the negotiations and hoped that the copyright protection bill might be favorably amended in the legislative process. On Yeutter's recommendation, President Reagan extended the suspension of 301 retaliatory action until the end of June 1987. Yeutter was charged with personally monitoring Brazilian actions and the progress of the negotiations.

In June, the Brazilian Chamber of Deputies narrowly passed legislation that provided copyright protection for software. The bill was still subject to approval by the Senate. Although Yeutter felt that the bill contained important loopholes weakening protection for intellectual property, he was satisfied with the general course of negotiations. Sarney's administrative changes appeared to be working. CONIN overturned several SEI decisions that had been unfavorable to U.S. firms; also, U.S. companies were now using the ad hoc group in applying to manufacture and sell computer-related equipment. But there was still no progress on the investment issue. According to several officials, the USTR understood Sarney's difficult position. "We had gone to the brink" to get copyright protection, said one official. The general belief was that a few more months of negotiations would produce an acceptable agreement. In view of this progress, Reagan again suspended 301 action, from June until December 1987. Speaking on behalf of the AEA's 3,300 corporate members, R. Wayne Sayer said:

The government of Brazil is to be commended for pushing this bill in the current domestic political environment. . . . In light of this progress we supported the administration's decision to suspend the 301 proceedings.[22]

Confrontation: December 1987–April 1988

By the end of 1987, negotiations had once again soured. Henry Kissinger told the *Los Angeles Times* that if the U.S.–Brazil conflict continued, "populist, anti-market, anti-U.S. forces will be dangerously strengthened just when a democratic constitution is being drafted."[23] The U.S. negotiators were mindful of the need to maintain a domestic constituency so that they would be seen as "defending American interests," which meant that they had to keep the U.S. computer industry on board since it was clear that there was no other domestic constituency. The USTR file on the case contained only one letter from a domestic manufacturer in another industry that hoped to benefit from the case, a small Massachusetts producer of disposable paint filters that expressed the hope that if the United States retaliated against the Informatics law, it would do so by raising tariffs on imported Brazilian paint filters.[24]

In September, Microsoft Corporation negotiated a deal to license a disk-operating system (DOS) to six Brazilian hardware manufacturers. SEI refused to approve the agreement, ruling that a Brazilian firm, Scopus, already manufactured a similar system. The ruling extended the range of the "rule of similars" to include software for the first time. U.S. industry and government officials contended that the Scopus system was far inferior to Microsoft's DOS. Just as Data General's CEO Edson De Castro had done ten years earlier, William Gates, CEO of Microsoft, tried to rally U.S. industry and the USTR against SEI's ruling.

Gates asked Yeutter to persuade the Ministry of Science or President Sarney to overturn SEI's ruling.[25] Should that fail, he wanted the Reagan administration to take action under the 301 finding. Gates argued that while the new software protection bill pending in Brazil's Senate might increase software protection, the functional equivalency preference as applied to software by SEI amounted to "an insurmountable barrier" that would keep U.S. software companies out of the Brazilian market.

Two of the Brazilian companies planning to license Microsoft's DOS appealed to CONIN to reverse SEI's ruling. Scopus and other Brazilian companies argued forcefully in support of the functional equivalency rule, claiming that they could not compete if Brazil opened its markets to U.S. software and thus Brazil would be forever dependent on foreign software. In further support of Scopus' case were indications that SEI had initially pressured Scopus to develop a DOS that would rival imports. Moreover, the Brazilian computer market had collapsed in 1987, and only one of the ten largest Brazilian computer and peripheral manufacturers had turned a profit that year. Against heavy U.S. pressure, CONIN and the Ministry of Science refused to overrule SEI.

At this time, U.S. negotiators realized that the Brazilian Senate was unlikely to pass an acceptable software protection bill. Although the copyright protection was considered adequate, the bill gave SEI "vaguely worded discretionary authority to define functional equivalence (for hardware and software) and levy a 200% tax," according to a USTR spokesman. The tax was to be used to fund the development of the Brazilian computer industry.

In 1987, major U.S. microcomputer manufacturers, already shut out of Brazil by the market reserve, had become alarmed by the increasing number of low-cost clones being produced in Brazil. Brazil's Unitron applied to SEI for permission to manufacture what Apple executives saw as a reverse-engineered clone of its Macintosh microcomputer, using pirated software. These firms, irritated at being locked out of Brazil, feared Brazilian exports that might undercut their own foreign sales. Thus they intensified pressure on Congress and the administration for some form of retaliation.

This pressure, along with Yeutter's report that negotiations had again deadlocked, set the stage for President Reagan to act. On November 13, he announced that the United States would impose $100 million worth of tariffs on Brazilian shoes, aircraft, and earthenware, and prohibit the importation of any Brazilian data-processing products. Reagan stated that he would remove the tariffs if Brazil reversed its policy. This was the first time that retaliation had been taken against a debtor country.

Within two days of Reagan's announcement, the Brazilian Congress voted to give Sarney discretionary authority to retaliate against the United States. Sarney stated that he would prefer to have GATT mediate a settlement. In the United States, firms such as Microsoft and Apple, along with CBEMA and the AEA, enthusiastically endorsed the sanctions. In testimony before the Section 301 Committee in December, R. Wayne Sayer, speaking for AEA, said:

> While we hope that Brazil will recognize legitimate U.S. interests, if this does not occur then sanctions are critical to emphasize to other countries that international trade rules and agreements must be respected. . . . We strongly support the President's decision to impose sanctions if SEI's decision on Microsoft is not immediately overturned, and if the problems associated with the software protection law are not corrected.[26]

William Krist, vice president of AEA for international trade affairs, also spoke out forcefully:

> A great deal of effort has gone into developing a set of international agreements to assure a measure of free trade, free markets, and property rights protection. These agreements constitute global guidelines which national governments can use to resist the pressure of special interest groups for special treatment and thus they promote the general interests of the country as a whole. Brazil's policies fly in the face of these international agreements and guidelines. I believe that the government was captured by an extremely narrow interest group which is running inefficient plants at enormous profit.
> We would like to see Brazil have a strong Informatic

capability, but it must be part of the world system. Their go-it-alone, reinventing the wheel strategy doesn't make sense. I must say that in recent years the policy has been moving in the right direction but it has a long way to go.[27]

Between November 1987 and January 1988, a rapid succession of events ensued. On November 27, the director of SEI announced, "Brazil is no longer interested in protecting or simulating basic computer programs similar to those produced by Microsoft."[28] On November 30, Sarney formally requested that GATT mediate the U.S.–Brazilian dispute. Brazil pledged to step up enforcement action against software pirates on December 10. Eleven days later, Sarney used a line-item veto to strike down the 200% tariff in the software protection bill, on the grounds that the taxing mechanisms were unconstitutional.

CONIN issued a clarification of the functional equivalency rule in January, following more bilateral talks and direct negotiation between Yeutter and CONIN directors. CONIN declared that Microsoft would not be allowed to sell its DOS 3.2 in Brazil, but would be allowed a license to sell its newer DOS 3.3, on the grounds that no functional equivalent existed. Microsoft executives announced that they were skeptical of the ruling, calling it "a PR move" and "a token concession that doesn't mean anything."[29]

Also in January, executives of Brazil's major exporters issued a public statement, after a month of behind-the-scenes pressure on the Brazilian government to ease restrictions that the United States found objectionable. The executives termed CONIN's action, "a great demonstration of [Brazil's] good faith."[30] The former head of the Brazil Exporters Association claimed that U.S. importers had already postponed $500 million worth of Brazilian orders. The group requested Reagan to resolve the trade conflict with Brazil.

More meetings between Brazilian representatives and the 301 Committee took place between January and March. CONIN appeared ready to retreat from the plan to license

Unitron's Apple clone. Sarney said that SEI would reformulate its operating guidelines concerning software regulation. Informed by Yeutter that negotiations were again progressing, on March 1, 1988, Reagan lifted the sanctions through the end of April 1988, at which time they were again deferred.

It would be logical to suppose that IBM's government affairs staff was following these events closely and helping the corporation to act. Perhaps the corporation's most important action was the evolution in its strategy during the early 1980s, which enabled it to enter into a number of joint ventures worldwide. Its venture with Gerdau was followed by others in 1988 and 1989, by which time Brazil's computer market registered annual sales of $4 billion, about half of the Latin American total.[31] We can imagine that governmental affairs managers, keenly aware of the political and ideological climate in Brazil, made an important contribution to that decision. IBM had to adjust to the problems Saur and his group voiced in 1974.

Clearly, too, IBM Brazil would have wanted to see a stable political climate and to encourage Brazil's democratic evolution. Reports indicated that leftist strength was rising. IBM would presumably like to see the moderates, with whom Sarney was associated, succeed. This meant no confrontations with Sarney and accommodation with SEI.

On the other hand, IBM Washington had to be concerned about President Reagan, who appeared to have initiated the 301 action primarily to keep an angry and protection-minded Congress at bay. "One Japan is enough," Congress appeared to be saying. The president and the USTR had difficulty garnering industry support for the 301 action; they were forced in the end to concentrate on software and copyright protection instead of the market reserve policy, at which Reagan's September 7 speech was aimed, because that was the only area where they had an industry constituency. Given IBM's global interests and continuing relationships with the USTR office, it could not afford to leave them in the lurch.

So we can imagine that IBM played an active role in developing a consensus within the industry associations that were involved, such as AEA and CBEMA, and working with the USTR to refine and implement it.

At the same time, we can imagine that IBM and other U.S. multinationals were actively helping the Brazilian government to shape its policies and state its case so as to avoid a head-on collision with an angry Reagan White House. (This role will probably be increasingly important in the future with respect to Brazil and a number of other countries. As the United States feels its power and hegemony slipping, it will become considerably more querulous. If it cannot punish the strong, like Japan, it will try to take it out on the weak, like Brazil. Such a turn of events would be a threat to the interests of IBM and many other firms that, it may be hoped, will quite openly and legitimately use their global influence to promote constructive relations.)

We may be giving IBM too much credit here, but in the Brazilian affair the moderating influence of the multinational computer companies is apparent. They appear to have done a good job, at least at rolling with the punches. Perhaps they did more. Perhaps they designed new and more lasting relations with and among the governments involved, helping Brazil and the United States to define and fulfill their community needs more effectively. Whether they have done enough remains to be seen. At this writing, Brazil is an economic disaster.

In Washington, the new USTR, Carla A. Hills, backed by a provision in the strengthened 1988 trade law known as "Super 301," was preparing for a shoot-out with a wide range of countries, including Brazil. Japan, Korea, and Taiwan, however, were her principal targets. They accounted for roughly half of the United States' $140-billion trade deficit. Japan's $50-billion surplus seemed to be *increasing* in spite of the lower value of the dollar. This was astonishing since reigning economists throughout the 1980s had confidently forecast that a decline in the dollar's value would set things right.

Hills, prodded by a petulant Congress, seemed to be saying, "We are tired of your promises and assurances; we want to see

results in market share." So the United States was joining the
rest of the industrial world in managing trade: Asians would
be expected to buy a fixed percentage of American goods if
they wanted to continue to sell in the United States. The
Asian reaction was indignant: "Americans don't bother to
learn our language. They don't make what we want. They are
unreliable suppliers. We resent being forced."[32] (Oddly, when
Hills announced her 301 targets in June 1989, Taiwan and
Korea were not among them. They were Japan, Brazil, and
India.)

The implications of the confrontation for companies like
IBM are far-reaching. Tensions, barriers, and retaliation resulting from a world of managed trade threaten the very lifeblood of the company. It is as concerned with its freedom to
import as it is with its ability to export. It does not want its
long and close relationships with Japan, where in 1989 it still
supplied 24% of all computers used, to be jeopardized by U.S.
retaliation for Japan's unwillingness to buy U.S. beef, for example.[33] IBM undoubtedly hopes that Hills will think strategically—that is, discretely—before wheeling out her 301 can-
nons. Furthermore, IBM and other companies will need an
even more precise understanding of how decisions are made in
Japan concerning their products. If they are being denied a
market, they need to know by whom and why. Without
such knowledge, frontal attacks by the U.S. government
may do more harm than good. Such knowledge is particularly important in the expanding world of telecommunications.

JAPANESE TELECOMMUNICATIONS POLICY

In 1984, Japan was exporting eleven times more telecommunications equipment to the United States than it
was importing. Nippon Telegraph and Telephone (NTT), a
government-owned company—the world's largest, with assets
valued at $300 billion and 320,000 employees—purchased all
its equipment from a select group of companies, known as the

NTT "Family": NEC, Fujitsu, Oki, and Hitachi. Following years of complaints by U.S. trade officials and companies like IBM and AT&T, in 1985 Japan vowed to liberalize its telecommunications market and privatize NTT. In 1988, the Americans were still complaining: Japan's telecommunications exports to the United States exceeded imports by seven times—$2 billion, compared to $278 million—and the Family still seemed to be the preferred suppliers.[34]

IBM's conception of public affairs is that it should align itself to the fullest extent with the objectives of government, "to do what is right." At the same time, it seeks open markets with free competition. These objectives are linked by an assumption: free markets will produce the best products at the lowest cost for consumers and thus will be perceived as being consistent with the objectives of government. The application of this logic to the Japanese telecommunications markets of the 1980s must have caused IBM and its issue managers some interesting moments.

No doubt they realized that the Japanese government, like most, does not speak with one voice. For all of its reputed coherence, it is, as much as any, riven with deeply rooted factions that erupt in bureaucratic turf battles of the most virulent kind. Entering the telecommunications market in the 1980s required a detailed and sophisticated understanding of the factions. As one U.S. trade official—one of the few who speak Japanese—said: "The real battle isn't between the Americans and Japanese. This [telecommunications struggle] is a gigantic turf fight between the Ministry of Posts and Telecommunications [MPT] and the Ministry of International Trade and Industry [MITI]. We Americans are like a little terrier, yipping at the heels of two giants. Every once in a while we get their attention, and they toss a bone."[35]

Chalmers Johnson writes that "for both MITI and MPT, the United States was not so much an independent player as a counter to be used in their domestic struggle."[36] The same goes for IBM. To discern governmental objectives, IBM had to perceive the quite different objectives of the two agencies. The differences were rooted in their histories and connected to their supporters in the ruling Liberal Democratic Party (LDP) and to their constituencies in the Japanese business community (who, of course, were major financial contributors to the party).

The bureaucratic battle was over the control of so-called value-added networks (VANs), electronic arrangements that enable companies using different computers to exchange and combine data over international telephone lines.[37] VANs could be a $40-million business in Japan alone by 1990. Eleven foreign companies, including IBM, had registered as international VAN suppliers. In the fall of 1987, MPT ruled that all VAN suppliers would have to adapt their equipment to a standard set of regulations. Meeting the regulations would add greatly to company costs and would also render worthless years of research and investment by many companies such as IBM.[38]

MPT's ruling was only the latest in a long series of actions designed to keep telecommunications under its control and the control of NTT and its family of firms. MPT's rival was MITI, which in the 1980s regarded its mission as "the promotion of high-technology industries of the future—telecommunications, new materials, and biotechnology."[39]

"It is on the basis of this vision," writes Johnson, "that MITI vice-minister Konaga [Keiichi] has sought to put his ministry almost totally in charge of administering research and development for high-technology industries." MITI's jurisdiction has always clearly included the computer industry, as we saw in Chapter 2, but a computer connected to a telephone circuit is a telecommunications network. Those circuits have always been under the jurisdiction of MPT. Thus, if MITI was to accomplish its mission it "must overcome its rival and bring telecommunications under its jurisdiction."[40]

MITI's prestigious history, its talented people, and high esprit de corps should have made for an easy victory, especially since it had an ally in the equally powerful and prestigious Ministry of Finance (MOF). (MOF had squabbled with MPT in the early 1980s over control of MPT's postal savings funds.) But MPT's strength was deceptive. Hardly an elite bureaucracy, it nevertheless had been—even before World War II—a political powerhouse, and a rival to MITI. With 23,000 post offices throughout the country, it directly controlled a large number of votes that were important to the LDP. Each year it ordered vast quantities of equipment, bicycles, uniforms, trucks, and so forth. And it runs "what is today the world's largest financial institution, the postal savings system, which is popular with the public because it pays higher rates of interest than the banks."[41]

Scandals and corruption in some of its offshoots ironically raised MPT's status, because politicians concluded it needed more power and responsibilities to prevent abuse. It also acquired new power from the trade friction between its charge, NTT, and the United States. Says Johnson: "After NTT president Akikusa was quoted to the effect that the only thing NTT would buy from the United States was 'mops and buckets', many in the Japanese government recognized that NTT's engineers and family members could not be trusted with international negotiations." MPT argued that in order to handle matters more smoothly it would need new policymaking powers. A third reason for its new status was as ironic as the other two. The privatization of NTT, which the West erroneously tended to assume would resemble the breakup of AT&T and lead to more "freedom," would in fact mean that MPT needed new powers to regulate it "and any other firms that might enter the telecommunications business in competition with it."

For all these reasons, by the mid-1980s MPT had emerged as a major rival to MITI in the business of high-technology policymaking and vision-setting. To keep and manifest its new-found authority, MPT was inclined to keep foreigners out, which it could easily do through endless licensing and regulatory requirements.

MITI, anxious about the threat of U.S. retaliation against its computer and semiconductor industries and eager to subvert MPT in any way, became a champion of liberalization in telecommunications, causing some people in the West to think MITI had had a dramatic change of heart. They were disabused of this notion when MITI came down hard on the protectionist side over the issue of computer programming. Until January 1, 1986, "there was no protection for computer software [in Japan]; and foreign programs were routinely pirated and rented or sold to personal computer owners."[42] The extension of protection to software meant a defeat for MITI by a coalition of MPT, the Cultural Affairs Agency of the Ministry of Education, and Americans. What all this goes to show is that MPT and MITI are neither liberal nor protectionist, says Johnson. First and foremost, they are preoccupied with retaining or expanding their power and influence and that of their industrial cohorts amid the shifting sands of LDP politics.

What conclusions can we draw from this story for government affairs management in a company like IBM?

First, corporate objectives must be sharp and clear. Talk of a level playing field, free trade, and fairness is meaningless and distracting. What precisely is the company after? Sales to the VANs, sales to NTT, protection of software?

Second, how can these objectives be achieved? Who is the company trying to influence? IBM must work with key people at MPT, NTT, and MITI; the U.S. president talking to the Japanese prime minister is not much help. IBM could use U.S. government help if it came from trade officials who spoke the language, who knew the history and the personalities, and who were on the job for longer than a few years at a time. The company must know the objectives and motivations of every key player. Then it can see whether MITI might help vis-à-vis MPT, and vice versa. The Ministry of Education might also be useful. Each agency has powerful LDP supporters, caucuses called *zoku*, whose members IBM should know and to whom it should explain its position. In short, where governmental objectives are so splintered, the company must help put them together, which it can do perfectly legitimately and in ways that promote its objectives.

Third, if the U.S. government is to be helpful—and IBM needs help badly—the government and the company must be close to one another. They must be aware of each other's full range of interests and concerns; they must have a shared strategy. IBM would like to see a far greater emphasis in Washington on the development of that strategy, and to see talented people working on it over a long period of time. As Clyde Prestowitz has written: "Americans can never hope to succeed if they always know less about what they are talking about than their Japanese interlocutors."[43]

Fourth, IBM would like to see U.S. trade negotiating teams speak with one voice. The Japanese, as Prestowitz points out, are experts at exploiting the differences between State, Defense, Commerce, Treasury and the USTR. The United States should be especially coherent and adept at exploiting divisions elsewhere.

Fifth, IBM can use the Japanese press to explain its position to some constituencies.

COMPARISONS WITH OTHER COMPANIES

Despite some similarities, the management of governmental affairs at other companies differs markedly from that at IBM. The differences spring from company histories and traditions.

AT&T

Before 1986, AT&T's Public Affairs Office (PAO), located in Washington, focused almost exclusively on relations with federal, state, and local governments in the United States. Reporting to the corporation's chief counsel, its primary function was to defend the company's interests in the halls of government. It was not seen as an architect of new relationships, nor was it expected to influence headquarters so as to align the company with governmental interests. This was hardly surprising, given the stormy relations between AT&T and government over the past decade.

After it was forced to divest by the Justice Department and the courts in 1984, AT&T launched a major campaign to penetrate international telecommunications markets. By 1986, AT&T's efforts in Europe and Asia had become the highest corporate priority. And, since the company's principal foreign customers were governments, government relations not only abroad but also in Washington became increasingly important. In 1986, public affairs professionals were assigned to the major foreign capitals as part of the AT&T international organization and reported to the operating divisions. The Public Affairs Office in Washington responded to ad hoc requests from unit managers, but until recently has not had a significant responsibility for long-run corporate strategy either in the United States or abroad.

AT&T's PAO and IBM's GPO perform similar functions, but the latter, perhaps having been at it longer, is more fully developed. Using the four categories of intelligence-handling employed by professionals in the field—targeting, collection, analysis, and dissemination—we can compare the two offices.[44]

In terms of targeting, IBM's thirty issue managers track specific topics on a continuing basis. The identification and assignment of topics ensures regular assessment and evaluation of whether the targets are appropriate. In contrast, AT&T's PAO has tended to focus more on tactical short-term business opportunities. It therefore runs a greater risk of missing important targets.

As for collection, both corporations tap into a broad range of public information, although IBM's GPO appears to be more centralized. IBM's use of non-American issue managers may tend to produce more objective and insightful information than AT&T's PAO, which has relied largely on Americans (AT&T is changing this). Furthermore, IBM makes a major effort to educate its issue managers as well as its global public affairs staff through annual training sessions at its Public Affairs Institute in Washington.

In analysis, IBM's issue-management system, at least at this writing, seems to offer clear advantages over AT&T's emphasis on technical business questions served up by operating managers. Furthermore, the issue managers develop historical memories and are more likely to discern shifting circumstances and potential crises. AT&T's PAO relies on a separate entity, the Information Resources Group, for research and analysis. It thus risks losing the richness of raw data in formulating conclusions and decisions, and its personnel lack the experience of data gathering and processing, experience that can often lead to important contacts.

Both companies have sophisticated networks for disseminating public affairs information. IBM's GPO emphasizes intimate, continuing relations with its clients in the operating divisions of the company. AT&T's PAO, on the other hand, appears to simply take requests from the operators or make recommendations to them, which does not foster the same continuity of intimate interaction as IBM seems to value.

French Telecommunications in the 1980s. AT&T's failure to break into the French digital switch market in 1987 was a major reason that the corporation is revamping its approach to governmental relations management.

In early April 1987, the French government of Prime Minister Jacques Chirac was seeking a foreign buyer for the state-owned telecommunications company, Compagnie Générale des Constructions Téléphoniques (CGCT). It was not much of a company, having lost money for five years, but three giants—AT&T, Ericsson, and Siemens—were anxious to acquire it because it represented 16% of the lucrative French digital switch market. The rest of that market— 84%—was held by CGE, the government-owned electronics giant, and its telecommunications subsidiary, Alcatel. For AT&T, acquisition of CGCT would mean a toehold in Europe from which it could expand internationally and gain a share of the world telecommunications market, which by 1990 would be more than $500 billion. In 1987, the world's switch market alone was $12 billion, of which a switching firm had to have 7% to 10% to survive. Thus, the stakes were high and AT&T's competitors were pressing hard for the French government's nod.

As part of the deal, the French government required each bidder to acquire a French partner. AT&T, which was negotiating through APT, its joint venture with Philips, chose

a small French electronics firm and five French union trusts owned by a Dutch-controlled bank and Morgan
Guaranty. Siemens chose Jeumont-Schneider, a substantial
French electronics firm, and Ericsson chose Matra, a leading
defense and electronics company headed by Jean-Luc Lagar-
dere, a Chirac confidant.

On April 23, the French government announced that CGCT
would go to the Ericsson/Matra partnership, a decision that
surprised many. All indications had been that AT&T would
win because of the great respect French technicians had for
Bell Labs and AT&T's technology. AT&T was shocked; it was
a bitter blow to an already faltering international strategy.

There are many views about what went wrong.

One view is that the French government had no choice: it
was pure politics. Chirac could not offend the Germans at a
time of growing European unity, and there was some evidence
that the German government had threatened to retaliate
against Alcatel's newly acquired ITT subsidiary in Germany
if Siemens did not get the deal. On the other hand, Chirac did
not want to make Washington angry, so choosing Ericsson
was the only way out of the dilemma.

Some say AT&T chose the wrong partner, that it disre-
garded French government advice to ally itself with Matra.
Others argued that it received conflicting advice on that score
from different officials of government. Some suggest that
Philips was not much help in the telecommunications field
because it was thought of as primarily a consumer electronics
company. Some say the U.S. government was late and ineffective in its involvement. The lack of cordial relations between
top AT&T officials and the U.S. government was seen as a
problem, as were the years of antagonism with the Justice
Department.

Many felt that AT&T had relied too much on the influence
of George Pébereau, CGE's chairman, in negotiating with the
French government. The Chirac government fired him soon
after it had come to power. Finance Minister Edouard Balladur apparently disapproved of his purchase of ITT's international division and was suspicious of his cooperation with

AT&T. Furthermore, Balladur had once worked for Pébereau and simply did not like him.

The AT&T government affairs office in Washington was only marginally involved. Essentially, it did the bidding of headquarters. It was not consulted on policy, and neither was AT&T Europe. As a result, the decision makers were cut off from a good deal of information they needed.

AT&T's loss must be seen at least in part as a failure in the management of business-government relations. Perhaps there was nothing that could have been done to alter the decision by the French government, but there is reason to believe that relations between AT&T, the U.S. government, and the French government were not well planned or coordinated. The company was caught by surprise too often, as illustrated by Pébereau's actions and firing. Its evaluation of the interests and motivations of different departments— Foreign Affairs, Industry, the Telecommunications Directorate, and others—was not what it might have been. Its judgment about its French partner was questionable. It did not get and maybe did not want the cooperation and participation of its European office, which seems odd.[45]

In 1989, AT&T scored a major success by defeating its rivals, Siemens and Ericsson, to win a contract from the Italian government to modernize its telecommunications system. Although the details of the negotiations have not been revealed, rumor has it that this time the Washington office was in high gear and governmental relations were effectively managed on all fronts. Hopefully, the vestiges of AT&T's litigious past have disappeared and the company and the American government have come to understand that they are not adversaries. In fact, of course, their interests are largely the same.

Mega Life Insurance Company

As the 1980s drew to a close, the insurance industry in the United States, as elsewhere, was highly regulated at the state level and was profoundly affected by federal policies on taxes, health care, and financial service regulation. Increasingly, it was also feeling the heat of international competition as Asian and European insurance companies fought for market share.

Mega is a pseudonym for one of the largest American insurance companies. Its GA office was well regarded by others in the industry and by the congressional staff people with whom it dealt. But, as in the case of AT&T, it had problems that required attention.

Like IBM's GPO, Mega's GA office was galvanized into significance by a watershed event—the 1982 tax bill, which included a section consolidating losses and gains abroad for tax purposes.[46] At the time the bill was passed, the undermanned and inexpert office completely overlooked the issue and the company paid a substantial price in lost tax savings. A year later, when Rep. Peter Stark, a senior Democrat on the Ways and Means Committee, organized a task force to overhaul the arcane insurance tax laws, Mega reacted by hiring Jacob Swirling, an experienced Washington operative, to take over the GA function. The company increased the office's budget to more than $2 million a year and gave Swirling a free hand in organizing it.

Swirling replaced the staff, all of whom had been insurance people, with a cadre of young, aggressive Washington experts. Disagreeing with IBM's approach, Swirling said, "You can always train a government guy to be a Mega person, but you can never train a business guy to be a government person." Many congressional staffers seemed to agree with him. Anne Zeppenfeld, tax counsel to Rep. Stark, said, "Business people often don't understand what kind of information we need and how we need it presented."

Swirling focused his staff on three issues: tax policy, health insurance, and the threat of competition from a deregulated banking industry. "We want to have leaders come to us for advice on these matters," he said. "That means both government leaders on policy issues and business leaders on corporate issues. If we accomplish that, then the bottom line—results for Mega—come much easier."

Swirling's performance has been impressive. A two-word provision in Rep. Stark's 1984 tax bill saved the company

$185 million; a section of the 1988 tax bill saved $45 million; and an amendment to a 1988 health care bill was worth $11 million. "Not bad for a $2-million annual investment," commented Jim Bond, one of Swirling's assistants. As another company representative put it, "God is in the details, and those guys understand the details of legislation, both the politics and the business." Zeppenfeld also respected Swirling and his staff. "I know that if [Stark] wants some information, they'll give me something I can take into him and be confident that it's correct."

Nevertheless, one wonders whether Swirling's approach is the correct one for the long run. It is inherently adversarial. What Mega gains in tax savings, the government loses. Both might benefit more if they took a longer view, looking for ways to raise the necessary funds with a minimum of economic distortion to the industry. This is hard to do if both sides spend their time bickering over minutiae.

As we saw in the case of the health equipment industry in Chapter 4, people on the industry side as well as in government fear being coopted. "Let's face it," said one Mega staffer, "if you get too close, neither side will trust you." Says Jim Bond, "Americans hate government. It's part of our culture." Maybe so, but such an attitude inhibits creative consideration of a number of issues that are critical for both the industry and the government: health coverage of the uninsured and competition in financial services, for example. It also may preclude the government help that Mega needs to secure and expand its market share outside the United States in the face of increasingly active foreign companies, many of which enjoy close working relations with their governments.

However, this adversarial approach in Washington is hard to change as long as it persists at headquarters in Chicago, where the prevailing attitude toward government is a mixture of fear and disdain. Government Affairs staffers risk being seen as having sold out to the enemy if they become too close to their governmental counterparts. In any case, they feel removed from the main line of company activities. Except for Swirling, who is a corporate officer, GA is not on the Mega career path. GA staffers can never expect to work in Chicago.

This is a serious disadvantage; among other things, it ensures that Mega will never have a CEO who knows much about Washington.

"I do a lot of hand-holding in Chicago," said Swirling. "When they are nervous about something in DC, they get this panicked look in their eyes and I have to keep them from going over the edge. Often, this means I must overstate my case, make them think we have the whole process wired and that any defeat we may suffer was just an inevitability. This, of course, raises performance expectations quite high and puts a lot of pressure on my staff."

In addition to difficult and sensitive relations with government and with corporate headquarters, Swirling also must manage relations between Mega and the rest of the insurance industry, whose Washington representatives often disagree among themselves. These three sets of relations today are troubled by more than the natural differences of opinion. They suffer from confused attitudes about the proper roles and relationships of government and business. They are clouded, that is, by ideology, which gets in the way of good-sense management. Chicago should not treat the GA staffers as slightly unsavory strangers or as field hands. Government Affairs is as important to the success of Mega as finance or marketing. It requires as much skill and professional attainment as any other function in the company, and it should be respected, not shunned. Moreover, government is not the enemy; increasingly, it should be a partner if the American insurance industry wishes to retain markets at home and expand abroad. The whole industry badly needs a strategy toward government. Swirling's job should not be made more difficult by management's failure to understand and accept reality.

W.R. Grace

Industries that are buffeted by crisis, as is the chemical industry, for example, understand well that there is no sensible alternative to a creative and cooperative relationship with government. At the end of 1988, W.R. Grace was a defendant in approximately 13,600 asbestos-related law suits, about twice as many as the year before. Speaking to a gathering of insurance executives in 1988, Peter Grace, the company's chairman, mentioned the need to reform toxic tort laws before "they ruin the private sector." But he said with equal emphasis that environmental concerns—ocean dumping, acid rain, the greenhouse effect, toxic waste—will "engulf us all . . . if we do not band together and do something about it. You can't replace land, water or air. Let the public and private sectors bring together common sense and science to secure reasonable and workable ways to preserve and improve our God-given right to" a liveable world.[47]

To lead Grace's environmental effort, the chairman established in 1987 a new Office of Environmental Policy (OEP) headed by former New York governor Hugh L. Carey. Carey was also named executive vice president and was placed at the same level in the corporate hierarchy as Grace's chief financial officer.

Carl Lorentzen, one of three group operating managers in Grace's Specialty Chemical division and its representative on the board of the Chemical Manufacturing Association, spoke of the effect of the environmental crisis on managerial and business purpose. "The chemical plant manager of 1995," he said, "will have to be someone who is a politician, a community activist, a medical specialist, an environmentalist, a media spokesman, a communicator, a lobbyist, and yes, hopefully, still a good businessman."

Alcan Aluminium in Brazil and the United States

Recalling our earlier discussion of Brazil–U.S. trade, let us finally, for the sake of comparison with IBM, take a quick look at Alcan Aluminium, Ltd., of Canada and its relations with governments.[48]

Alcan is the largest producer of aluminum in the world, operating in more than thirty-three countries. In 1987, it produced 1.59 million tons of primary aluminum, which represented 13% of the world total outside the Soviet bloc. Total sales reached $6.5 billion, and 32% of all its products were sold in the United States. The company is highly decentralized and each company president reports directly to the chief executive officer. Alcan enjoys close relations with the host government in each country where it operates. It has also emphasized good relations with the community, especially in matters of safety and environmental protection.

Alcan's Brazilian subsidiary, Aluminio do Brasil, is the country's largest foreign producer with capital investments of $800 million and 8,000 Brazilians in its employ. Thirty percent of its 120,000 tons of annual production is exported to the United States. Brazil has high hopes for its aluminum industry, whose exports reached $1.5 billion in 1988, 50% more than the previous year. With state support, the industry has planned a ten-year expansion program.

On the other hand, aluminum imports into Brazil from the United States in the late 1980s were steadily declining in the face of a plethora of tariff and nontariff barriers, some of which, it was alleged, violated GATT rules.

Alcan's U.S. subsidiary, headquartered in Cleveland, Ohio, is the world's second-largest recycler of aluminum beverage cans, handling 11.5 billion containers per year. Its Rolled Products division employs 6,300 people in thirty-one states. Its president is eager to increase market share and sales, but also wants to gain acceptance, support, and respect from the federal government, whose environmental policies are critical to the company's future.

Alcan's James P. Monaghan has been the company's only government relations representative in Washington, DC for the past seventeen years. He sits on the board of the Aluminum Association, which includes eighty-nine companies and operates on a budget of $1 million per year.

The dilemmas facing Alcan's CEO in 1989 were clear. Alcan Brasil, in place for forty years, was an important long-term source of revenues for the firm and a major contributor to Brazil's struggling economy. At the same time, the company hoped to expand its U.S. subsidiary and build a variety of product plants, including new recycling plants for which government approvals would be essential. In Washington, Jim Monaghan and the Aluminum Association strongly supported the actions of the USTR to compel Brazil to adhere to GATT trade standards.

Thus, there were conflicts between Alcan's Brazilian and U.S. subsidiaries whose resolution required a more sophisticated government relations strategy than had been needed in the past. Such a strategy cannot be built quickly. It must be based on a history of mutual understanding and analysis, and on extensive communications within the company, especially between Canadian headquarters, Brazil, the U.S. operation in Cleveland, and the Washington office. Alcan's decentralized management of government relations may have made good sense in the past, but it is a system that was unable to take sufficient account of events in the 1980s. The company needs close relations with the governments of Brazil and the United States, but there are tensions between the two governments that may damage Alcan unless they are recognized and managed carefully. Alcan is a player in an international marketplace whose rules are changing. A more proactive approach to government relations will give Alcan a greater opportunity to help design those rules.

CONCLUSIONS

Managers of governmental relations walk a number of fine lines that mark the boundaries of diverse interests within and among governments and industries, and within their own companies. The extraordinary complexity of their task is compounded by the ideological blinders frequently worn by those with whom they must deal at headquarters, among subsidiaries, and in government.

They are too often regarded as outsiders in their own companies, less important than those engaged in finance, marketing, or production, mere order-takers who cannot hope to reach the higher levels of corporate management, and dangerously tainted by proximity to the enemy. Not surprisingly, government officials often hold a similarly jaundiced view. They assume that the governmental affairs manager is bound by a single-minded devotion to the short-term profits of the company, with little objective understanding of the requirements of government or desire to align the company with those requirements.

There are, of course, exceptions to this norm on both sides. Hopefully, government and business will develop more creative and cooperative relationships in the future, but this will require the active involvement of the highest levels of corporate and governmental management. The roles and relationships of both business and government are in fact in transition, and the management of that transition should be a high priority for every CEO as well as for the White House and the leaders of Congress.

NOTES

1. This section is based on a paper, "Governmental Programs at IBM," presented by Charles E. McKittrick, Jr., vice president, governmental programs, IBM, at the Harvard Business School colloquium on Comparative Business-Government Relations, July 8, 1988, published by Harvard Business School (#389-109), 1989.
2. Emanuel Adler, "Ideological 'Guerrillas' and the Quest for Technological Autonomy: Brazil's Domestic Computer Industry," *International Organization* 3 (Summer 1986): 674–705, as excerpted in George C. Lodge, "Brazil's Informatics Policy: 1970–1984," #389-044. Boston: Harvard Business School, 1989; Peter B. Evans, "Declining Hegemony and Assertive Industrialization: U.S.–Brazil Conflicts in the Computer Industry," *International Organization* (Spring 1989): 207–238; Chalmers Johnson, "MITI, MPT, and the Telecom Wars: How Japan Makes Policy for High Technology," working paper, published by the Berkeley Roundtable on International Economy, University of California, Berkeley, 1986.
3. José Sarney, "Brazil: A President's Story," *Foreign Affairs* (Fall 1986): 103, quoted in Frits van Paasschen, Joel Szabat, and George C. Lodge, "The USTR and Brazil: 1985–1988," #389-046. Boston: Harvard Business School, 1989, p. 4.
4. Lodge, "Brazil's Informatics Policy," p. 1.

5. William R. Cline, *Informatics and Development: Trade and Industrial Policy in Argentina, Brazil, and Mexico* (Washington, DC: Economics International Inc., February 1987), p. 3.
6. Lodge, "Brazil's Informatics Policy," p. 1.
7. Ibid.
8. Cline, *Informatics and Development,* pp. 4, 65.
9. Lodge, "Brazil's Informatics Policy," p. 15.
10. Interview with Helen Shapiro in George C. Lodge, "Brazil's Informatics Policy: 1970–1984, Supplement," #389-045. Boston: Harvard Business School, 1989, pp. 2, 3.
11. White House press release of President Reagan's radio address of September 7, 1985, quoted in Evans, "Declining Hegemony and Assertive Industrialization," p. 207.
12. Evans, "Declining Hegemony and Assertive Industrialization," p. 217.
13. Ibid., p. 228.
14. Paasschen, Szabat, and Lodge, "The USTR and Brazil," p. 7.
15. AEA letter filed with USTR, Case 301-49, October 11, 1985, quoted in ibid., p. 7.
16. CBEMA letter filed with USTR, Case 301-49, October 11, 1985, quoted in ibid., p. 7.
17. Paasschen, Szabat, and Lodge, "The USTR and Brazil," p. 7.
18. Evans, "Declining Hegemony and Assertive Industrialization," p. 223, quoting a Brazilian businessman.
19. *Mercantile Journal of Brazil (Journal Mercantil do Brasil),* October 20, 1985.
20. Paasschen, Szabat, and Lodge, "The USTR and Brazil," p. 8.
21. "USTR-Brazil 301 Trade Case," Washington, DC: USTR, October 1985.
22. Testimony by R. Wayne Sayer to 301 Committee, December 17, 1987.
21. Quoted in Evans, "Declining Hegemony and Assertive Industrialization," p. 223.
24. Ibid.
25. Letter from Gates to Yeutter, September 24, 1987.
26. Sayer, Testimony to 301 Committee, December 17, 1987.
27. Interview with William Krist, March 1988.
28. *Journal of Commerce,* November 27, 1987, p. 3A.
29. Interview with Martin Taucher, Microsoft, May 1988; also *Seattle Times,* January 15, 1988, p. 1C; and *Financial Times,* January 21, 1988, p. 5.
30. *Journal of Commerce,* January 25, 1988, p. 3A.
31. *The Wall Street Journal,* April 13, 1989, p. 19.
32. "The Asians Are Bracing for a Trade Shoot-Out," *BusinessWeek,* May 1, 1989, p. 40.
33. *Japan Economic Journal,* June 24, 1989, p. 16.
34. "Japan Sends Out a Disconnect Notice," *BusinessWeek,* June 13, 1988, p. 46.
35. Johnson, "MITI, MPT, and the Telecom Wars," p. 13, quoting Michael Berger in *BusinessWeek,* March 11, 1985, p. 67.
36. Ibid.
37. "Japan Sends Out a Disconnect Notice," p. 46.

38. Ibid.
39. Johnson, "MITI, MPT, and the Telecom Wars," pp. 3, 4.
40. Ibid., p. 4.
41. Ibid., p. 6.
42. Ibid., pp. 19, 20.
43. Clyde Prestowitz, "The Nine Commandments for Negotiating with the Japanese," *The International Economy* (September/October 1988): 94–97.
44. Based on Ron Seckinger, "The Role of Intelligence in International Business," unpublished CBGR Research Paper, May 3, 1989.
45. See Barbara Jenkins and George C. Lodge, "French Telecommunications in the 1980s (A) and (B)," #388-160 and #389-037. Harvard Business School, 1988, 1989, respectively.
46. This section is drawn from Mark Usellis, "The Mega Company Government Affairs Office," unpublished CBGR research paper, May 2, 1989.
47. Taken from Paul Butler, "Case Study in Diversified Management: W.R. Grace and Co.," CBGR research paper, May 3, 1989.
48. This segment is based on Cynthia B. Carroll, "Alcan Aluminium Corporation in Brazil and the U.S.," unpublished CBGR research paper, May 3, 1989.

CHAPTER 6

Recovery

The recovery of U.S. competitive strength is important to the country and the world. The country's standard of living—and those of the many nations that export to it—depends on it, as does its ability to work its will in the world. A weak America *could* be a dangerous one, prone to vindictiveness and resentment. Presuming power that it may not possess, it might launch missions that are doomed to fail, wasting its resources and those of its allies, losing its self-respect and the regard of others, spiralling downward, angry and resentful. This is the sad story of recent decades: Vietnam, frustrations in Central America, and continuing losses to Japan and other countries of what once had been competitive leadership in the technologies of tomorrow. It is not preordained that America be number one—or two or three—but there is good reason to make the best of ourselves. That we are not doing.

The failure is systemic, reaching into many related areas of American life—education, Wall Street and the capital markets, human resource management, and government policies. I am concerned here with one particular area: business-government relations. The old ideas, which shaped and legitimized those relations, are now obsolete and present a serious barrier to the recovery of competitiveness. What must be done?

Government must be organized to think coherently about the industrial priorities of the future. It is no longer valid—if indeed it ever was—to suppose that government should not treat some industries as more critical to the nation's interest than others. American supremacy in aerospace, agriculture, and other fields has derived from policies that for one reason or another assigned priority to those industries. It is an essential role of government to assign those priorities. Furthermore, it does not seem particularly difficult to do. Where do we want to be in the year 2000 and beyond? We want to be strong in the high-value-added, high-profit, high-income industries of the age—electronics, telecommunications, biotechnology, advanced machine tools, and so on. These industries are more important than clothes pins. They contain the promise of our youth. They are the source of our economic strength.

If assigning such priorities is government's role, then government must be organized accordingly. Whether this means a Department of Industry, as virtually all other nations have, an expanded DARPA, an enhanced USTR, or an integrative council or committee to synthesize the interests of separate departments, coherence within the executive branch and a more effective bridge between the executive and the legislative on economic priorities is clearly needed.

More effective and creative industry organizations and interindustry associations are also essential, not so much to lobby for members' interests, but to help government define and implement the national interest; to serve as bridges between the public and private sectors; to make the most of their common interests; and to shape strategies for particular industries, including relations with other industries. We saw that in microelectronics, for example, a healthy industry depends on a food chain that includes consumers, manufacturers, and suppliers in many areas. HIMA, SIA, AEA, and SEMI are associations that exemplify this trend.

These changes will work only if the purpose of business is clearly aligned with the national interest—the long-run needs of the community—and this alignment must be understood and accepted by the banking community and by other providers of capital. The old attachments, derived from the notion of individualism, no longer work as well as they once did. While profit is more important than ever, the uses of profit and the incentives that determine those uses need examination. A competitive economy requires that profit be invested for innovation and future growth, not squandered to meet short-run expectations.

Considered in these terms, business and government are not adversaries; they are partners.

The examples given in this book demonstrate a drift in the direction of restructuring the business-government relationship. But just as the Soviet Union finds its perestroika retarded by the old ideology and those who derive solace, profit, or prestige from its hymns, so does the United States suffer from the mindless clutch of old assumptions. Where is the pragmatism that we as a nation have traditionally exhibited? (It was, after all, invented here.) Will it be reasserted in time to save us from crises of catastrophic proportions? An optimist would say *yes,* it will: business leadership will force the political order to abandon illusions of supremacy and face reality before it is too late. A pessimist would say *no,* there will be no such concerted effort: our competitiveness will continue to erode; the budget and trade deficits will continue to grow; our creditors, especially Japan, will become restless; we will lose control; interest rates will rise; inflation will soar; recession will come; and economic collapse will follow. An already inflammatory social disintegration will worsen, leading to widespread violence if not outright urban warfare.

Some will say that the course I suggest emulates Japan's, and they will hasten to add that the United States is different, which of course it is. But Japan has learned much from the United States since World War II, so theoretically, at least, there is no cultural reason why we cannot learn as much from Japan.

In a sense, this book advocates doing unto Japan what Japan has so effectively done unto us. This is not a hostile suggestion; in fact, in many ways Japan needs a strengthened America. Its strategy requires a carefully orchestrated reciprocity, especially in trade matters. But U.S. calls for reciprocity abroad without broad-based systematic restructuring at home will not be sufficient. Rather, they will be the whining of a toothless tiger.

Japan is not an enemy. Demands that it change its system—i.e., level the playing field—will not make the United States more competitive. To avoid increasing the economic disparity between Japan and the United States and to prevent the irrational antagonism—bashing—that serves neither's interest, it is necessary for the United States to know its priorities and to organize and allocate its resources so as to fulfill them. Naturally, its priorities may conflict with those of other nations, including Japan. When they do, negotiations make sense. But negotiations can only succeed if the United States knows its interests and has fully developed its own capacity to fulfill them.

RECOMMENDATIONS FOR LEADERSHIP

I have described relations between government and—for the most part—a rather special category of business: large, publicly held firms in industries that are increasingly exposed to intensifying global competition: computers, semiconductors, telecommunications, earth-sensing, health equipment, and so forth. Firms based in countries that have winning systems are more competitive than those from countries that do not.

My focus has been on the United States, and my purpose has been to help those who are aware of the awesome challenges and changes confronting American companies in such industries to manage business-government relations more effectively. (For advice on what to do inside the firm, I recommend the works of my Harvard colleagues Kim Clark, Robert Hayes, Ramchandran Jaikumar, David Garvin, Robert Kaplan, Rosabeth Moss Kanter, Quinn Mills, Richard Walton, and Shoshana Zuboff, among others.)[1]

Industries that are exposed to foreign competition have the choices described in Chapter 2: to leave the United States in one way or another, or to stay and change themselves, their relationships with government, and government itself. Many firms, of course, are doing both. And let me emphasize that it may very well be in the interest of the United States, the employees of an American company, and its shareholders for the company to go abroad. Indeed, it may be essential for many reasons: to seek new markets, gain more intimate relationships with customers and suppliers, circumvent tariff barriers, and derive the benefits of lower-cost labor, for example. But it must be acknowledged that sometimes there is tension between the choices, marked on the one hand by the short-run interests of shareholders—or at least those who speak for them—and on the other by the long-run interests of the country and employees. I have concentrated on the forms of change being undertaken by those who have opted to stay.

On the industry side, the first prerequisite for survival is clearly the production of superior products at competitive prices with superior after-sales service and support; that is, the ability to compete in a completely open and free world marketplace. Because such a marketplace is rare, however, further measures are required. They include: cooperation among rivals to pool resources in order to generate the knowledge required for competitive innovation (e.g., Sematech); greater cooperation with government in order to achieve a definition of and a connection with community need that would justify funding and other forms of assistance; greater use of industry associations (e.g., HIMA) to devise and execute industry strategies for dealing more effectively with government; and ascribing new importance and status to the function of managing business-government relations in the firm.

On the government side, the changes include: perceiving industry as vital to the achievement of community need—the national interest; defining community need to give high priority to industrial competitiveness along with other needs such as safety, health, defense, a balanced budget, and strong consumer spending; developing coherence among governmental departments and agencies to allow a reliable and systemic

definition of community need; and achieving sufficient cooperation between the Congress and the executive to permit a
close working relationship between business and government
agencies.

As the 1980s drew to a close, the American system was
failing to compete successfully with those centered in Asia
and Europe. The cause lay partly in the slowness with which
these changes were being introduced. As the crisis mounted,
there was a tendency—fruitless at best—to blame the competitors for America's failure.

In industry, the changes were impeded by traditional ways.
If government is to regard industry as an essential contributor to community need and provide it with assistance to
that end, then business must in fact be such a contributor. Its
leaders must help politicians to define community need in a
manner that is clearly rooted in the interests of the community and to align the purpose of business with the fulfillment
of that need. Such a conception, however, strains an older one,
namely, that the purpose of business is only to satisfy shareholders. The strain is especially severe if those shareholders
are represented by Wall Street traders or LBOers whose time
horizons are very short. Under such circumstances, a firm is
understandably tempted to sell off temporarily losing ventures, as Perkin-Elmer is attempting to do with its equipment
business, regardless of the impact on the nation. Although
this may be good for the shareholders in the short run, it is not
good for the competitiveness of the country, or indeed for
those same shareholders, in the long run.

"The only pressure I have on me is short-term pressure,"
said Andrew C. Sigler, chairman and CEO of Champion International Corp. "I announce that we're going to spend half a
billion dollars at Courtland, Alabama, with a hell of a pay-out
from redoing a mill and my stock goes down two points. I
finally caved in and announced I'm going to buy back the
stock, which makes no sense. If the economy is supposedly run
by corporations and corporations are supposed to invest and
be competitive, buying back your own stock, if you have alter-
natives, makes no sense."[2]

Some 60% of companies on the Standard & Poor's 500 list are owned by institutions, among them employee pension funds. New York state's public-employee fund owns a million shares of Champion. "In many respects," said Sigler, "they're my only long-term owners. That doesn't mean they're looking long term, it just means they are going to be around awhile."[3]

So if Mr. Sigler wants to invest for long-run competitiveness, he must convince the people who manage those funds, and perhaps the public employees themselves. If managers cannot be owners and if owners are to retain the rights of property, there seems to be no alternative. If, however, that is too cumbersome and unreliable, other changes in the system need to be made. The investment banking industry as a whole might produce a national strategy for competitiveness. Or a variety of carrots and sticks might be legislatively arranged to enable business managers to serve long-run community needs.[4]

Oddly perhaps, the old idea that management authority comes from the owners has become uncompetitive. In the industries with which we are concerned, such authority is coming increasingly from the community as well as from those who are managed, as reflected in contemporary changes in human resource management. The success of community-derived authority depends on how well the community defines the purposes it wants the corporation to serve. The corporation cannot do everything. For the new system to work, government must be adept at defining and assigning priorities to the community needs it wants business to serve: global competitiveness, military security, a clean environment, full employment, safety, health, and so forth.

A successful system of business-government relations diminishes the natural friction among conflicting community needs; that is, defense requirements can be met in ways that enhance commercial competitiveness. But political leadership must demand coherence and the several agencies of government must be organized to achieve it. Safety and effectiveness in health care can be harmonized with the need for economy and competitiveness if the FDA, HCFA, the USTR, Commerce, and the industry work together. Washington in 1989 had a long way to go. For example, global competitiveness was not even a factor in determining which biotechnology products received "fast track" treatment from the FDA, EPA, and USDA. Neither was it considered by the woefully under-staffed Patent Office. Looking at the examples we have discussed—semiconductors, high-definition TV, health equipment, earth-imaging from space—industry has a significant role in helping government to coordinate its activities better, and especially to recognize the thrust of global competition. Recall the case of health equipment. The industry success-fully opposed OMB efforts to deny the FDA the inspectors it needed to provide timely product approvals, and at the same time sought to bring the approval process closer to the aims of those at HCFA who sought more economical health care.

Defining Community Needs

Once community needs are defined, care must be taken to select the best method of aligning business with them. As I discussed in Chapter 1, there are four methods for doing so. In many areas—retailing, for example—free market competi-tion, safeguarded by the antitrust laws, works best. In others, such as food and drugs, regulation is essential. But business-government partnerships appear increasingly to be the most competitive method. Such partnerships have been tried in a number of states in the past decade with some success.[5] And, as we have seen, they are now inching their way forward at the federal level. For partnership to work, especially in a hos-tile ideological climate, its terms must be carefully de-lineated: who the "senior partner" is; what the terms of the partnership are; who is in and who is not. If America is going to develop a strategy to regain competitiveness, a broad range of interests, including the investment community, environ-mentalists, and labor and consumer groups, must join in. A consensus is required. A potentially debilitating legitimacy gap opens as business and government depart from tradi-tional ideology; it must be closed by calling up a new ideology as justification. If not, the traditionalists will defeat the innovation with cries of fascism, corporate-statism, and loss of freedom.

Defining community need and aligning business with it does not mean planning by a bureaucratic elite and imposing the results on the economy. Not only is this approach ideologically repellent, but it does not work, as experiments in the USSR, Eastern Europe, France in the 1960s, and elsewhere have clearly shown. Although government undeniably has the *authority* to define community need, business equally undeniably has the *competence* that is essential for a wise definition and for its implementation. Industry leadership in governmental initiatives to foster competitiveness is essential. Sematech will not work without such continuing leadership. And there must be mutual respect—government for business, and vice versa.

Industry associations are crucial to the organizing of business leadership for new and more creative relationships with government. It is uneconomic, inefficient, and ineffective for each company by itself to attempt to design and conduct a partnership with government. This can be handled far better by associations of companies with permanent staffs whose task is to draw from each side—business and government— what the other needs. These associations manage cooperation, set vision, and make strategy. Their task will increasingly demand the best and most talented people. Industry associations are the bridge between business specialists on one side and politicians and government officials on the other.[6] That bridge, as we have seen, is becoming increasingly crucial to competitiveness. In the mid-1980s, for example, Motorola, working with the Semiconductor Industry Association, succeeded in obtaining significant U.S. government help in gaining access to Japanese markets for its microelectronics products. John Mitchell, the company's president, said: "It seems that the harder Bob [Galvin, Motorola's chairman] pushes in Washington, the more sales Motorola gets. The U.S. government is the greatest ally of Motorola."[7]

At the same time, within the firm the function of governmental affairs management—to inform corporate policymakers of the community need in those communities the corporation affects and to alert the communities to the requirements of the corporation—is crucial to success. If a high purpose of the competitive corporation is to serve the community need, then it must know what that need is. If the community is slow to define an aspect of that need, the corporation through its GA staff should lead, helping government to arrive at a definition. In the case of earth imaging from space, for example, it was the responsibility of General Motors and General Electric to use their appreciable influence in Washington to inform government as early as possible of the need for a coherent and long-term strategy. Resigning oneself to the role of order-taker from an ill-informed bureaucracy is not good business-government relations.

The Dangers of the Business-Government Alliance

In all of this there are many dangers. Inefficient corporations may be coddled. Instead of winners being helped to win, losers may be insulated from the competition that should invigorate—or eliminate—them. Government may provide assistance without making its expectations of business clear and firm. The status quo may be protected for its own sake; essential change may be delayed; crises may worsen.

Changes that are so radical and so ideologically abhorrent to so many will proceed slowly, with great ambivalence and substantial inadvertence. The full implications of what is happening might not be faced. We could try to sneak it in, pretending that nothing is being changed,[8] but in such circumstances, the legitimacy gap will widen as business and government behave in ways that differ radically from the traditional norm. Unless the new norm is set forth clearly, in all of its communitarian dimensions, pressure will grow to close the gap by reverting to the old norms and crises will mount to catastrophic proportions. The changes will be made, but clumsily, in haste, desperation, and confusion. Ultimately, they will be deemed illegitimate.

The new ideology justifying what the United States is doing and what it must do is a version of communitarianism. Although it threatens cherished features of individualism, it can, with care, be constructed to preserve them. Ironically, in fact, the protection of individual freedoms and rights in this age requires a communitarian shift.

Is the world witnessing an end to ideology? Absolutely not. But it is witnessing the end of antique ideological constructs: socialism, capitalism, and communism. These words should be abandoned to history. They are worse than useless; they are misleading. They are not accurate descriptions of the evolving ideological forms that are shaping the economic and political lives of nations and the world. The new forms are emerging out of the need to adapt to the inexorable realities of international competition, technological change, and ecological strain. Managing them effectively requires, above all, that our vision be uncluttered by myths of the past.

A final word is necessary on the virus of nationalism with which some may feel I am infected. They may find it indeed strange that I argue for invigorating business-government relations at the national level at a time when nations and corporations are becoming more tightly laced in a complex network of interdependence. But nation-states show no signs of dying gracefully: rather, their power seems to be increasing. They are a fact of life now and for the foreseeable future. Unelected business leaders will never be allowed to define community need by themselves. National governments will battle among themselves to control business and to bend it to their will.

As the decade of the 1990s unfolds, formidable business-government coalitions in Asia and Europe face a fragmented, incoherent, and divided United States. The U.S. response has been partially constructive, insofar as it is gearing itself to become more competitive; but it has also been petulant and vindictive, chastising and seeking to punish those whom it considers cheaters. This is a useless course. What is clearly desirable is a new system of transnational government, one that includes a more effective General Agreements on Tariffs and Trade with real dispute-settling powers; an expanded International Monetary Fund/World Bank with the capacity to bridge the chasms of world debt; agreements and covenants such as those being fashioned in Europe to provide reliable definitions of global needs regarding property rights, fair trade, hunger, disease, and the environment. But even though the United States cannot participate effectively in this movement from a position of weakness, and certainly cannot lead it, there is no appetite in Congress or elsewhere for the magnanimity—or the objectivity—that leadership requires. So the USTR is required to wield the clumsy club of Super 301, and the country is distracted from its real—its own—problems. Ironically perhaps, the emergence of a more sensible global pattern of relationships depends on the United States straightening itself out along the lines I have suggested. With strength and confidence restored, American leadership will be effective in moving the world away from competitive nationalism and toward a more fruitful consciousness of its oneness.

Central to this task is improved business-government relations that rest on a redefinition of the roles of each and the design of new mechanisms and procedures for bringing them together. This means change and controversy. It will take time: hopefully not too much because with time comes crisis, and crisis is expensive. It is a shame to waste it. To repeat: The overriding task of leadership in government and business is to make maximum use of minimum crisis for maximum change.

NOTES

1. Following are the latest books by some of my colleagues at the Harvard Business School describing the changes required inside the American corporation to increase its competitiveness: Kim Clark, Robert Hayes, and Steven Wheelwright, *Dynamic Manufacturing: Creating a Learning Organization* (New York: Free Press, 1988); David Garvin, *Managing Quality* (New York: Free Press, 1988); H. Thomas Johnson and Robert S. Kaplan, *Relevance Lost: The Rise and Fall of Management Accounting*

(Boston: Harvard Business School Press, 1987); Rosabeth Moss Kanter, *When Giants Learn to Dance* (New York: Simon and Schuster, 1989); D. Quinn Mills, *The New Competitors* (New York: John Wiley, 1985); Richard E. Walton, *Up and Running: Integrating Information Technology and the Organization* (Boston: Harvard Business School Press, 1989); and Shoshana Zuboff, *In the Age of the Smart Machine* (New York: Basic Books, 1988).

2. *The Wall Street Journal,* June 6, 1989, p. A29.

3. Ibid.

4. Bruce R. Scott, *As If by an Invisible Hand* (preliminary title), forthcoming.

5. David Osborne, *Laboratories of Democracy* (Boston: Harvard Business School Press, 1988).

6. See Joseph L. Bower, *Two Faces of Management: An American Approach to Leadership in Business and Management* (Boston: Houghton Mifflin, 1983).

7. David B. Yoffie and John J. Coleman, "Motorola and Japan: Supplement III," #388-059. Boston: Harvard Business School, 1988, p. 2.

8. See Don E. Kash, *Perpetual Innovation: The New World of Competition* (New York: Basic Books, 1989), Chapter 1 and elsewhere.

APPENDIX I

Some Government Policies Affecting Business

Let us look in more detail at some of the more important ways in which government policies affect business.

FISCAL POLICY: THE REVENUE SIDE

Budget deficits require governments to borrow at home or abroad, which raises interest rates, increases the cost of capital, and discourages business investment. Higher interest rates also tend to raise prices and increase the cost of exports in global markets.

FISCAL POLICY: THE EXPENDITURE SIDE

Policy decisions on government expenditures affect economic growth, prices, and employment. In the 1960s, the U.S. decision to fight the Vietnam War and pursue the Great Society without raising taxes contributed to inflation, recession, and unemployment in the 1970s. The effects were especially severe on business because at the same time the Japanese government was using government expenditures to sustain "miracle growth" by encouraging its companies to acquire world market share, and the Japanese economy was greatly stimulated by U.S. war-related expenditures.

The processes a government uses to determine expenditure levels and priorities tend to determine outcomes. The United

States relies heavily on the free play of interest groups in the halls of Congress. Other countries, such as Japan and Germany, look to other institutions: powerful and prestigious government agencies, coupled with banking institutions, that are relatively well insulated from interest group pressures.

MONETARY POLICY

Policies of the Federal Reserve Board and the Treasury affect the value of the dollar in foreign exchange markets, making American exports cheaper or more expensive and encouraging or discouraging imports. Government policies of other countries such as Japan are used to help firms adjust to such exchange rate changes.

Government policies also control the cost of money by their impact on interest rates. Some governments, such as Japan and Germany, coordinate fiscal and monetary policy to achieve desired levels of economic growth and price stability. By linking the two with credit policy, they are also able to control the flows and the cost of capital to key sectors of industry. Plainly, this capability affects the competitiveness of those sectors vis-à-vis others in the world economy.

TAX POLICY

U.S. tax policies have traditionally encouraged consumption over savings and investment. If American products are competitive with those of foreigners, this helps business. If they are not—indeed, if U.S. firms have abandoned important sectors such as consumer electronics to foreigners—then tax incentives to consume become subsidies to America's competitors. Such policies have a particularly powerful impact when competitors pursue the opposite course of encouraging savings and investment and discouraging consumption. For close to twenty years, America has had among the lowest rates of savings and investment in the industrial world. This is not a cultural quirk; it is the direct result of government policy.

Tax incentives can also help certain businesses and industries more than others. Housing and real estate in the United States, for example, have greatly benefited from friendly tax policy, as has agriculture and shipping.[1] In other countries, high-tech manufacturing for export receives tax breaks.

FINANCIAL POLICY

Tax policy also reaches into the financial markets, encouraging debt over equity as a source of investment capital in the United States. Interest payments are deductible and dividends are taxed twice. Tax laws thus subsidize leveraged buyouts, which have questionable effects on the economy and its competitiveness.

Some countries allocate credit to important industries engaged in international competition; others, like the United States, allocate credit to domestic sectors such as agriculture and housing, which have political priority.

When it deregulated financial markets, the U.S. government greatly increased the volume and reduced the costs of equity trading. This intensified the short-run outlook of traders, investors, and managers, making even more important the quarterly performance numbers of American corporations. At the same time, America's competitors were paying increasing attention to long-run market share. The result: American corporations showed higher profits, but their foreign competitors gained market share.

TRADE POLICY

Governments may adopt trade policies that are designed to promote free trade, as does the United States, or that protect infant industries, promote exports, and discourage imports, as do most other countries. Ironically, in the name of free trade—that is, punishing the cheaters, as in the case of European steel—the United States has secured sixty-two so-called "voluntary restraint agreements" to protect certain industries, including steel and automobiles. Thus, trade policies can also have the effect of protecting uncompetitiveness—propping up losers—or promoting competitiveness.

The 1988 Omnibus Trade and Competitiveness Act allowed the president to prohibit foreign investments or acquisitions in the United States if they adversely affect the "national security," a term broadly defined in the act. This government policy now affects a U.S. company's ability to sell itself as a subsidiary to foreigners.

INDUSTRIAL ORGANIZATION POLICY

Antitrust laws constitute the basic American approach to industry organization. Designed to prevent or prohibit restraints on competition in the marketplace, they have discouraged cooperation, consolidation, and rationalization, which other governments not only permit but encourage.

In 1984, the National Cooperative Research Act suggested a possible new approach. It allowed cooperation for joint research, presumably, although not explicitly, in order to promote U.S. competitiveness. In 1989, there was doubt about what government policy was in this area.

GOVERNMENT PROCUREMENT POLICY

Government procurement has a substantial impact on business. Both U.S. and non-U.S. defense contractors are helped. Defense procurement alone amounts to $300 billion a year in the United States. The nature of defense procurement and the procedures followed can also affect the commercial competitiveness of firms. Today, the commercial uses of defense-funded research and development and procurement are less than they once were. In fact, in many high-tech products such as semiconductors, commercial developments are ahead of military ones. In addition, the Department of Defense can encourage or discourage the export of U.S. military products. The U.S. portion of world military sales fell from 49% in 1976 to 20% in 1986. And the Defense Department's decision to join with Japan in the production of a new fighter plane, the FSX, was thought by some to erode U.S. leadership in the aerospace industry.[2] DOD procurement policies can also encourage or discourage innovation, risk-taking, and human resource management policies that make firms more or less competitive in the world economy. The trade balance seems to suggest that in recent years DOD policies have had a negative effect on business performance.

Furthermore, government procurement is used as a way of promoting social and political ends as well as economic ones. In the 1970s, the Japanese government purchased Japanese computers to boost the country's fledgling computer industry and help it compete with IBM. French policies in the telecommunications area in the mid-1980s were shaped by the desire to build European strength vis-à-vis Japan and the United States. The United States uses procurement as a means of encouraging small business, especially small business owned by minorities and women. This is the thrust of Section 8a of the Small Business Act, which mandates "set-asides" to enable such firms to obtain government work without competitive bidding.

Occasionally, a government may actually launch an industry, as France and the United States did when they established private companies to generate commercial markets for images of the earth received in space by government-owned satellites. The success of such ventures, as we have seen, depends almost entirely on government-business relationships.

EDUCATION POLICY

All governments devote substantial sums to education. Some tie these expenditures to performance, insisting on standards, discipline, and course structures, while others leave such decisions to locally elected officials. Some— Germany, for example—augment schooling with elaborate apprenticeship and training programs to equip people for jobs in industry; others leave skill training to the free interplay of schools and business.

LABOR POLICY

The U.S. government has tended to shape its labor policy to practice as it evolved. The National Labor Relations Act (NLRA), for example, endorsed the practice of adversarial collective bargaining as it was developing in the 1930s. By the 1980s, different practices were emerging—employee involvement, quality of work life, and organizational development— practices that emphasized consensus in the workplace over the legal contract envisaged by the NLRA. Government policy, however, remained essentially unchanged. In other countries, government policy plays a more active role in shaping relations between managers and the managed, whether it is the various schemes for involving workers in management in Europe or the human resource management policies of Japan.

REGULATORY POLICY

All governments regulate the practices of business to ensure some measure of safety and health as well as other outcomes regarded as essential to the needs of the community, outcomes that the free play of market forces do not ensure. There is, however, considerable variation in how community needs are defined and how business is brought into line with them. Some governments, like that of the United States, are so internally divided that the definition of needs that regulations are supposed to serve is slow, uncertain, and unreliable. In the matter of health equipment, for example (see Chapter

5), the Food and Drug Administration, which is supposed to ensure safety and effectiveness, is frequently at odds with a Congress that is eager for strictness and with an Office of Management and Budget that is concerned with frugality. The FDA also proceeds with little or no coordination with its sister agency, the Health Care Financing Administration, which is charged with deciding whether a particular medical device is worth paying for under the Medicare program. (Both agencies, incidentally, are in the same department, Health and Human Services.) And in the United States, tradition has meant that relations between the regulators and the regulated tend to be adversarial, marked by suspicion and mistrust.

Other governments seem to be more adept at defining community need and working out cooperative relations with business to fulfill it.

NOTES

1. Robert B. Reich, "Why the U.S. Needs an Industrial Policy," *Harvard Business Review* (January–February 1982): 74–81.
2. Bruce Stokes, "Beat 'Em or Join 'Em," *National Journal,* May 25, 1989, pp. 459–464.

APPENDIX II

Japan versus America

Five-Year Changes in the Level of Japanese Technology and Ability to Develop High-Tech Products

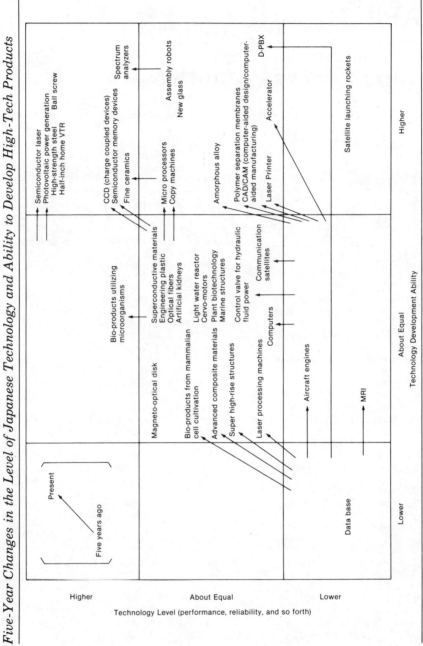

Source: Ministry of International Trade and Industry, Tokyo, September 1988.

224

INDEX

ABICOMP. *See* Brazilian Computer Industry Association
Adler, Emanuel, 161, 165
Advisory Group on Economic Structural Adjustment for International Harmony (Maekawa Commission), 50–51
AEA. *See* American Electronics Association
Akikusa, Tokuji (NTT president), 185
Alcan Aluminum, Ltd., 195–197
Aluminum Association, 196, 197
American Electronics Association (AEA), 69, 70
  Brazilian informatics policy and, 172, 175–176, 178–179
American myths, and government policy, 6–7
Antitrust concerns
  cooperative research and, 68, 79–80
  industrial associations and, 129
Apple Computer, 177, 178
AT&T
  French telecommunications market and, 189–191
  Public Affairs Office (PAO) at, 187–189, 191
  Sematech and, 82
Augustine, Norman, 81, 82
Authority
  of Brazilian technocrats, 166
  governmental affairs management and, 159, 161
  sources of, for management, 6–7, 10, 40–41, 97–98, 206–207
Automobile industry, 54–56

Baker, James. 114
Baldrige, Malcolm, 83, 113, 114, 115, 116

Balladur, Edouard, 190–191
Balog, Stephen J., 88
Benson, James, 132–133
Bessey, Edward C., 145
Biotechnology industry
  global competition and, 123
  military vs. commercialization issue and, 71
  role of industrial association in, 129
Bond, Jim, 193
Bower, Joseph L., 76
Brazil
  Alcan Aluminum and, 195–197
  on individualistic-communitarian continuum, 16
  informatics policy in, 163–165 (*see also* Brazilian informatics policy)
Brazil Exporters Association, 179
Brazilian Computer Industry Association (ABICOMP), 173–174
Brazilian informatics policy
  Brazil–U.S. confrontation on, 176–182
  characteristics of technocrats responsible for, 165–167
  IBM's issues manager and, 165–167, 169–170, 171–172, 174, 180–181
  negotiations following *301* action, 172–176
  statement of, 163–165
  U.S. Sec. *301* action on, 167–168, 170–172
Brazilian Secretariat of Informatics (SEI), 168, 174, 175, 176, 179, 180
Bristol-Myers, Medical Device Improvement Act of *1988* and, 141, 143–144
Brooks, Harvey, 118
Budetti, Peter, 143
Bureaucracy. *See also specific Japanese ministries; specific U.S. government agencies*

Bureaucracy (*continued*)
  in France, 35–36
  in Germany, 34
  in Japan, 33–34, 183–186
  need for coherence among agencies in,
    38, 133, 205–206, 207–208
  relationship between bureaucrats and
    politicians, 148–150
Bush, George, 65, 91
Business
  changes needed in, 205
  impediments to change in, 206–207
  leadership by, in industrial policy,
    67–68, 209
  options for dealing with global compe-
    tition and, 204–205
  roles of, 40–45
  structures of, 45–47
Business–government alliance
  in chemical industry, 194–195
  community needs and, 208
  Comsat and, 122
  dangers of, 210–212
  industrial strategy and, 68–72, 208–
    209
  industry associations and, 148, 209
  national competitiveness and, 50–57
  U.S. industrial policy and, 68–72
Business–government relationships,
    47–59. *See also* Business–govern-
    ment alliance
  forums and, 47, 50–51
  in France, 107, 112–113
  in Germany, 34–35
  global industries and, 25–26
  increased emphasis on management
    of, 56–57 (*see also* Governmental
    affairs management)
  in Japan, 21, 50–53, 134
  multinational corporations and, 13
  process and, 47–48
  restructuring of, and ideological as-
    sumptions, 203
  RSS competition and, 105–119
  size of government and, 20
  substantive issues and, 48–57

Campos, Roberto, 164
Career tracking, governmental affairs
    staff and, 193–194
Carey, Hugh L., 195
Carter, Jimmy, 113
Castro, Edson De, 176
CBEMA. *See* Computer and Business

Equipment Manufacturers Associa-
    tion
Center for Strategic and International
    Studies report, 90
Central Intelligence Agency, 79
CFIUS. *See* Committee on Foreign In-
    vestment in the United States
CGCT. *See* Compagnie Générale des
    Constructions Téléphoniques
Challenger disaster, and EOSAT, 116–
    117
Champion International Corporation,
    206–207
Chemical industry, 194–195
Chirac, Jacques, 189, 190
Cline, William, 164–165
COBRA, 166, 167–168
COCOM. *See* Coordinating Committee
    for Multilateral Export Controls
Collaboration. *See* Business–govern-
    ment alliance; Partnership; Re-
    search consortia
Collis, David, 3
Committee on Foreign Investment in
    the United States (CFIUS), 87–88
Communications, and Brazilian tech-
    nocrats, 166
Communitarianism
  role of government under, 15–16
  structures of government under, 27–
    28
  transition from individualism toward,
    7–8, 211
Community needs
  alignment of business with, 10, 21,
    158–160, 202–203, 208–209
  importance of business to, 97–99, 205,
    206
  managerial authority and, 7, 97–98
  regulation and, 222–223
  vs. shareholder interests, 9
  in U.S. vs. Japan, 68
Community needs, definition of, 22, 25–
    26, 208–210
  role of government in, 7, 95, 97–100,
    207
  role of industry in, 146–147, 206,
    209–210
Compagnie Générale des Constructions
    Téléphoniques (CGCT), 189–191
Competence, of Brazilian technocrats,
    166
Competition. *See* Free markets; Global
    competition
Computer and Business Equipment

Manufacturers Association (CBEMA), 172, 178
Computer industry
Brazilian informatics policy and, 163–182
development of, in Japan, 74–77
Comsat, 122
Congress
agency oversight and, 149, 151
1985 protectionist legislation in, 171
Sematech and, 83
Toshiba matter and, 52–53
CONIN. See National Council on Informatics and Automation (CONIN), in Brazil
Conner, Gerald R., 143–144
Cooperation. See also Business–government alliance; Partnership; Research consortia
between HIMA and HCFA, 139–140
Japanese VLSI/TRA and, 74–77
mechanisms for, 47–48
Coordinating Committee for Multilateral Export Controls (COCOM), 52–53
Copyright protection, and Brazilian trade case, 173, 174–175
Corporate management
government experience of Japanese personnel, 33–34, 50, 53
issues facing, 57–59
recommendations for, 204–212
sources of authority for, 6–7, 10, 40–41, 97–98, 206–207
Corporate objectives. See also Community needs; corporate management
ranking of, in U.S. and Japan, 43
Corruption
governmental affairs management and, 153
in Japanese agencies, 185
Cost-cutting, and governmental affairs management, 154
Council on Competitiveness, 91, 96
Credibility, and governmental affairs management, 159–160
Crisis, costs of, 122–123

DARPA. See Defense Advanced Research Projects Agency
Data General Corporation, Brazilian informatics policy and, 165, 167–168
DEC. See Digital Equipment Corporation
Decentralization, 197

Decision making, 159–160
Defense Advanced Research Projects Agency (DARPA)
funding role of, 96–97
HDTV and, 70
military vs. commercialization issue and, 70–71
Sematech and, 84–85
semiconductor industry and, 71–72
superconductivity (HTS) research and, 98, 99
U.S. industrial policy and, 88–89, 91–92, 95–97
Defense Science Board (DSB), 81, 82, 91
Department of Commerce
EOSAT and, 115–116
Health Industry Manufacturers Association (HIMA) and, 140–141
Landsat and, 106
Sematech progress and, 85, 87
U.S. RSS capability and, 106, 110, 111
Department of Defense. See also Defense Advanced Research Projects Agency
cuts in budget of, 92
DARPA and, 92
EOSAT's decline and, 108
government procurement policy and, 220–221
industrial policy and, 90–91
machine-tool industry and, 4
military vs. commercialization issue and, 20–21, 70–71
Sematech and, 82, 83, 84–85
Department of Health and Human Services. See Food and Drug Administration; Health Care Financing Administration
Developing countries, 107–108
Developmental state, 16–17, 21
Diagnosis-related groups (DRGs), 136, 138
Digital Equipment Corporation (DEC), 82
Dingell, John B., 141, 144
Domínguez, Jorge, 24
Dondoux, Jacques, 14
Dorsey, Tom, 83–84
Dove, Grant A., 79
DRAM chips. See Dynamic random access memory (DRAM) chips
DRGs. See Diagnosis-related groups
DSB. See Defense Science Board
Dyer, Davis, 54

Dynamic random access memory (DRAM) chips, 73–74, 87, 93

Eaton, Robert J., 56
Economic Policy Institute, 93
Education policy, 221–222
Ehrlichman, John D., 27
Eisenhower, Dwight D., 11
Encarnation, Dennis, 48
Environmental issues
  chemical industry and, 195
  governmental affairs management and, 195, 196
  myth on specialization and, 7
  technological threat and, 14
EOSAT
  creation of, 106
  decline of, 107–108, 110–112, 113–118
  funding for, 115
  lack of business leadership and, 121–122
  lack of govement support for, 114–116
Espionage, and Japan, 52n
Europe
  government policies in, 3–4, 5
  Health Industry Manufacturers Association and, 140
  industrial associations in, 46
  industry–government microelectronics consortium in, 85
  joint ventures within, 104–105 (see also JESSI)
  research consortium (JESSI) in, 89–90
  semiconductor industry in, 73
  transnational agreements and, 212
European Commission, 104, 105
European Community, 5
Evans, Peter B., 161
"Extraterritoriality," 156

FDA. See Food and Drug Administration
Federal Food, Drug, and Cosmetic Act of 1938, 1976 amendments to, 131, 141–142. See also Medical Device Improvement Act of 1988
Federal Trade Commission (FTC), 54–56
Felker, Lansing, 68
Feudal traditions, and governmental structures, 28
Fields, Craig, 70, 84, 88, 97

Financial policy, 219
Fiscal policy, 217–218. See also Tax policy
Food and Drug Administration (FDA)
  approval time, 131
  function of, 130–131
  HIMA and, 124, 125–126, 130–135
  Medical Device Improvement Act of 1988 and, 141–146
  medical device regulation and, 131, 222–223
  relationships with Health Care Financing Administration (HCFA), 133
Foreign investment
  government competition for, 25–26, 48–50
  ownership philosophy and, 49
Foreign policy, 107–108
Forums, 47, 50–51
France
  business–government relations in, 107, 112–113
  government policies on auto industry in, 54
  on individualistic–communitarian continuum, 16
  policy reevaluation and, 24
  SPOT Image in, 107–108, 109, 111, 112–113
  state power in, 35–36
  telecommunications in, and AT&T, 189–191
Free markets
  Japanese telecommunications markets and, 183
  political issues and, 104
  trade policy and, 219–220
  U.S. auto industry and, 55
  world competition and, 17
FSX (Fighter Support Experimental) deal, 66, 98, 99–100, 221
FTC. See Federal Trade Commission

Galvin, Bob, 209
GA management. See Governmental affairs (GA) management
Gates, William, 176–177
GATT. See General Agreements on Tariffs and Trade
General Agreements on Tariffs and Trade (GATT)
  powers of, 211–212
  U.S.–Brazil dispute and, 171, 173–174, 178, 179, 197

General Dynamics, 65
General Electric, 121
General Motors, 41, 55–56, 121
Gephart, Richard, 170–171
Germany, 41–42, 45
  government policies on auto industry
    in, 54
  on individualistic-communitarian
    continuum, 16
  role of controlling banks in, 44–45
  state power in, 34–35
Gilmartin, John A., 126, 129
Global competition
  business-government partnerships
    and, 50–57
  business structure in U.S. and, 46–47
  coordination of industry competition
    for research and development and,
    20–21
  governmental intervention and, 17–
    18
  government priorities and, 130, 208
  importance of U.S. strength in, 201,
    212
  industry's options for survival and,
    204–205
  intensification of, in the 1980s, 13, 14
  national interest and, 103–105
  regulatory policy and, 191–192
  U.S. government regulations and, 123
  U.S. medical technology industry and,
    138–139
Globalization of business. See Global
  competition; Multinational corporations (MNCs)
Godown, Richard, 129
Gomes-Casseres, Benjamin, 49
Gorbachev, Mikhail, 16, 92
Government
  changes needed in, 205–206
  reorganization of, for industrial
    priorities, 201–202
  role of industry and, 207–208
  size of, and business–government re-
    lations, 20
  strong vs. weak, 31–38
Government, roles of
  ideological paradigms and, 15–26
  industrial strategy and, 95–97
  purposes and, 22–25
  U.S. ambivalence about, 111
Governmental affairs (GA) management, 8–9, 153–200
  access to decision-making apparatus,
    159–160
  as adversarial, 192–194
  at Alcan Aluminium, 195–197
  analytic process in, 161–163
  at AT&T, 187–191
  company objectives and, 186
  conflicting interests and, 160–162
  credibility and, 159–160
  decentralization and, 197
  education and, 160
  environmental concerns and, 195
  European experience in, 105
  function of, 8–9, 209–210
  government objectives and, 186
  at IBM vs. AT&T, 188–189
  increased emphasis on, 56–57
  industrial strategy and, 186–187
  in insurance industry, 191–194
  internal politics of foreign countries
    and, 186–187
  obstacles for, 153–155, 160
  relationship of lobbying and issues
    management in, 157–158
  remodeling process and, 8–12
  response to 301 actions and, 169–170
  role of industry associations in, 130
  Washington location and, 157
Government banks, in Japan, 50, 53
Government–business forums, in Japan, 50–51
Government intervention
  myths about, 6
  problems with, 18–19
  as reality, 2–5
Government policies
  affecting business, 217–223
  effect of, 2–5
  influence of industrial associations on,
    146–147
  national differences among, 5–8
  role of business in shaping of, 9
Government relations staff. See Lobbyists
Governments
  competition for global industries and,
    25–26, 48–50
  methods for meeting community
    needs and, 21–22
  national differences in priorities of,
    158–160
  priorities of, and governmental affairs
    management, 160–161
Government structures, 26–39
  in individualistic vs. communitarian
    societies, 17
  vs. strategy, 38–39

Grace, W.R. (company), 194–195
Gramm-Rudman-Hollings legislation, 116
Gravatt, Cary, 113–114, 115, 116
Grove, Andrew S., 54
Gundaker, Walter E., 134–135

Haney, H. Glen, 78
Harbison, Earle H., Jr., 71, 147
Hatch, Orrin, 141, 144
HCFA. *See* Health Care Financing Administration
HDTV. *See* High-definition TV
Health Care Financing Administration (HCFA), 135–140, 223
Health equipment industry. *See also* Health Industry Manufacturers Association (HIMA)
   business–government cooperation in, 123, 124
   Medical Device Improvement Act of *1988* and, 141–146
Health Industry Manufacturers Association (HIMA), 68, 123, 124–141
   concern with global competition in, 124, 125
   Food and Drug Administration and, 130–135
   HCFA and, 135–140
   Japan and, 140
   Medical Device Improvement Act of *1988,* 141–146
   membership of, 124
   mission of, 128–129
   obstacles for, 129–130
   organizational purpose, 124–128
Hewlett-Packard Medical Products Group, 127–128
High-definition TV (HDTV), 69–72, 87
High-temperature superconductivity (HTS). *See* Superconductivity
Hills, Carla A., 181
HIMA. *See* Health Industry Manufacturers Association
Holmes, Ben L., 127–128, 129, 145–146
HTS (high-temperature superconductivity). *See* Superconductivity
Huntington, Samuel, 28
Hutcheson, Jerry, 88

IBA. *See* Industrial Biotechnology Association

IBM
   Brazilian informatics policy and, 165–167, 169–170, 171–172, 174, 180–181
   control of subsidiaries and, 49, 50, 164
   Future System concept, 75–76
   Governmental Programs office at, 155–163
   internal politics of foreign countries and, 186–187
   MCC and cooperative research in U.S. and, 78, 80
   open markets and, 183
   Sematech and, 81, 82, 95
   U.S. Sec. *301* actions and, 182
"Ideological guerrillas," 165
Ideology. *See also* Communitarianism; Free markets; Individualism
   attitudes toward shift in, 7–8
   business structures and, 45–47
   erosion of myths and, 6–7
   governmental affairs management and, 153–154
   individualistic vs. communitarian societies and, 15–16
   new forms of, 211
   restructuring of business–government relationship and, 203
   shift in, and definition of community need, 97–100
Income security, as welfare concern, 23
India, foreign investment in, 49
Individualism
   role of government and, 15
   structures of government under, 28
   transition toward communitarianism, 7–8, 211
Industrial Bank of Japan, 53
Industrial Biotechnology Association (IBA), 123, 129
Industrial policy, U.S., 65–102
   beginnings of, in *1985,* 80–85
   business–government alliance and, 208–209
   choices for, 67–68
   collaboration and partnership and, 68–72
   before FSX debate, 65–67
   impact on business, 220
   industry-led, 67–68
   role of DARPA in, 88–89
   Sematech and, 80–85
   subsidies and, 47–48

trade policy and, 90–91
White House opposition to, 91, 94
Industrial Policy Council, 91
Industry. *See* Business
Industry associations. *See also* Aluminum Association; American Electronics Association; Computer and Business Equipment Manufacturers Association; Health Industry Manufacturers Association; Industrial Biotechnology Association; Sematech; Semiconductor Industry Association
conditions for success of, 147–148
critical role of, 122–141
difficulties facing, 125–127, 129–130
in Europe, 46
functions of, 146
industry strategy and, 68–69
in Japan, 46
management of, 148
mission of, 128–129, 147–148
need for, 146–147, 202
organization of business–government relationships and, 209
U.S.–Brazil dispute and, 172, 173–174, 180–181
Information
analysis of, 188–189
collection of, 159, 188 (*see also* Remote satellite sensing)
dissemination of, 189
Inman, Bobby Ray, 79
Innovation, Health Care Financing Administration procedures and, 138
Insurance industry
governmental affairs management in, 191–194
management of relations between companies in, 194
Interest groups, in Germany, 34
Interindustry associations, need for, 202
International Monetary Fund, 212
Ishihara, Shintaro, 100, 104
Issues management
governmental affairs management and, 159–160
lobbying and, 157–158

Japan
administrative guidance in, 50, 51–53
auto industry in, 54
bureaucratic influence in, 33–34

business-government relations in, 21, 50–53, 134
business structure in, 45–46
computer industry in, 74–77
conflict among government agencies in, 183–186
controlling banks in, 44–45
dedication to national interest in, 103–104
as developmental state, 21
five-year changes in technology, compared to U.S., 215–216
Health Industry Manufacturers Association (HIMA) and, 140
on individualistic-communitarian continuum, 16
industrial policy in, 19–20, 94
influence of Ministry of Finance in, 32–33
lessons to be learned from, 203–204
machine-tool industry in, 4
management authority in, 42–44, 45
national strategy of, 17–20
RSS market and, 110
semiconductor industry in, 73–74
state power in, 31–34
structures vs. strategy in, 38–39
telecommunications policy in, 183–187
USTR actions against, 181–182
welfare concerns in, 23
Japanese Development Bank, 53
Japan Robot Leasing Company, Ltd. (JAROL), 52
JAROL. *See* Japan Robot Leasing Company, Ltd.
Jensen, Michael, 44
JESSI. *See* Joint Submicron Silicon Initiative
Johnson, B. Kristine, 126–127
Johnson, Chalmers, 16, 19–20, 21, 183, 184, 185, 186
Johnston, James, 55
Joint Submicron Silicon Initiative (JESSI), 85, 89–90, 104–105
Joint venture
IBM strategy and, 180
among Japanese companies, 52
between Landsat and SPOT, 111
Julyan, David, 112–113

Kane, Sanford L., 79, 81, 82, 84, 85, 87
Katzenstein, Peter, 34, 36

Keidanren, 46
Keiichi, Konaga, 184
Keiretsu, 46
Keith, Steven, 144
Kelman, Steven, 30
Kennedy, Edward M., 141, 144
Kissinger, Henry, 176
Krist, William, 178–179
Krugman, Paul, 17–19, 119

Labor organizations, role of, 34, 37
Labor policy, 222
Land Remote Sensing Commercializa-
   tion Act of *1984*, 109
Landsat program, 106. *See also* EOSAT
Latham, Donald C., 108, 111, 116
Laxalt, Paul, 115
LBO. *See* Leveraged buyout (LBO) cor-
   poration
Legitimacy gap, 10, 29–30, 210
Leveraged buyout (LBO) corporation,
   44–45
Libero, Robeli, 164
Light, Jay O., 44
Lilly, Ely (corporation), 141, 143–144
Limited state, myth of, 6
Lobbyists, 56, 157–158, 160
Lorentzen, Carl, 195
Lowi, Theodore, 48

McCormick, Janice, 35
McGroddy, James C., 20
Machine-tool industry, 3–4
McKittrick, Charles E., Jr., 156–161
McLain, Patrick M., 142
Maekawa, Haruo, 50–51
Mahini, Amir, 50
Management. *See* Corporate manage-
   ment; Governmental affairs (GA)
   management
Mannen, Ted R., 125
Market reserve policy, in Brazil, 163–
   164, 174, 177, 180
MCC. *See* Microelectronic Computer
   Technology Corporation
Medicaid, 151
Medical Device Improvement Act of
   1988, 141–146
Medical technology industry
   global competition in, 138–139
   innovation in, and Medicare, 136–138
Medicare, 124, 135–136, 137, 151
Meese, Edwin, 114
Mega Life Insurance Company [pseud.],
   191–194

Meiji modernization, 43–44
Mexico, 16, 24, 28, 49
Microelectronic Computer Technology
   Corporation (MCC), 77–80
Microsoft Corporation, 176, 178, 179
Military–commercial applications con-
   flict, 70–72, 99, 220–221
Miller, Jim, 116
Ministry of Finance (MOF), in Japan,
   32–33, 50, 51, 184
Ministry of International Trade and In-
   dustry (MITI), in Japan
   administrative guidance and, 51–53
   control of telecommunications indus-
      try and, 183–186
   goals of industrial policies of, 19–20
   government–business forums and, 50,
      51
   influence of, 31–32
   VLSI/TRA and, 75–77
   "White Paper on Industrial Technol-
      ogy," 19–20
Ministry of Posts and Telecommunica-
   tions (MPT), in Japan, 183–186
Mitchell, John, 209
MITI. *See* Ministry of International
   Trade and Industry
Mitsubishi Heavy Industries Ltd., 65
Mitsui, 42–44
MNCs. *See* Multinational corporations
MOF. *See* Ministry of Finance
Mohan, Kshitij, 133–134
Moliter, Robert M., 127, 140, 144
Monaghan, James P., 196, 197
Monetary policy, 218
Monsanto, 72–73, 87–88
Mosbacher, Robert A., 66
Motorola Corporation, 209
MPT. *See* Ministry of Posts and Tele-
   communications, in Japan
Multinational corporations (MNCs). *See
   also specific companies*
   Brazilian informatics policy and, 164,
      167–168, 181
   business–government relations in
      1980s and, 13
   coordination of foreign subsidiaries
      and, 50
   government competition for, 48–50
   government objectives and, 103–105,
      186
   government relations and, 25–26
   Japanese, and MITI, 53
   strategic trade policies and, 26
   U.S. Sec. *301* actions and, 182

NASA. *See* National Aeronautics and Space Administration
National Advisory Committee on Semiconductors, 93–94
National Aeronautics and Space Administration (NASA), 106
National Cooperative Research Act of *1984,* 68, 79
National Council on Informatics and Automation (CONIN), in Brazil, 174–175, 177, 179–180
National interest. *See* Community needs
Nationalism
  Brazil's informatics policy and, 165, 166
  world interdependence and, 211–212
National Labor Relations Act (NLRA), 222
National Oceanic and Atmospheric Administration (NOAA)
  EOSAT and, 115, 116, 117–118
  Landsat and, 106
  RSS development and, 111
  U.S. RSS capability and, 106, 110, 111
National Recovery Administration (NRA), 29
National Science Foundation, 99
National Semiconductor, 82
National Space Policy and Commercial Space Initiatives directive, 109
National strategy. *See also* Industrial policy, U.S.
  conditions for success of, 18
  in Japan, 17–20
  relative success of, in *1980s,* 13
  vs. structure, 38–39
NCR Corporation, 67
New United Motors Manufacturing, Inc. (NUMMI), 55
Nippon Telegraph and Telephone (NTT), 182–183
NLRA. *See* National Labor Relations Act
NOAA. *See* National Oceanic and Atmospheric Administration
Nonstatist communitarianism, 34
Norris, William, 77–78, 80
Noyce, Robert, 83, 85, 88, 97
NRA. *See* National Recovery Administration
NTT. *See* Nippon Telegraph and Telephone

NUMMI. *See* New United Motors Manufacturing, Inc.

Office of Management and Budget (OMB), 83–84, 110–111
OMB. *See* Office of Management and Budget
Omnibus Trade and Competitiveness Act of *1988,* 220
"Open skies" policy, 107, 111
Oversight committees, 149, 151n12

Packard, George, 100
PACs. *See* Political action committees
Palmer, Robert, 116
Partnership, between U.S. and French firms, 189–190
Paster, Howard, 55
Pébereau, George, 190–191
Perkin-Elmer, 72–73, 87, 88
Pfizer, 141, 143–145
Philips, 89, 105
Pickens, T. Boone, 40
PMA. *See* Premarket approval
Policymaking, bureaucratic vs. political, 150
Political action committees (PACs), 57
Politicians, relationship with bureaucrats, 148–150
Porter, Michael, 13, 25
Postal savings system, in Japan, 185
Power, of Brazilian technocrats, 166
PPS. *See* Prospective payment system
Premarket approval (PMA), of medical devices, 131
Prestowitz, Clyde, 187
Procurement policy, 220–221
Property rights. *See* Shareholders
Prospective payment system (PPS), in Medicare, 135–136
Protectionism, U.S.
  effects of policies, 4–5
  1985 legislation and, 171
Putnam, Robert, 149

Quality, industry concern with, 134–135
Quayle, Dan, 91, 110, 112

Reagan, Ronald
  EOSAT and, 113–114, 117
  industrial policy and, 65
  RSS competition and, 106, 109, 110, 122
  trade conflict with Brazil and, 167, 171, 173, 175, 176, 177–178, 180

Regulatory policy. *See also* Food and
     Drug Administration (FDA)
  auto industry and, 55
  business and, 208, 222–223
  global competition and, 123, 191–192
  health equipment industry and, 123,
     125
  industry associations and, 130–135
  national objectives and, 125
Regulatory state, 16, 21
Remodeling
  effective management of, 2
  necessity for, 1–2
Remote Satellite Sensing (RSS), 105–
     119
  business-government relations and,
     105–119
  civil applications of, 108, 109
  French development of, 107
  functional characteristics of, 108–109
  international consortium in, 111–112
  U.S. decline in, 107–108, 109–111,
     113
  U.S. development of, 106, 109
  U.S. leadership in, 107, 109–110
Research consortia
  antitrust laws and, 79–80
  clarity of purpose of, 80
  elements for success of, 86
  government as coordinator in, 95
  Japan's VLSI/TRA and, 75–77
  MCC and, 77–80
  movement toward collaboration and,
     68
  nationalistic exclusivity and, 88–89,
     90
  strategic trade policy and, 90
Roper, William, 138–140
Ross, Ian, 93
RSS. *See* Remote Satellite Sensing

Salter, Malcolm S., 54
Samuel, Frank E., Jr., 124–127, 130,
     139–140, 141, 150
Sarney, José, 163, 167, 173, 174–175,
     176, 178–180
Saur, Ricardo, 165–167
Savings, and tax policy, 218–219
Sayer, R. Wayne, 175–176, 178
Scheuer, James H., 109
Schroeder, Leah, 127
Scopus (Brazilian firm), 176–177
SEI. *See* Brazilian Secretariat of Infor-
     matics

Sematech
  duality of purpose and, 83
  inadequacy of, and trade policy, 90–
     91
  origins of, 72, 74, 80–85, 89
  role of government in, 82, 84–85, 92,
     93, 95–97
Semiconductor industry, U.S.
  business leadership in, 122
  food chain in, 72–74
  HDTV and, 69–70
  industrial policy and, 65
  market share of, 73–74
  merchant vs. captive manufacturers
     in, 72
  military vs. commercialization issue
     and, 70–72
  need for developmental role of govern-
     ment in, 20
  origins of Sematech and, 80–85
  rate of restructuring in, 1–2
  structure of, 46
Semiconductor industry, world
  change in leading chip producers rev-
     enues in, 94
  production by region, 74
Semiconductor Industry Association
     (SIA), 68, 82, 83, 209
Shareholders
  community needs and, 206–207
  management authority and, 40–41
  myth on ownership by, 6–7
Shinohara, Myohei, 19
Shockley, William B., 72
Shonefield, Andrew, 24
SIA. *See* Semiconductor Industry Asso-
     ciation
Siemens, 89, 105
Sigler, Andrew C., 206, 207
Slayton, Deke, 114
Small Business Act, 221
Smith, Hedrick, 57
Software protection
  Brazilian trade case and, 176–177
  in Japan, 186
Space Council, EOSAT and, 110
Space imaging industry, 121–122. *See
     also* Remote Satellite Sensing
Specialization, myth of value of, 7
Spector, Leonard, 107–108
Sporck, Charles, 81–82, 83
SPOT (Satellite Pour l'Observation de
     la Terre) Image, 107–108, 109, 111,
     112–113

Stark, Peter, 192–193
Steel industry, 3
Stockman, David, 113, 114, 115, 116
Streimer, Robert, 136
Subsidies, in U.S., 47–48
Superconductivity, 98–99
Sweden, 30–31
Swirling, Jacob, 192–194

Takeyoshi, Kawashima, 51
Targeting, 188
Tax policy
    business and, 218–219
    financial markets and, 219
    global competition and, 156
    governmental affairs management
        and, 192–193
Technology, politicization of, 13–14
Technology transfer, within cooperative
    consortia, 79
Telecommunications industry, issues for
    managers in, 57–59
Terashima, Jitsuro, 53
Texas Instruments, 79, 87
Thomson, 89
Toshiba Machine Company, 52–53
Trade policy
    business and, 158, 219–220
    contingent protectionism and, 62n57
    defense-sponsored industrial policy
        and, 90–91
    reciprocity and, 204
    U.S. negotiating teams and, 187
    U.S. Sec. 301 actions and, 168–169
Trades Union Council (TUC), in Brit-
    ain, 37
Transnational government bodies
    Japanese violation of COCOM regula-
        tions, 52–53
    standards and, 211–212
Trust
    governmental affairs management
        and, 159
    industry associations and, 148
TUC. See Trades Union Council

Union of Soviet Socialist Republics
    (USSR), 16, 52–53
United Kingdom, 16, 24, 36–37
United States
    balance of power in, 28
    business structure in, 45–47
    danger in weakness of, 201, 212

foreign trade issues in 1985 in, 170–
    171
impediments in government plan-
    ning, 37–38
on individualistic-communitarian
    continuum, 16 (see also Ideology)
as regulatory state, 21
sources of management authority in,
    40–41, 45
state power in, 36, 37–38
U.S. Memory (consortium), 87
United States Trade Representative
    (USTR)
    actions against Brazil, 165, 167, 171–
        176, 180
    actions against Japan, 181–182
    HDTV standards and, 69–70
    Health Industry Manufacturers Asso-
        ciation and, 140
    Sec. 301 and, 167–168, 170
    U.S. industrial policy and, 91
Unitron (Brazilian firm), 176, 179–180
USTR. See United States Trade Repre-
    sentative

Value-added networks (VANs), 184
Van Wolferen, Karel, 61n32
Very Large-Scale Integrated Circuit
    Technology Research Association
    (VLSI/TRA), 75–77

Waste, 118–119
Waxman, Henry A., 141, 142, 143, 144,
    145
Waxman committee, 141–143
Webber, Alan M., 54
Welfare role of government, 22–25
Wells, Louis T., Jr., 48, 50
Williams, Charles, 114, 115, 117–118
Williamson, Gilbert, 67
Wolff, Alan, 3
Woods, Rose Mary, 153
World Bank, 212
Wysocki, Bernard Jr., 39

Xerox, 50

Yamashita, Eme, 53
Yeutter, Clayton, 168, 175, 176, 177,
    179, 180
Yoffie, David B., 4–5, 62n57

Zeppenfeld, Anne, 192, 193
Zysman, John, 35